AN UNFORGETTABLE DALIT VOICE

AN UNFORGETTABLE DALIT VOICE

Life, Writings and Speeches of M.C. Rajah

Edited, with an Introduction by
SWARAJ BASU

MANOHAR
2026

First published, 2012
Reprinted 2026

ISBN 978-81-7304-966-8

Published by
Ajay Kumar Jain *for*
Manohar Publishers & Distributors
4753/23 Ansari Road, Daryaganj
New Delhi 110 002

Printed and bound in India

Contents

Preface

More than sixty years after Independence Dalits in India are still fighting for rights and social justice in spite of having constitutional and legal provisions to ensure social equity and justice. The present-day Dalit movement needs to be understood in a historical perspective. In the late nineteenth and early twentieth century a number of Dalit leaders in different parts of India made valuable contributions in mobilizing Dalits to assert for new social identity as well as for their legitimate rights in education, employment and governance. M.C. Rajah deserves to be remembered as one such important Dalit leader from Tamil Nadu, who was a contemporary of B.R. Ambedkar and played a significant role in organizing Dalits and raising their issues and concerns in various forums to protect their interests. He was the first Dalit leader nominated in the Madras Legislative Council and the Central Legislative Assembly and for about twenty years continuously M.C. Rajah represented Dalits in legislative bodies. In course of my research on caste movements I felt that the writings, speeches and letters of M.C. Rajah were yet to be explored adequately by scholars. Way back in 1930, J. Sivashunmugam Pillai wrote a short book entitled, *The Life, Select Writings and Speeches of Rao Bahadur M.C. Rajah, M.L.A.*, which covers few of the speeches of Rajah and his correspondence till 1930. Recently the publisher Critical Quest of New Delhi has reprinted M.C. Rajah's book, *The Oppressed Hindus*, written in 1925. It is therefore necessary to acquaint ourselves with the works of M.C. Rajah who fought a relentless struggle for freedom of Dalits. I have made an effort by visiting National Archives, Central Secretariat Library and Nehru Memorial Museum & Library, New Delhi to collect his speeches, writings and correspondence. This book is a collection of M.C. Rajah's works which include his book, memorandum, letters, speeches, etc., so that researchers can critically analyse the significant role played by him towards the liberation and empowerment of Dalits.

The idea of doing this work came from my own research interest on caste movements and identity politics in India. My discussions with colleagues Kapil Kumar, Darvesh Gopal, Salil Mishra, Sashi Bhusan Upadhyay and Debal SinghaRoy at Indira Gandhi National

Open University, New Delhi helped me in giving this collection a shape. I am grateful to all of them. I thank the staff of National Archives, Central Secretariat Library and Nehru Memorial Museum & Library for providing required assistance in the collection of documents. Finally I wish to thank Ramesh Jain, Manohar Publishers, Delhi for the timely publication of this book.

School of Social Sciences,
Indira Gandhi National Open University,
New Delhi

SWARAJ BASU

Introduction

> The exclusion of Dalits from the main body of society is symbolized on many fronts. Physically the cheris are located outside the main village; semantically they are referred to as "untouchables"; spiritually, Dalits are denied access to temples, told that they are impure…; materially Dalits are alienated from resources and land; culturally their skills are demeaned; and socially they are served in different receptacles in restaurants.[1]

The condition of Dalits[2] in contemporary Tamil Nadu, as portrayed by Hugo Gorringe, may help in imagining the trauma and stigma with which they lived in the past. Today's struggle of Dalits for equal rights and justice has its roots in history. By late nineteenth- and early twentieth-century Dalits in Tamil Nadu, as in other parts of India, raised their voices for social equality, justice and political rights and at the same time challenged the given identity to them as 'untouchables'. One major Dalit voice of early twentieth century was of Rao Bahadur Mylai Chinnathambi Rajah (popularly known as M.C. Rajah, 1883-1943) who at the regional as well as national level raised his voice for freedom, justice and equal rights of Dalits. It is a different story that in spite of being the first Dalit leader in the Provincial Legislative Council and also the first Dalit leader in the Central Legislative Assembly we hardly come across any reference to the works of M.C. Rajah and his struggle for the cause of Dalit's emancipation. It is more painful when a scholar like Gail Omvedt in her study of Dalit movement in colonial India introduces M.C. Rajah as the 'Hindu Mahasabhite Dalit', failing to locate M.C.Rajah's ideas and life long struggles for the empowerment of Dalits.[3] The recognition he deserves because of his forceful voice within and outside the legislative bodies to give back Dalits their lost dignity and rights hardly finds mention in the narratives of Dalit movements. The big presence of Ambedkar as an erudite scholar, ideologue and the great fighter for Dalit empowerment possibly engaged most of the scholars of Dalit studies leaving in the margin leaders like M.C. Rajah and others, whose efforts in bringing the issue of equality, justice and rights for Dalits in the agenda of administrative reforms remained mostly unnoticed. Every body knows that Ambedkar strongly advocated social democracy before talking about political democracy and he stood for equality, liberty and fraternity. But very few know that M.C. Rajah much before Ambedkar wrote in 1925 that 'freedom of person is a pre-requisite for the development of nationality. Freedom should not be given to the people of India before our social wrongs have been set right. Social equality, social liberty and social fraternity should be enforced among the people who clamour for political equality, political liberty and political fraternity.'[4] Being in public life as representative of Dalits in the provincial and central legislature for about two decades, M.C. Rajah fought for the empowerment of Dalits through various administrative reform initiatives of the British government in India. Being a contemporary of Ambedkar, Rajah's leadership to Dalit struggle as President of All India Depressed Classes Association and his writings on Dalits speak about his relentless struggle and concern for the rights of Dalits. This book is an attempt to compile important writings, letters and speeches of M.C. Rajah at one place to facilitate further research in this area.

LIFE SKETCH

Presenting the Sanad of Rai Bahadur to M.C. Rajah on 15 December 1922, the collector of Madras made the following remarks:

> You are such a well known public man that it is almost unnecessary for me to say much about you. No doubt you have received this title because of the work you have done for and the esteem in which you are rightly held by the members of your own important community of the Adi-Dravidas. During the labour troubles you did yeoman service in restraining them from violence and in protecting them effectively from law-breakers.
>
> You have represented your community in deputations to the Right Honourable the Secretary of State and to His Excellency the Viceroy. You are the first Adi-Dravida to enter the Legislative Council and you have the interests of the depressed and poor always at heart.
>
> I understand that your grandfather was an Indian Mutiny Veteran. The courage and endurance which he displayed in times of war are evinced by you in times of peace.
>
> The Government are well aware of the public services you have thus rendered and have therefore conferred on you this title.[5]

M.C. Rajah's concern and tireless efforts for freedom, equality and rights for Dalits were recognized by the British government by conferring on him the title of Rai Bahadur. His commitment to liberate and empower Dalits was the guiding force behind his struggle at the local as well as the national level against the oppressive upper caste domination. Born in 1883 in a family of Pariahs, a Dalit community of Tamil Nadu, M.C. Rajah was fortunate to have access to education. He studied in Christian Missionary School and then the Madras Christian College which according to him helped in learning the spirit of tolerance. Being born in a Dalit family he could feel the sufferings of Dalits from his own experiences and was enlightened enough to understand that how in the name of caste system a vast section of Indian society was denied of social justice and equal rights for such a long period. He worked as a teacher-trainer at Teacher Training College, Saidapet and as a lecturer in Voorhees College, Vellore. Realizing the importance of education as the liberating force he appealed to the government for providing better opportunities for education to children of Dalit families. His concern for education of Dalits caught the attention of the government and he was nominated in various committees of government education department. He was instrumental for securing scholarships, building hostels for Dalits and also setting up a Dravidian School in 1936 at Nungambakkam.[6]

Being influenced by the on-going non-Brahmin movement which challenged the Brahminical domination in different spheres of life in Tamil Nadu, Rajah initially joined the Non-Brahmin movement. But having felt that the leaders of the Non-Brahmin movement were not taking up the cause of Dalits he disassociated himself from the Non-Brahmin movement and reorganized Adi-Dravida Mahajana Sabha in 1916 to mobilize Dalits for abolition of untouchability and to demand for socio-political and economic rights. He said that Madras Legislative Council under the leadership of the Justice Party had not done anything for the welfare of Dalits and nor had they done much to ensure the representation of Dalits in local bodies and municipal councils. Taking the cue from the Dravidian movement he demanded the usage of Adi-Dravidas to refer Dalits in Tamil districts. He was critical of caste Hindus whom he considered responsible for the oppression of Dalits. M.C. Rajah was of the opinion that without abolishing caste there would be no freedom for Dalits. He wrote,

> We are not bricks or stones. We have feelings and ambitions and national pride. We have suffered all sorts of tyranny, exploitation, insult and injury. You have trampled on our national honour and dignity and also heaped outrageous insults on us, added to grave injuries, economic and political . . . we do not want any patronage. We want social emancipation, economic emancipation and political emancipation.[7]

To draw general attention to the past glory as well as present oppression of Dalits in Tamil Nadu he wrote a book in 1925 titled as *The Oppressed Hindus.*

M.C. Rajah's leadership to Dalits for emancipation from social oppression influenced the British government to nominate him as a Dalit representative in the Madras Legislative Council and thus he earned the honour of being the first Dalit leader to be nominated in the Provincial Legislative Council. Again he had the unique distinction of becoming the first Dalit representative nominated by the government to the Central Legislative Assembly. On behalf of Dalits he gave representation to the government committees for administrative reforms to safeguard the interests of Dalits. On the issue of joint or separate electorates for Dalits he supported the joint electorates although at the beginning he was demanding separate electorates. He differed with Gandhi and Ambedkar on various issues concerning Dalits and at the same time where needed he also joined them for the cause of Dalits. He was president of the All India Depressed Classes Association for many years and disagreed with the views of Ambedkar on religious conversion. Initially Rajah maintained an independent line of action on issues pertaining to the rights of Dalits and he had ideological differences with Ambedkar. But at a later stage both the leaders joined hands and gave a joint representation to Sir Stafford Cripps demanding socio-political rights for Dalits. At the core of his ideology was to emancipate Dalits from social oppression and to empower them socially, politically and economically with the cooperation of government and by mobilization of Dalits at the regional and national level.

SOCIO-POLITICAL CONTEXT

It would not be out of place to refer to the socio-political context in which M.C. Rajah developed his ideology for the empowerment of Dalits. The three major social groups of Tamil Nadu were Brahmins, non-Brahmins and Dalits and by the beginning of the twentieth century, due to the contribution made by European and Indian scholars, a dominant view emerged that non-Brahmins were Dravidians and original settlers of the land and Brahmins were Aryan invaders who imposed Sanskrit culture over Tamil land. Brahmins because of their dominant socio-cultural position occupied most of the administrative and educational jobs in government although they comprised only 3.2 per cent of the total population of Tamil Nadu. This domination of the Brahmins was skilfully used by non-Brahmin leaders to create a separate Dravidian cultural identity with the tacit support of the British government in the early years of the twentieth century. Eugene F. Irshik's study of the non-Brahmin movement in south India between 1916 and 1929 illustrates the issues and complexities of the non-Brahmin movement. In the opinion of Irshik the serious rift between Brahmins and non-Brahmins was because of 'the drive for political power, for administrative position, and for economic security'.[8] The opposition to Brahmin domination by non-Brahmins in Tamil Nadu had two distinct strands, one under the banner of Justice Party and the other, of the Self-Respect movement. Explaining the emergence of non-Brahminism in Tamil Nadu, Narendra Subramanian has argued that as a result of colonial intervention and the importance given to *varna* framework, Brahmins became more powerful compared to pre-colonial society in Tamil Nadu. In his opinion 'the memory of greater autonomy in pre-colonial times and the residual autonomy that many non-Brahmin groups enjoyed even into the twentieth century aided the growth of non-Brahminism'.[9] The idea of Brahmins as Aryans coming from outside and non-Brahmins as the descendants of the Dravidian who are culturally rooted in Tamil Nadu was gaining ground and culminated in the formation of the Justice Party (1916-17). Leaders of the Justice Party emphasized on educational development of non-Brahmins along with their demand for social justice. By mobilizing members through provincial conferences, the Justice Party demanded representation of non-Brahmins on a communal basis in the Legislature. In the successive elections of Madras Legislative Council in 1920 and 1923 the Justice Party secured majority and brought changes in favour of non-Brahmins in government service and educational opportunities. To safeguard the rights and interests of non-Brahmins, Madras Legislative Council suggested the appointment of a 'Protector'. However, it is argued that the Justice Party was unable to connect with the masses and the Party failed to address many grievances of the non-Brahmin masses.[10] The Self-Respect Association formed in 1926 tried to accommodate the common grievances of non-Brahmins.

E.V. Ramaswamy Naicker, popularly called Periyar, was instrumental in giving a new dimension to non-Brahminism in Tamil Nadu. Initially being influenced by Gandhian principles and encouraged by C.

Rajagopalachari, Periyar joined the Congress party in Tamil Nadu in 1920 with the hope of addressing the concerns of non-Brahmins through the Congress platform. He participated actively in non-cooperation, Khilafat and Khadi movements launched by Gandhiji. In 1924 at Kerala he participated in the Satyagraha movement at Vaikom for the entry of all castes in the prohibited street leading to the temple. But Periyar was opposed to Gandhiji's paternalistic approach and Gandhiji's version of *varnashrama dharma*. He demanded communal representation for all elected bodies. When Periyar's demand for greater political representation of non-Brahmins did not find favour from the Congress leadership, he decided to leave Congress and form the Self-Respect Association in 1926. Through a series of articles in the journal *Kudi Arasu* he attacked Brahmin orthodoxy and caste oppression. He and his followers through public meetings tried to mobilize public opinion against Brahminism but he did not identify himself with the Justice Party. At the core of Periyar's ideology was 'Destroy god; destroy religion; destroy Congress; destroy Gandhi; destroy the Brahmin'.[11] Besides these two main groups there were also non-Brahmins within the Congress who were also raising voices for the rights of non-Brahmins.

Besides Brahmins and non-Brahmins, Dalits comprised a large social group mostly living in rural areas on the mercy of the upper castes. Most of the Dalits were unskilled and were paid very less. This economic condition of Dalits was due to the fact that hardly 1 per cent of them were literate in the first quarter of the twentieth century. Dalits living in villages had no right to use the streets where the Brahmins lived. Since late nineteenth century the British government took special interest to improve the condition of Dalits through land grants and educational facilities. The Madras government created the office of the Protector of the 'Depressed Classes' to provide required assistance. Disparities prevailing between Dalits and non-Brahmins in terms of social status and other opportunities made Dalits critics of non-Brahmins and demand separate social and political identity. Dalits claimed them as Adi-Dravidas and tried to prove their cultural superiority as the original inhabitants of Tamil land. There were references to conflicts between Dalits and other castes over respective social power and status. When there was labour unrest in Madras in the early 1920s Dalit leadership refused to support the strike call given by the upper caste Hindus on the ground that they had no other means of livelihood except working in the mills. As the non-

Brahmin leadership failed to take note of the complexity of interests of different social groups, the British officials fully capitalized on the situation and projected themselves as the real protector of the interests of Dalits. Dalit leadership was sceptical of the intention of non-Brahmin leadership for liberating Dalits from social discrimination. References to conflicts between Dalits and the Kallars, non-Brahmins, are found in the study of non-Brahmin movement in south India.[12] Thus from the picture that we get of late nineteenth- and early twentieth-century Tamil Nadu, one can make out the growing resentment against Brahminism for various reasons. It is equally true that the anti-Brahmin voice was not united and Dalits were very much concerned to ensure their independent socio-political and economic identity. We have to situate the ideas of M.C. Rajah in the backdrop of these developments.

ADI-DRAVIDIAN IDENTITY

It is important to refer here that the late nineteenth and early twentieth century witnessed the growth of anti-caste ideology, particularly in Maharashtra and the sustained efforts made by Dalit intelligentsia during this period to question the given social identity of Dalits. In Tamil Nadu leaders of non-Brahmin movement giving reference to history argued for the dominant position that the Dravidians enjoyed in the province. Taking lesson from the Dravidian ideology, M.C. Rajah argued that Dalits were the original inhabitants of the region before the Aryans came down from northern India. The very names by which the caste Hindus refer to them show their contempt towards Dalits. Therefore, M.C. Rajah on behalf of Dalits of the province requested the British government to address them as Adi-Dravidians as the non-Brahmin Hindus were referred to as Dravidians. In fact, before M.C. Rajah, it was Iyodhi Das (1845-1914) in Tamil Nadu who was critical of caste system and felt that social emancipation was only possible by embracing Buddhism. He started a journal called *Tamizham* through which he tried to give vent to the sufferings of Dalits. The consciousness which was gaining ground for freedom from social oppression in the name of caste system got further momentum under the leadership of M.C. Rajah. He strongly felt that the Dalits who formed majority should first get socio-economic and political equality and justice, otherwise any other freedom becomes meaningless in India. M.C. Rajah played a pioneering role in the creation of Adi-Dravidian ideology through his book *The Oppressed Hindus.* He wrote,

> No greater wrong can be done to a community endowed with human feelings and human capacities than to place it in such circumstances as to force it or lead it to believe that its members are eternally and for all time to come doomed to a life of ignorance, servitude and misery and that any sort of ambition in them for betterment or improvement is sin.[13]

With the help of Tamil literature and other references he argued that the Adi-Dravidas were the original inhabitants of southern India and before the advent of the Aryans, the Adi-Dravidas had their own social institutions and administrative set up. In support of the greatness of Adi-Dravidas he wrote that Thiruvalluvar, the author of *Thirukkural* was an Adi-Dravida, the famous Adi-Dravida saint Thiruppan Alwar is worshipped in all the Vaishnavite temples in south India. He also wrote that Adi-Dravidas had a well developed administrative system before the Aryans came in and the power of the monarch was checked by five councils having representatives of the people, priests, physicians, astrologers, astronomers and ministers. Adi-Dravidas were a martial race and were brave soldiers. Thus through his writings he wanted to reinforce the idea that how the Adi-Dravidas lost their dignity and rights as a result of Aryanization. Liberation of Adi-Dravidas from the present state of exploitation was only possible through education, jobs and representation in various representative bodies. He advocated for educational opportunities of Dalits and wrote that to encourage children for attending schools and colleges there should be more free hostels and scholarships for Dalits. He believed that so long Dalits remain oppressed and are denied equality and social justice no reform towards self-government will be supported by Dalits. He also demanded reservation of jobs in government offices and reservation of seats in various representative bodies for Dalits. He urged the government to ensure that no legislation affecting Dalits should be incorporated in the Statute Book unless two-thirds of Dalit representatives support this and the government must ensure that the proposed legislation is not against the interest of Dalits.

EMPOWERING DALITS

M.C. Rajah strongly believed that Dalits did not gain by the transfer of power from the bureaucracy to the representatives of Indian people following the Montague-Chelmsford Reforms of 1919. He argued that any grant of self-government at that stage would lead to concentration of power in the hands of those Indians who were not concerned for Dalits. He felt that Swaraj had no meaning for Dalits unless they were given their due share of rights in the society. He urged upon the government to appoint one representative from Dalits to the Provincial Cabinets and also one to the Executive Council of the Viceroy. He also urged upon the government to create separate electorates for Dalits and to widen the franchise to enable Dalits to elect their representatives. His concern for Dalits made him realize that supporting the Congress-led national movement would not help Dalits. Rather it would be prudent to urge upon the British government for reservation of seats in legislative bodies and reservation of government jobs that would really empower Dalits. When the Congress gave the call for boycotting of the Simon Commission as the President of the All India Depressed Classes' Conference, held in Delhi on 26 February 1928, he welcomed the appointment of the Simon Commission and requested Dalits in different provinces to submit their representations to the commission.[14] He took active part in the process of franchise reforms initiated by the Simon Commission. He had differences with Ambedkar on the issue of separate or joint electorates and to find a solution on the issue of Dalit representation, on which there were different views expressed by the Congress and the Hindu Mahasabha, M.C. Rajah's concern was not to disturb unity within Hindu community. Taking part in the debate in the Central Legislative Assembly on the Round Table Conference and the issue of representation of Dalits, M.C. Rajah said that 'The communalists, especially, at the Round Table Conference, were able to persuade the two delegates of the Depressed Classes in the Conference to join them and prepared a pact, called the "Minorities Pact" to which they were able to secure the signature and support of the Depressed Classes delegate.'[15] After studying the pact it was found that Dalits were getting less number of seats in most of the provinces based on their population strength compared to Muslims. This disparity in representation proposed in the pact made M.C. Rajah convinced of the futility of separate electorates and to opt for joint electorate with the majority community through reservation of seats. This might have been a reason for his signing a pact with B.S. Moonje, President of Hindu Mahasabha. He argued, 'It is by engaging in a common task with others that we can break down prejudices however deeply rooted they may be and not remain untouchables in a separate electorate roll. As a minority community with a separate electorate our influence will be circumscribed, whereas, as a strong section of a general electorate our influence will be unlimited'.[16] His central concern was to ensure adequate representation of Dalits in legislatures proportionate to their numbers in each province. When Ambedkar suggested for conversion of Dalits to any religion other than Hinduism M.C. Rajah objected to this and wrote,

> Hinduism is our religion and it is sacred to us. It is our duty to preserve it and purify it. We do not want to cut away from the Hindufold. We want a better recognition—recognition of the fact that we are men equally with themselves, the caste Hindus. Our goal is the removal of untouchability and our aim is to become an unsegregated and unquarantined part of the Hindu society.[17]

He also did not support Moonje's suggestion on this count and wrote to him saying,

> Your solicitude for the place of the Depressed Classes in the political scheme not only exposes the interested nature of your concern for these classes, but is like placing the cart before the horse. One would expect you as President of the Hindu Mahasabha to ameliorate the social condition of the Depressed Classes by removing civic and social disabilities of these classes, not to speak of securing for them the right of worship in Hindu temples on an equal footing with other worshippers, and to further the Harijan movement started by Gandhiji all over the country. Instead of doing this, what is it that you are doing? You are dissecting the Depressed Classes. . . .[18]

Gandhiji endorsed the views of M.C. Rajah and wrote that 'I do not at all understand Dr. Moonje's or Dr. Ambedkar's position. For me removal of untouchability stands on a footing all its own. It is to me a deeply religious question. The very existence of our religion depends on its voluntary removal by Savarna Hindu in the spirit of repentance. It can never be a question of barter for me. And I am glad you take nearly the same position that I do'.[19] M.C. Rajah also shared Gandhiji's concern for the abolition of untouchability and expressed the need of everybody's help for the protection of Dalit's interests. But he declined to join the Congress before the elections of 1937 when the Congress approached him. Later on he wrote to Gandhiji that after the election of 1937 in Madras, the Caste Hindus were forcing Dalits within the Assembly to vote with the Congress even in cases affecting the interests of Dalits. In the debate on the Temple Entry Bill in the Madras Legislative Assembly, Dalit members within the Congress in the Assembly were asked to vote against the Bill proposed by Rajah. He requested Gandhiji to intervene in the matters pertaining to Harijan upliftment in Madras presidency. He was upset with the Madras Congress on the issue of the Temple Entry Bill and reminded Gandhiji to the assurances given by him to Dalits during Gandhiji's epic fast. M.C. Rajah wrote to Gandhiji that

> We do not wish to remain betrayed any longer. . . . It is no pleasure for me to differ from you, but when I see the cause which is so dear to you and me betrayed in action by one in whom you have implicit faith and whom you have helped to place in a position of power which may be used for good or for evil, for large ends or narrow purposes, I have no alternative but to say that your faith in which you wish me to share is misplaced.[20]

His differences with the Congress ministry in Madras province on issues concerning Dalits led to change in his attitude towards the Congress. This was the time when he came close to Ambedkar and made joint representation to Sir Stafford Cripps for empowerment of Dalits.

M.C. RAJAH AS LEGISLATOR

Beginning with 1919 till 1939 M.C. Rajah was a member of either provincial or central legislature. He raised the issues in the legislature primarily for the empowerment of dalits. He demanded for deletion of terms like 'Panchama' and 'Paraya' from government records and usage of 'Adi-Dravida' in the Tamil and 'Adi-Andhra' in the Telugu districts for the ancient Dravidian community in southern India. He moved resolutions in the house for financial aids to the Dalit students and also exemption of examination fees. His interventions in the discussion on the annual budget in Madras Legislative Council show his command over the economic issues and by eloquent speech in the Council he proved the point that the needs of Dalits are not addressed properly in the budgetary provision. Taking part in the debate on a bill for the reorganization of the Madras University M.C. Rajah said,

> . . . I owe a duty to my people and when I find that their immediate and distant progress is bound up with elementary education, how can I support a Bill whose effect, sure and certain, will be to divert funds which ought to be spent on education suitable to their needs, and which will thus lead to the neglect of my peoples' educational interests? . . . the process of developing the non-brahman movement into an oligarchic and anti-democratic movement

will be complete, when funds which might be spent on elementary education are spent on university reform.[21]

He said in a general discussion on the budget in the Council that Indianization of services in India should be commensurate with the progress of Dalits, otherwise in India where caste still rules, people belonging to upper castes would monopolize public services.

In a speech in Imperial Legislative Assembly M.C. Rajah said,

> Well, Sir, as a matter of fact what has this Legislative Assembly done all these years to alleviate the sufferings of these voiceless millions? What have the provincial councils done for them? There was a time when it was said that once the people of India get power into their hands they would help forward the oppressed classes in India. Are we any nearer to the time when the caste Hindu will think with shame of such atrocities having once existed in this country? . . . Can India get self-government before our social wrongs have been set right? Social equality, social liberty and social fraternity should be enforced among the people who clamour for political equality, political liberty and political fraternity. . . . Nation-building should be directed towards the amelioration of the condition of the one-sixth of the population of the country that have been kept down for ages. Nation-building will all be tall talk if the activities are not directed towards the uplift of these waiting millions, the real sons of the soil.[22]

Taking part in the debate on the Statutory Commission Rajah spoke in the Assembly that it is due to the Britishers that the Dalits got their representatives in legislative bodies otherwise the Congress men were not supportive of Dalits. He strongly felt that the Congress had done nothing for removing social inequalities and giving proper representation to Dalit voices. He expressed his confidence in the house hoping that in all future negotiations and collaborations with the government, the views of Dalits should be given due weightage. In the course of debates on constitutional reforms in the Assembly in 1932, M.C. Rajah stated that the caste Hindus have acknowledged the sufferings of Dalits and he argued that remaining within the Hindus there will be the end of Dalits' sufferings and not by segregating Dalits from caste Hindus. At the same time he was critical of orthodox Brahminical culture which was opposed to the entry of Dalits to Hindu temples.

> The question of temple entry is only one of the many items in the campaign for the eradication of the curse of untouchability. . . . The opening of temples to the Depressed Classes will give a new life and a new hope to them. You call them unclean. Their unclean habits are entirely due to you, as you keep

them away and give them unclean quarters and not give them light, water enough to drink and bathe. You are the sinners.[23]

He moved a motion for the abolition of untouchability among the Hindus. During the course of debate on the untouchability abolition bill when Krishnamachariar said that Ambedkar was not in favour of temple entry, M.C. Rajah referred to a letter written to him by B.K. Gaikwad, Secretary of the Satyagraha Committee, Nasik. The letter says,

> I hope you are aware of the Kala Ram temple Entry Satyagraha of Nasik conducted under the leadership of Dr. Baba Saheb Ambedkar, last year. . . . Now, the Committee, with the full consent and a sort of order from Dr. Baba Saheb Ambedkar, who is just now sitting on the Round Table Conference, decide to begin again Satyagraha. But this time we do not care to have it only as a local show. It is an all-India question, and the honour of all-Indian untouchables is in the scales. And I write this letter on behalf of the Committee to request you very strongly that you please take up the question and use all your resources for the cause.[24]

In his speech at the 9th session of the All India Depressed Classes conference held in the Punjab on 31 October 1931, M.C. Rajah asked, 'Why does not Mahatma Gandhi direct his energies to removing the oppressive features in our social structure, and in particular, to removing the canker of untouchability before he makes any further attempt for Swaraj, since he himself had wisely admitted on more than one occasion that this reform should precede Swaraj.'[25]

Being elected in the Madras Legislative Assembly in 1937, M.C. Rajah moved a motion for introducing a Bill for the removal of social disabilities among certain classes of Hindus and he succeeded in getting the support of various parties on this. In 1938, M.C. Rajah introduced a Bill in the Assembly to remove disabilities of Dalits in regard to entry into Hindu temples. He said in the Assembly,

> There seems to be, sir, absolutely no justification for the Congress government to ask me to withdraw this Bill. This Bill has been most widely circulated and public opinion has been received in its favour. . . . I wanted to tell you the reason why we subscribed to the Poona Pact. We thought there will be total removal of untouchability. That was the promise given to us then. But now, sir, we understand from the attitude of the Government that the Poona Pact was intended only as a political manoeuvre and not for the eradication of the wrongs. . . . I am only concerned about my friends, the members of the Depressed Classes belonging to the Congress party, because I was in a way instrumental in making some of them join the Congress, because I then

agreed with Mahatma Gandhi and his conditions. The condition is this; Harijan members of the Congress party will have full freedom of opinion and vote in respect of matters specially affecting the Harijan community where they differ from the policy adopted by the party should any such difference arise. I say this, Sir, because some of the Harijan Congress members came and told me that they were not in agreement with the Premier.[26]

LEGACY

M.C. Rajah by creating an alternative history of Dalits in Tamil Nadu questioned the legitimacy of Brahminical hierarchy. He realized that without education Dalits would not be able to compete with the upper castes. Therefore his immediate concern was to promote education among Dalits. He firmly believed that education, employment, social equality, right to land and representation in decision-making bodies can only emancipate Dalits from various forms of exploitation. His disillusionment with the ongoing non-Brahmin movement of Tamil Nadu was due to the failure of non-Brahmin leaders to mitigate the sufferings of Dalits. The Congress-led national movement also failed to evoke much response from M.C. Rajah because he firmly believed that without the emancipation of Dalits from their present state of exploitation political freedom from the British is not desirable. M.C. Rajah said that

> the Depressed Classes are in no way behind any other section of this country's inhabitants in their desire for political advance. Rather they appreciate freedom more than anybody else, just as the caged bird longs for freedom all the more keenly because it has known the limitations of a cage or restrictions on its liberty. I may go further and say that we are more anxious for the freedom of this country than others, because we are the original inhabitants of this land, and the country's interests and ours are closely associated.[27]

He was supportive of Gandhiji's movement for abolition of untouchability and temple entry but later on after the 1937 election when the Congress formed the government in Madras he felt that the Congress government in the province was not giving the desired response to Dalit issues. This made him very critical of the Congress party as well as Gandhiji. He was opposed to the caste system but he was not opposed to the idea of remaining within Hinduism. His response to Ambedkar and Moonje on this issue of religion makes it clear that he wanted to fight for the rights of Dalits by not leaving Hinduism but by bringing change in the attitude of orthodox Hindus. This approach of M.C. Rajah definitely does not deserve to be characterized him as a 'Hindu Mahasabhite Dalit'. He was very clear that without social equality and justice, mere political freedom was not going to liberate Dalits from their present state of oppression. Dalit leaders did not speak in one voice although all were fighting for the empowerment of Dalits. M.C. Rajah had his own understanding of Dalit problems and in consultation with like-minded people he tried to address those problems. He was very flexible in his approach to negotiate with others for the protection of Dalit interests and never hesitated to take a position in disagreement with Gandhiji or Ambedkar. It is therefore essential to make a proper assessment of M.C. Rajah's contribution towards the empowerment of Dalits, situating him in the context of prevailing socio-political developments and his tireless efforts to organize Dalits at the local as well as national level and to register their demands forcefully in various forums. The great legacy of M.C. Rajah lay in his relentless efforts to organize Dalits against different forms of oppression they were subjected to by the upper caste Hindus and to pressurize the government for necessary amendments in its policy to protect the rights of Dalits.

NOTES

1. Hugo Gorringe, *Untouchable Citizens: Dalit Movements and Democratization in Tamil Nadu*, Sage Publications, New Delhi, 2005, p. 73.
2. As in contemporary studies the term 'Dalit' is much in use to refer the social groups who are at the bottom of caste hierarchy so in this collection of M.C. Rajah's works I have used the term 'Dalit' in place of 'Depressed Class' which referred to 'untouchable' in the colonial official records.
3. Gail Omvedt, *Dalits and the Democratic Revolution: Dr. Ambedkar and the Dalit Movement in Colonial India*, Sage Publications, New Delhi, 1994, p. 10.
4. M.C. Rajah, *The Oppressed Hindus*, The Huxley Press, Madras, 1925, p. 52.
5. Cited in J. Sivashunmugam Pillai, *The Life, Select Writings and Speeches of Rao Bahadur M.C. Rajah*, Madras, 1930, pp. 8-9.
6. Ibid., pp. 3-4; Report on the Birth Anniversary of M.C. Rajah, source: http://insightyv.com.
7. Rajah, *The Oppressed Hindus*, op. cit.
8. Eugene F. Irshik, *Politics and Social Conflict in South India: The Non-Brahman Movement and Tamil Separatism, 1916-1929*, University of California Press, Berkeley and Los Angeles, 1969, p. 26.
9. Narendra Subramanian, *Ethnicity and Populist Mobilization: Political Parties, Citizens and Democracy in South India*, Oxford University Press, New Delhi, 1999, pp. 95-6.

10. Ibid., p. 98.
11. Ibid., p. 115.
12. Indu Rajagopal, *The Tyranny of Caste: The Non-Brahman Movement and Political Development in South India*, Vikas Publishing, Delhi, 1985, pp. 136-9.
13. Rajah, *The Oppressed Hindus*, op. cit.
14. *The Indian Annual Register*, January-June 1928, rpt., Delhi, 2000, pp. 428-9.
15. *Central Legislative Assembly Proceedings*, 5 September 1932.
16. Ibid.
17. *The Indian Annual Register*, July-December 1935, rpt., Delhi, 2000, p. 318.
18. *The Indian Annual Register*, July-December 1936, rpt., Delhi, 2000, p. 279.
19. Ibid.
20. Letters to Gandhiji, M.C. Rajah Private Papers, Nehru Memorial Museum & Library, New Delhi.
21. *Madras Legislative Council Proceedings*, 15 November 1922.
22. *Central Legislative Assembly Proceedings*, 4 March 1927.
23. Ibid., 23 August 1934.
24. *Central Legislative Assembly Proceedings*, 1 February 1934.
25. Ibid.
26. *Madras Legislative Assembly Proceedings*, 17 August 1938.
27. *Central Legislative Assembly Proceedings*, 7 March 1931.

PART I

THE OPPRESSED HINDUS

by

M.C. Rajah

The Huxley Press, Madras, 1925

DEDICATED

to

The Members of British Parliament and their representatives here, the Government of India, for their earnest endeavours to promote the interests of the Depressed Classes in India.

Contents

The Oppressed Hindus

I. INTRODUCTION

No epoch in the history of South India is so interesting or so important as the present period of transition after the Montagu-Chelmsford dispensation of 1919 when forces which have lain quiescent during a hundred and odd years of the British Reign of Law have come up again to the surface with apparently renewed vigour and vitality. For whatever may be said about the sins of omission and commission of the British Administration during the period, the outstanding fact remains that from the prince to the peasant, the high-caste Brahmin to the "Depressed Indian," the people were made equally 'powerless' and subject to the same machinery for the administration of justice in its widest sense and the machinery itself was thoroughly imbued with the British notions of Justice, Equity and Good Conscience. The promise of absolute "religious neutrality" in the gracious Proclamation of Queen Victoria of blessed memory was the first surrender which His Brittanic Majesty's Indian Government has had to explain away and circumvent whenever they had to legislate, for the correction of social abuses or in the highest interests of morality and humanity. The tendency of the British Indian Courts to accept the legal binding force of long-standing custom and the wholesale Indianisation of the subordinate judicial machinery tended to crystallize age-long social abuses into a rigid social system upheld by law and every small attempt to remove even a single social disability by Legislation has been checked by the cry of "Religion in Danger" and the apparent anxiety of the state to steer clear of even a suspicion of infringing the sacred promise of Queen Victoria.

The Indian *personnel* of the administration were mostly drawn from the lower middle classes who were the first to take the advantage of the educational facilities offered by the Universities established under the Act of 1854. That educational system modeled on the old University of London, a mere examining body, has now been condemned as soulless and as having produced merely sensitized specimens of humanity. The products of that system were types that had cut themselves adrift from all their old moorings of "Dharma and Ahimsa" and had not assimilated the British ideals of Justice and Fairplay. They were with a few honourable exceptions, merely free-lances abroad armed with a smattering of Western knowledge in a vast population of varying degrees of culture from the fifth century to the fifteenth and mostly took to the predatory professions and fished in troubled waters of their own creation. Those of them that got into the subordinate branches of the administrative machine, from the highest Deputy Collector or Commission and Subordinate Judge to the lowest Urban Police Constable or Village Headman carried on the merry game of tyranny and oppression of the common people, for both they and people knew full well that behind the meanest policeman stood all the absolutism of the Indian Government backed by the full might of the British Empire. The people who were too poor and spiritless to attempt to bring home to the erring officials his heinous acts committed under the cloak of authority and the British agency were too few in number and the individual officer had too great an area under his control to maintain any effective supervision over his entire jurisdiction.

All this fell with the greater intensity on those classes that are classified as the "Depressed" and riveted their social disabilities on them, for the Indian official was almost entirely drawn from the higher castes with their notions of inherent superiority.

II. THE OPPRESSION

According to the latest Census Report, the total population of the Madras Presidency is 42,794,155. Out of this, the Depressed Classes alone number about 7,503,475 slightly more than a sixth of the total population of the Presidency. The term "Depressed Classes" should not be confused with the term "Backward Classes". Backward Classes are those communities that are really high up in the social, economic and religious scale.

On the other hand, communities that are called "Untouchable Classes" and are educationally, economically and socially backward come under the term "Depressed Classes". These people have been kept down by the Caste Hindus, through the ages, by systematic tyranny and social oppression. The present submerged condition of these people is due to the organized age-long oppression of the so-called superior classes. Sometimes it is argued that the existence of such a class is not peculiar to India. But caste in the form and under the circumstances in which it exists in India does not exist anywhere else. It should be remembered that the Submerged Tenth of other countries owe their condition chiefly to economic causes, but in this Presidency the Submerged Sixth or the Adi-Dravidas and Adi-Andhras owe their miserable condition to social and religious rules, operating against them through the centuries. The peculiarity in the case of India does not consist in the existence of such a submerged class, but rather in the means employed to keep that class permanently under the blockade set up by the usurpers of power and influence. How these are regarded as Untouchables or rather Unapproachable – to approach whom is pollution – is a matter in which Social Workers should take a deep and abiding interest. You may touch your horse, you may pat your dog, you may stroke your cat, but you may not touch an Adi-Dravida or an Adi-Andhra. You may breed cows and dogs in your houses, you may drink the urine of cows and swallow cow-dung to expiate your sins, but you shall not even approach an Adi-Dravida. The following is found in Sonnerat's *Voyage to the East Indies*:

> When an Indian of any other caste permits a Pariah to speak to him, this unfortunate being is obliged to hold his hand before his mouth, lest the (Caste) Indian may be contaminated with his breath; and if he has met on the high way, he must turn on one side to let the other pass. If any Indian whatever even a Choutrie by accident touches a Pariah, he is obliged to purify himself in a bath.

This account is one hundred and fifty years old.

They are denied access to public wells, tanks and roads. They cannot enter temples. They cannot obtain admission even into certain state-aided Schools and Colleges. They cannot even get into certain Post Offices either to post letters or to get a stamp. They are not allowed into choultries; although these houses of charity are solely intended for giving relief to the poor, the needy and the suffering, yet, these classes are not allowed their benefit. They are denied even the rights permitted to dogs, cats, pigs, asses and buffaloes. Man's inhumanity to man makes countless thousands mourn. How long is such a state of things to continue?

No greater wrong can be done to a community endowed with human feelings and human capacities than to place it in such circumstances as to force it or lead it to believe that its members are eternally and for all time to come doomed to a life of ignorance, servitude and misery and that any sort of ambition in them for betterment or improvement is sin. These voiceless millions are ground every day into the dust, and treated with contempt, a barbarity that is not accorded even to the vilest of animals. Hungry, naked, dispirited, living in wretched hovels, cringing in their attitude through long oppression, driven often by hunger to eat anything they get, abandoned religiously, morally, mentally and physically, they remain utterly miserable and helpless. Is this not a great nation iniquity?

The social condition of the Outcastes of India is tragic. The very manhood has been altogether crushed out of them, as the result of long centuries of oppression. High-handed lawless oppression overtakes the outcastes in a thousand forms as soon as ever he attempts to assert the freedom of his manhood or the elementary rights of a citizen, and he is thrust back into his old place, worse off and not better for the effort he has made. Being illiterate and socially downtrodden, his Caste Hindu neighbours prey upon him without compunction.

Now the Depressed Classes feel their smallness. They feel keenly that they have been deprived of their ancient heritage. They feel that it is the perverted judgment, purblind sectarianism, caste pride and caste arrogance in the so-called Caste Hindus, that is the cause of their starvation, ignorance and oppression. They also feel that they are the children of the soil and citizens possessing equal rights and privileges with their Caste-proud Hindu brethren.

When they compare their present condition with that under Indian Rulers, prior to the advent of the British, the dominant feeling is one of gratitude and thankfulness. With the advent of the British, their emancipation commenced. But the emancipation is by no means complete; it has just commenced. We hear people speak of the foreigner with a certain amount of dislike. But after all, is it not to the foreigner that these people owe what little of education, material prosperity and personal liberty they possesses, and not to their selfish countryman, the Caste-proud Hindu, who calling himself their kith and kin, exploited their labour for the fulfilment of his selfish ambition and greed, giving them a pittance. Moreover the Adi-Dravida field labourer in many districts, is so tied up by debt to his master, who is a Caste Hindu and who takes care that the debt shall not be redeemed, that he is practically in the position of a serf and the system of man-mortgage by which the labourer binds himself and frequently his heirs to service till the debt is redeemed is well-known.

In most districts if a member of the Depressed Classes aspires to acquire a piece of Government waste land, the jealousy of Caste landholders is aroused. Then what happens? He has to reckon from the very start with a strong and deep seated conspiracy of the hereditary landholders and "there is often no meanness, no lying dishonesty, no low creeping craftiness to which that conspiracy will not descent to deceive and destroy its victim".

Being almost invariably illiterate and socially down-trodden, it is a common thing for the village Munsiff (a public officer) to collect excessive taxes from these people, who are cultivators, to withhold their receipts and charge them twice or thrice, denying the first payment and staying the reaping of their crops, or even putting their lands to auction, if the unjust demand is not met. Sometimes they are made to pay wet rates for dry cultivation.

It will no doubt interest the readers to know how applications for assignment of Government *Darkhast* lands from the members of Depressed Classes are at present disposed of. Invariably these applications are put down on the irrelevant and frivolous grounds of tank-bed-land, water-storage, village common, etc. These are mere pretexts for reserving these lands for well-to-do Caste Hindus. In the disposal of these applications, the remarks of the village Karnam and the village Munsiff (petty Government village officials) go a great way almost to decide their fate. These Government village officials are in almost all cases Caste Hindus, and they have no sympathy whatsoever towards these people. Another objection very commonly urged against the grant of such lands is that they are required for grazing purposes, for the grazing of the cattle of the Mirasdars and other land owners who are all Caste Hindus. These wealthy Caste Hindus have vast areas of lands of their own. Instead of setting apart a portion of their own lands for the gazing of their own cattle they want Government to provide free grazing ground for their cattle, and think that the members of the Depressed Classes are lower in the scale of creation than their cattle. This is the very reason why the application for lands is being treated in this summary and contemptuous fashion. It will be strange to hear that in certain cases these applications have been rejected simply because the applicant did not possess a pair of bullocks and a plough of his own. This is like putting the cart before the horse. How on earth could one expect a poor Depressed Class man who has not even an inch of land of his own to possess a pair of bullocks and a plough. If by chance a piece of land is assigned to the applicant, he is asked to pay for the trees growing on it. When a poor farmer of the Depressed Classes starts life practically, it is hard to expect him to have money with him to pay for these trees.

Another feature in the assignments made to these people is the introduction of caste distinctions even in classifying waste lands. In this caste-ridden country even lands are divided into High Caste Lands and Low Caste Lands, the high caste lands being better lands reserved for so-called high caste people and the low caste lands being inferior lands reserved for so-called low caste people; for instance, when a member of the Depressed Classes applies for an elevated place for house site he is offered site on a low marshy ground and when he applies for a piece of cultivable waste land, he is offered a piece of land – barren, rocky-waste or saline in nature.

The following extracts from the Rev. T.B. Pandian's brochure *The Slaves of the Soil in Southern India* will show what oppression really means with the Adi-Dravida.

A poor pariah started from his native town in the Madras Presidency to one of the British Colonies in quest of a fortune. He landed safe on colonial soil and was soon able to eke out an existence as a coolly labourer on the wharfs. His daily hire amounted to on the whole about 20 cents – a little over six annas – and this was ample to keep body and soul alive; but economy-stern economy-he soon pulled up in his exchequer. After the lapse of five years he one day said to himself: – "I will now sail home to India, and see what I can do there." Yes, the very idea of home, sweet home, caused his heart to palpitate; for it seems difficult to a man to keep away from those near and dear to him. There was joy, when he arrived at the doorstep of his cozy little rustic mansion. The wife and the little ones welcomed him with shouts, and with words of love, and everything within that rustic home was full of life. The poor man for some days enjoyed the quietness of home life, and in course of time set himself up in a petty trade. This alarmed the caste people of the village and it was an "eyesore" to the "swellish snobs", when they looked on the freaks of Dame Fortune. To find Raman, the swine feeder, a petty tradesman, was too much for the mirasdars (landlords) to behold. In fact, it gave swine-feeder, an ascendancy, which was detestable, for the very fact that he was a Pariah. So oppression was the order of the day. They soon resolved to wreck Raman's independence, "petty independence", and a criminal case was most dexterously weaved to enmesh the man who had been the architect of his own fortunes. Raman was placed before a tribunal for theft, convicted and lastly thrown into a felon's cell. Now, all was darkness within that rustic dwelling. Smiles turned into tears, and after the lapse of a few months, poverty once more spread her hideous black pall over the poor household. It was all starvation, sheer starvation, and then sickness. One by one, the little ones – sweet flowers, drooped down to die as the rays of poverty were too sharp for them and they fell to mother earth never to rise, never to see the face of their father after his release. What about the wife? Sorrow and starvation were also her portion and she also succumbed as a pauper. The husband after his release traces his steps to the old homestead, but vacant is the old home, and the only portion left to him is the profession of a mendicant; but keen sorrow and privation soon end his days also. Such was Raman's lot.

I have to tell you again in my own homely style another incident, where a poor labourer was deprived of his cow, the sole means of support of himself and his wife. This labourer was an exceedingly poor man of the lowest caste and one who had a large family. His sons, young men, went in search of labourer to distant parts, leaving their parents to live the best way they could. The cow was therefore their only sustenance, but the headman of the village (a caste Hindu) was rather fascinated with the beast and ordered some men under him to fetch the animal. The animal was taken by force; and the husband and wife both pleaded to the effect that the cow was their only support in life, and if it was taken away from them, they would necessarily suffer from poverty. But to appease them the headman drove the couple away, promising to give them the sum of 8 annas a month for their up-keep. Such instances as these occur almost every day in country places, and it is oppression unpardonable, to rob the poor who cannot defend themselves. Is it not cruel to trade on the poor earth-worm and to treat it as we would treat the Cobra? Cruelty, in whatever phase we may view it, should be sternly put down, and to those who devastate poor homes, no punishment administered by the law can be too severe.

Here is another instance, where the Karnam (village accountant) of a village utilizes the poor Pariah to his benefit. The Karnam has by some mysterious way become a land holder, but he is still not satisfied. He wishes to add to his possession and in some respects to cope with petty Zemindars, and thus finding a waste piece of land near to an extensive cultivated plot of his own, he holds a private "Panchayat" Council among half a dozen of his own Pariah slaves, and strives his utmost to make some of them believe that waste lands can be monopolized without the consent of Government, and if the tax be regularly paid, no suspicions of any nature would arise. Upon this the Pariah soon toils at the sweat of his brow, first he clears the land of all its weeds, and the next thing is he borrows a country plough and ploughs for a few annas, and turns over the hard crusted soil. Pic-cottahs (water lifts) are next built on a loan from the Karnam himself, and flocks of sheep may be seen here and there scattered to manure the soil. All this means money, and the poor Pariah borrows it, so that at the end he may recover four-fold in the produce of the land. Well, after the soil is prepared to receive the seed, the poor and deluded Pariah husbandman is induced to apply for Government "Pattah", as this secures to the land owner a right to his possession, and thus keeps him safe and well-protected from the interference of other "land-grabbers". But he finds that no sooner is an application made for a "Pattah" than the Karnam opposes the application, or in other words, turns out to be the most inveterate foe of the man whom he pretended to protect. The Karnam in his evidence informs the authorities concerned that the Pariah occupied the land of his own sweet will and without his permission. The decision then is, that the land should be made over to the Karnam, since the "Pattah" was *sub rosa* made in his name. This is what the Karnam wished to obtain; that is, waste land, well cleared of its refuse by the brow-writhing labours of the poor Pariah, who under dupery toiled hard to benefit himself, but in the long run was ousted and was destined not to enjoy the fruit of his labours. Such is the injustice and the law sanctions it.

Here is another similar instance, where rude oppression has its iron sway, but here we find the Pariah husbandman a little fortunate. He has cultivated land without Government permission and interference for over ten years and holds Revenue receipts to show that he has been a regular taxpayer, but he thinks it far safer to make a move and asks the Karnam to put in an application for a "Pattah". But the Karnam is a "wide awake", and informs his salve to toil on for another couple of years. After the lapse of another six years, the Pariah put in a second application direct to the authorities for "Pattah" and this time he is opposed by a mirasdar, in whose name the "Pattah" was originally made without the knowledge of the Pariah. While the Pariah is thus in the vortex of litigation a drove of cattle is wantonly driven into the 'Cumboo' fields of the Pariah, and the whole field is laid bare in a few hours. Whereupon, the Pariah launches another case in court, and receives a fair compensation for damages done, but the "Pattah" made on the mirasdar's name was produced, and the Pariah after so many weary years of honest toil is caste upon the open world, with no means whatever to defend himself. This is the iron-hand of oppression.

Swami Sahajanandam, an Adi-Dravida Saint, a highly cultured Sadhu, applied for a piece of Government waste land for his Nandanar Free School in Chidambaram. His application for the grant of this land was sent to the subordinate Government Revenue Officials. These caste-ridden officials did not recommend the assignment. Whereupon, the application of Swami Sahajanandam was rejected. The Swami did not stop there. He went up to the District Collector who is an Officer of the Indian Civil Service, and requested him to personally inspect the site, before finally rejecting his application. The District Collector was a sympathetic officer, he went up to the spot, inspected the site and assigned it to our Swami and wrote the following proceedings, which will clearly show how the British Collectors are thwarted in their attempts to benefit the Depressed Classes by their Caste Hindi subordinates:

D. Dis. No. 2395-20-A-4.
Proceedings of the Collector of South Arcot dated 3-9-1920.
R.F.B.L. Guppy Esq., I.C.S.
Read: Correspondence ending with report No. 112-S.C. of 1920, dated the 2nd August 1920 of the Revenue Divisional Officer, Chidambaram.

ORDER.

Assignment – land – Chidambaram Taluk – Kallipadi village – Sahajanandam – Manager – Nandanar School – Chidambaram.

* * * *

I therefore resolved to inspect the land and did so. All reports in the file are misleading. More correct reports are found in another file not shown to me before inspection. The northern portion is the highest and is no use for storing water. The middle portion is low, and is required for draining off surplus water of Kunamangalam tank.

* * * *

The mirasdar Mr. V. Velayudam Pillai is the chief opponent of the alienation. Knowing that I inspected the land he gave up the contention that the Northern portion is required for water spread and says that it is required for village site. The contentions of persons who offer contradictory arguments of this kind are worth nothing.

(Sd.). F.B.L. Guppy,
Ag. Collector.

III. CHRISTIANS AND CHRISTIANITY

Sometimes the European Christian Missionary who is their Good Samaritan is blamed for giving them religious instruction, or rather these people are looked down upon for receiving religious instruction at his hands. But what did the so-called patriotic Caste Hindu do for these, his fellow countrymen, by way of moral and religious instruction? The Christian Missionary opens his doors wide to all and especially to the outcaste and down-trodden, following his Masters saying "Come unto me all ye that labour, and are heavy laden, and I will give you rest" and fulfilling His teaching "He that is least among you the same shall be great." Is it not a fact that some among the Depressed Classes, being unable to endure the treatment at the hands of the so-called higher castes, are becoming Christians? Is it not a fact the Caste Hindus show greater respect and give better treatment to those that have become Christians than to those that remain within Hindu fold? When Raman or Ramaswamy becomes Mr. Ramsay, he is respected by the Caste Hindus. Thousands and thousands of Depressed Classes are becoming converts to the Christian faith. This is due to the inhuman treatment of the Caste proud Hindu.

IV. PAST AND PRESENT

Of the former greatness of the Adi-Dravidas, it is not for me to speak. But it may be stated that they cherish the memory of their former greatness and delight in asserting that they were the original inhabitants of the soil.

The Adi-Dravidas represent the earliest civilization of South India. They were once a very great and powerful community that played a conspicuous part on the historical stage of India, and had developed a complete civilization of their own, with their democratic form of Government, their priests, their astronomers and astrologers, their fine arts and a religion and philosophy of their own. Long before the Aryans came down to South India, the Adi-Dravidas had their own political and social institutions: upon them they (the Aryans) sought to impose their civilization. Even now when a Foreign Missionary comes into our midst and begins to expound the Gospel, those that are educated, independent and in good circumstances do not go near him, but resist his attempts and call him "Milecha". On the other hand those who are in adverse circumstances and who are not well versed in the Hindu religion, approach him, listen to his teaching and become his disciples. So also, when the Aryan missionaries came to South India some Adi-Dravidas followed them and listened to their mantras, tantras and religion, and some others resisted their attempts. The Adi-Dravidas of to-day are the descendants of those who strongly and successfully resisted the attempts of the Aryans. As missionaries the Aryans received into their fold anybody who agreed to accept their spiritual guidance and leadership and acknowledged their superiority. Having succumbed to the teaching of the Aryans and not resisted them in their attempts, the Dravidas of to-day were taken into their fold and were converted into Caste Hindus, and for having resisted and stood aloof from their system, the Adi-Dravidas of to-day, left out to sink in the social scale, as the Aryans became powerful. By their cunning the Aryans gradually became the lords of the soil and the Adi-Dravidas were punished with social degradation and were made serfs and slaves. When the Aryan immigrants came into India, there was a paucity of women in their clan, probably there were none. So the immigrants were forced to take wives from the indigenous people and miscegenation discontinued as soon as each mixed tribes had a sufficient number of women to provide itself with wives. Then the Adi-Dravidas were the Vellalas (weavers and tillers of the soil) in times of peace and Kshatriyas (armed warriors) in times of war. F.A. Steel in *India Through Ages*, says, "A time before this, when the Aryans came to India, they found a people in India civilized enough to have towns and disciplined troops, to have weapons and banners, women whose ornaments were of gold, poisoned arrows whose heads were of some metal that was probably iron." These were the Adi-Dravidas, a tawny race as compared with the white-skinned Aryans. They did not perform sacrifices, their rites were different from those of the Aryans. The Aryans called the, "The wealthy barbarians", "the neglectors of sacrifices" who "decorated with gold and jewels", and "dwellers in iron cities". The Aryan invaders got from the Adi-Dravidas, servile work, debarred them from meddling with matter religious and denied them the privilege of carrying arms. It was the centuries of serfdom that made them depressed, but the spirit is still dormant in them.

The Adi-Dravidas were the ancient sons of the soil. They were so highly cultured that their advanced civilization had the vitality to spread as far as Ancient Babylon. They were also a great commercial people, sending their ships all over the known world and carrying on a great commerce. Their refusal to submit to the influence of the Aryan immigrants from the North gave the death-blow to their advanced civilization. There was no caste system among the Ancient Dravidians. But when the Aryans first came, a system of caste existed among them. There were already groups within the Aryans, – Brahmins, Kshatriyas and Vaisyas. To this they added the fourth section and admitted into it all the Adi-Dravidas, the Dravidas of to-day, who tamely submitted to their influence. This fourth section was given the name of "Sudras". Those Adi-Dravidas who strongly resisted their influence and refused to submit to their teaching were left out and condemned as outcaste. They, the Aryans, adopted towards these people an attitude similar to that usually assumed by the white races towards the coloured races in tropical colonies.

For the crime of having stood aloof from the system of the Aryan foreigners these Adi-Dravidas were not only punished with social degradation, but were also stigmatized as untouchables and unapproachables. It is this despicable caste system that imposed various social and economic disabilities upon them. But the Caste Hindus could not get on without their assistance, for it was they that supplied the labour and the Caste Hindus enjoyed the fruits thereof, giving them a mere pittance in return.

A historical survey of the caste system will not be out of place here. The four castes gradually developed a number of sub-castes. During the time of Sandracottes, the Greek Ambassador Magasthenes noticed the existence of only seven Hindu castes: 1. Philosophers, 2. Husbandmen, 3. Shepherds and Hunters, 4. Labourers or those who trade or vend wares, 5. Fighting men, 6. Inspectors charged with the supervision of all that goes on, 7. Councillors and Assessors of the King. There was no slavery then. Now instead of the original four or the latter seven, we have about 2,400 Main Castes and Tribes and about fifty Races or nationalities in South India. From the cradle to the grave the monstrous "Caste", encourages repulsion between man and man, sways every movement of the Hindu as it exists in India to-day, brings on physical degeneracy and national poverty, crushes individual liberty, stunts the growth of nationality, sows disunion and discord, degrades the race of man to the low level of brutes, hardens the heart of one against the sufferings of another and fills a few with pride and arrogance which makes them imperious in their demeanour towards their fellowmen.

The outcaste people were called Pariahs, Pallas, Valluvas in the Tamil Districts, Malas and Madigas in the Telugu Districts of the East Coast, and Pulayas and Cherumas and Holeyas in the Districts of the West Coast. Pariah was a common name used to indicate all these untouchable classes. For the first time the word "Pariah" occurs in a poem of Mangudi Kilar, a poet of the second century A.D. This term Pariah is not found either in any earlier Tamil Literature or in any ancient inscription. The term "Pariah" is derived from *Para* or *Parai,* a drum. The inference is drawn that they were the drummers and have obtained their name from the instrument, the Parai or drum, that they were supposed to use. The word Parai or Para, is not found in any other Dravidian language in the sense of drum, but Tamil and Malayalam. If the Pariahs were really the drummers, they would be called by the same name wherever they were found in India. But these people were called and are called Holeyas in Kannada and Malavadu in the Telugu country. Now the so-called Pariahs do not beat drums. Those that beat drums and play the band during festivals, marriages, etc., are called Ambattans and they belong to the Barber Caste, a sub section of the Sudras. The Pariahs were in actual possession of the fields which were subsequently taken from them and made over to the Aryans. Thus the lord of the soil became the serf attached to the soil.

The outcastes in the Telugu country are called Mallas. The Mallas are repeatedly mentioned in the *Mahabharata* and the various Puranas as a nation. The outcastes in Northern India are called Mars or Mhars. The Mallas are the same as Maras, who are known as Mars or Mhars, transformed into Mahar. Mallabhumi and Mallarashtra which refer to the Northern parts of India, occur in *Ramayana* and *Mahabharata*. Mallarashtra and Maharashtra are identical in meaning. Although the term Mallarashtra dropped into oblivion, yet these two names indicate the connection of Mallas and Mahars with the land, Mallarashtra the country of the Mallas and Maharashtra the country of the Mahars. From this also it is very clear that these people were once the Lords of the Soil.

The word Pariah may as well be a corruption of the word Paharias, a race of mountaineers. When the Aryans came to the country, these people were probably then living in mountains and hills, and attacked the Aryans with all the ardour of the mountaineers in defence of their independence and liberty. Again the word Pariah split into *Par* plus *Iyan* in Tamil; *Par* meaning land and *Iyan* meaning lord, may mean the owners of the land and the lord of the soil (India). So the Pariahs were then probably the rulers of the land, cultivators and weavers in times of peace and warriors in times of war. Thus you come across the two divisions Uzavu (ploughing) and Nesavu (weaving).

Going further still into their subdivision we see such a section as Valluvas (priests and state heralds who proclaimed the news by beat of drum from on the back of caparisoned elephants). The words Kottai (fort), Kottaram (granary where in ancient days the land tax levied in kind was stored), Sambu (God Siva), Virabhahu (a General of Siva), Panikan (teacher), Kolyan and Solyan (weavers), and Ambu (arrow) in their language point to the fact that these people were once a great nation, occupying a high position, having priests, heralds, tax gatherers, religious devotees, and solicitors and owning forts. The Adi-Dravidas were then a flourishing nation with a language, religion and art, occupations and a political status of their own.

They had their kings even as late as the 2nd or 3rd century A.D. These kings were reigning at Vellore, Ambur and other places, with all the pomp of Eastern Rulers. In Vincent A. Smith's *Early History of India*, it is stated that "the Chandeis, like several other dynasties first come into notice early in the ninth century, when Nannuka Chandel, about A.D. 831, overthrew a Parihar (Adi-Dravida) chieftain (King), and became lord of the southern parts of Jejakabhukti". He further describes Jejakabhukti as the province between the Jumna and Narmada, now known as Bundelkhand.

The Caste Hindus have called them for a long time Pariahs. Whatever be the derivation of the name, this word uttered by a Caste Hindu tongue, conveys everything that is mean and despicable today and means the opposite of all that is holy and respectable. Awakened to a sense of self-respect they protested against this opprobrious name and agitated for a better one. Some of the Caste Hindus suggested the name of Panchama meaning one belonging to the fifth class. In their eagerness to get rid of the name of Pariah, they accepted the name Panchama. But as their sense of self-respect grew, they came to realize the sinister implications of the name Panchama. When there are only four Hindu Castes to call them Panchamas or men of the fifth class or caste, is really to call them "outcastes".

So they sought for a name which would indicate that they were the first inhabitants of Southern India and had nothing to do with that most inhuman of human institutions, Caste. They wanted a name which would point to their racial and territorial origin. Disliking the name Eurasian, the Eurasian community took to themselves the name "Anglo-Indian". The non-Brahmin caste Hindus, disliking the name Sudra took to themselves the name Dravidian.

When the question of a name for the community was considered some thirty-two years ago, it was decided that they should be called Adi-Dravidas to distinguish them from "Sudras", who had now taken the name Dravidians or Dravidas.

Adi means original, pure and unalloyed as in "Adi Saivas, Adi Sankaracharìar, Adi Lakshmi, Adi Bagavan, Adi Sivan, Adi-Narayan, Adi-Kesavan, Adimulam" etc.

There are at present day some relics of their ancient rights and privileges which show beyond doubt the former greatness of these people, which are still to be found in the village organizations. Their decision in disputes concerning ownership of land is regarded as final. In an inscription of the eleventh century A.D., we find recorded the decision of one Vesali Parian and his Councillors to be a final one in a civil case concerning the ownership of a piece of land belonging to a temple in the village of Mudepakavar. Even in the North it is so, for the evidence of the Mhar is required in every dispute. "Should two cultivators quarrel respecting the boundaries of their fields" says Mr. R.N. Goddine, "the Mhars' evidence ought to decide it, and should a similar quarrel happen between two villages, the Mhars are always the chief actors in it and to their decision alone it is sometimes referred". Mr. W.F. Sinclair calls the Mahar as the guardian of boundaries and of public peace and health.

The lower offices in villages are held by the Adi-Dravidas and wherever there is any dispute about the boundaries of land, the Adi-Dravida walks over the true boundaries with a pot of water on his head. They are wonderful experts in the matter and unerringly point out where boundaries should run, even when the demarcation stones have been removed. This also shows that the Adi-Dravidas' connection with the land is of longer standing than that of any other caste. Moreover the admitted proprietary right which they have in site, known as *Cheri-natham*, on which their huts stand is a confirmation of this. It is not so well known that the Brahmin who considers himself polluted by the touch, the presence or shadow of an Adi-Dravida, will not be allowed to enter the *Cheri-natham*. Should a Brahmin venture into a *cheri*, water with which cow-dung has been mixed, is thrown on his head and he is driven out. Some Brahmins consider a forsaken *cheri*, an auspicious site for an *Agraharam*. It is also stated by Captain J.S.F. Mackenzie in the *Ind. Ant. II*, 1873, that "Brahmins in Mysore consider that great lunch will await them if they can manage to pass through the Holeya quarters of a village unmolested and that should a Brahman attempt to enter their quarters, they turn out in a body and slipper him."

The special privileges that the Adi-Dravidas enjoy even to this day, point to their former greatness. At the annual festival of the tutelary Goddess of George Town in the premier city of Madras, the *thali* or marriage badge is tied round the neck of the Goddess by an Adi-Dravida in the name of the entire community. The Adi-Dravida in question is clothed gorgeously and fed in the temple as the accepted bridegroom of the Goddess as long as the festival lasts. Drums are beaten in his honour when the idol of the Goddess Egathammal is carried round the city and a copper coin is placed in his hand and another copper coin on the hand of the Goddess by the officiating priest when the *Kappu* ceremony is performed. The Adi-Dravida officiates as priest at the Bull Games at Dindigul. During the great Hindu annual festivals at Conjeeveram, one of the sacred cities of

India, and at Srivilliputtur, Kumbakonam, Tiruvottiyur and other holy places, Adi-Dravidas are permitted to pull the ropes of the huge cars containing the idols. Rev. A. Andrews rightly remarks "A special license is given to the Pariahs on such great religious festivals and this shows how accommodative Hindus can be when it suits their purpose." Yes, they can be very accommodative when it suits them. During the festival of Siva at Tiruvalore in the Tanjore District, the Adi-Dravida headman is specially honoured by being placed on the temple elephant along with the God and made to carry the *chowry* in his hand to fan the idol.

Adi-Dravidas according to the *Indian Antiquary*, vol. III, p. 191, are accorded special privileges even in famous Krishna Temple in Melukote in the Mysore State. Melukote is the chief seat of the Sri Vaishnavite Brahmins and the residence of the Sri Vaishnavite high priest. It is the place where Ramanuja the famous Vaishnavite Reformer lived for fourteen years in the 12th century and is therefore regarded as a very holy place by Ramanuja's followers. It is recorded that a certain Adi-Dravida pointed out to him a certain image of which he had been dreaming and for this act he conferred on the Adi-Dravida community the privilege of entering the temple for three days in the year for all time to come. This Andrews points out, is a very extraordinary privilege when we consider how rigid and strict the Vaishnavite Brahmins are with regard to ceremonial purity in things pertaining to worship and social intercourse. They also enjoy a similar privilege at Sriperumbudur in the Chingleput District, for having sheltered an image of Vishnu during the Mussalman raid.

There is no doubt that the Adi-Dravida community was once a very important community and that it had a glorious past. It had its own Government and its own courts. Each village elected five men and these formed the Panchayat, the Council of the Elders. A Panchayat is a court presided over by five men; it was something like the *Witanagemot*. Out of these five men one was elected as the headman and he was called the Natamaikaran. Even to-day we see the remnant of this institution in the villages. All disputes of the village so far as they are arbitrable were tried by the Panchayat, an admirable instrument of decision. The Valluvans, a section of the Adi-Dravidas, were priests to the Pallava Kings, before the introduction of the Brahmins, and even for sometime after it. The late Sir Harold Stewart in the Census Report for 1891 quotes an unpublished *Vatteluttu* of the 9th century in which the following sentence occurs:

Ithani Uvachan srivalluvampuvanavan, niyamam aaralittu uvachchappani seibavan,

which means, Sri Valluvan Puvanavam, the Uvachan (or temple minister) will employ six men daily and do the temple service. The inference is that the Valluvan a member of the Adi-Dravida community was a man of recognized priestly rank and of great influence. Not only this, the Valluvans were the astrologers and astronomers and physicians and surgeons. Even to-day there are Valluvans, who are expert astrologers and capable physicians practising the Ayurvedic and Siddah system of medicine.

There is however, evidence to show that these people were intimately connected with the important temples. Mr. Gustav Oppert in his work *On the Original Inhabitants of Bharatavarsha or India*, says "Valli is a well-known female name common among the Pariahs and Pallars." Subramanya, the son of Siva, is credited with having chosen a South Indian girl called Valli as his wife. She was an Adi-Dravida. Parvati, the wife of Siva is even worshipped as an Adi-Dravida woman in her disguise as Matangi. Among the twelve *Alwars* of Vaishnavaism, the famous Tirupan Alwar was an Adi-Dravida. Among the sixty-three *Nainars* of Saivitism, the well-known Nanda was an Adi-Dravida. In the sacred work *Manushya Panchakam* of Jagat Guru Sree Sankaracharya, the founder of the four *Sankara Pedams*, the seats of learning, it is stated that this Great Jagatguru publicly accepts one Visvanathan as his guru and received initiation from him. This Visvanathan is an Adi-Dravida and is held in high esteem by his followers who are Smartha Brahmins. In *Bakthavijayam* – Lives of Vaishnavite Bhaktas or Devotees of North India – Chokka melar, the great bhakta who was accepted as a guru by the learned Brahmins of Pandaripur, was an Adi-Dravida. So also Nambaduwan and Maraneri Nambi whose lives are recorded in that sacred standard work *Guruparamparai* – Lives of Vaishnavite Saints and Devotees of South India. Among the *Sanga Pulavars*, the most ancient Tamil Academy of Poets, the world-famed author of the immortal *Thirukkural*, Thiruvalluvar, one of the greatest didactic poets in the world, was an Adi-Dravida. Avvai, the popular poetess was an Adi-Dravida. Arundhathi, the wife of Maharishi Vasishta belonged to the Depressed Classes. The origin of the famous Jagannath Temple at Puri, is also closely connected with the outcastes.

In this connection a few words about the Adi-Dravida luminaries referred to above will not be out of place. In the galaxy of the eminent poets and scholars of the period the holy Thiruvalluvar stood first and foremost. His famous work *Thirukkural* is a code of morals expressed in poetical aphorisms. Even after a lapse of more than 1800 years it has lost none of its original admiration and popularity among the Tamil people and it is still considered as a standard authoritative work in Tamil literature. This masterpiece is prescribed as a textbook for the B.A. and M.A. Degree examinations of the University of Madras.

Thiruppan Alwar is one of the most prominent among the twelve Alwars. The famous work of Thiruppan Alwar, *Amaran Adhiparan* in Tamil verse, is chanted in all Vaishnavite temples side by side with the Sanskrit hymns or Upanishads. It is accepted by all, Brahmins included, that this Adi-Dravida saint has become one with God Sree Ranganatha, at Sreerangam in the Trichinopoly District. Even to-day the image of Thiruppan Alwar is seen in all the Vaishnavite temples of South India and is universally worshipped.

Nanda was a Saivite saint. He was a ryot under a Smartha landholder. This Nanda was eager to go to Chidambaram to worship the God Nataraja. But the Brahman was an obstacle to this and would not allow him to do this. Nanda persisted. His master with a view to stop him from going to Chidambaram to worship Sree Nataraja imposed on him several impossible tasks and wanted him first to finish them and then go. Being a bhakta, God Siva himself did all the work for him without his knowledge in a single night. His master struck with the devotion of Nanda, immediately prostrated himself before him, adored him and permitted him to go to Chidambaram. Nanda went there and became one with Siva. His image is found in all the Siva temples and is worshipped by the devotees.

The famous Tamil poetess is Avvai. Her poems are read by every beginner in Tamil. Her two books of aphorisms, *Athichudi* and *Konraiventhan*, were considered by the learned Reverend Beschi as 'worthy of Seneca himself'.

Arundhathi is the wife of Vasishta, the Brahma Rishi, one of the *Saptha Rishies* and a *Vathaparangadha*. She is famous for her chastity and that is why she is worshipped by the bridegroom and the bride of all Hindu communities on marriage occasions. When Arjuna's son Abhimanyu was hit by an arrow and was at the point of death, his mother Subhadra invoked the blessing of Arundhathi and her son recovered. This shows the high veneration with which she was held by women of all classes. She is now said to exist in the form of a star.

Again according to *Nanavethi* the Adi-Dravidas have eighteen titles and possess also the same insignia.

Among these insignia are mentioned the following: White, earth-circle umbrellas; lion, swan, green and white, monkey (Hanuman), cuckoo, plough-handle, wheel and lion faced flags; a trumpet; closely carried torches (aruku) and day torches; victorious bells, two white chowries, white elephant; white horse; ivory palanquins; cuscus fan, flute; white long robe, two poles with cloth stretched across the street (makaratorna), golden pot, etc.

Samban is also a title borne by some Adi-Dravidas in the Tamil country. The word Samban is a corruption of the word Jambavan, who though described in *Ramayana* as a bear and having a following of his own species, is said to be the first borne of the God Brahma, the creator. It is also found in *Ramayana* that Jambavan, the Adi-Dravida, was the custodian of all ancient learning and was a mighty warrior though called a bear in *Ramayana* by the Aryan poet in his conceit. Jambavathi, a daughter of Jambavan, was married to King Krishna. God Sree Krishna, the black (*'karian', 'kariyameni', 'karmeni'* as said by Nam Alwar, Peri Alwar and Sree Andal) is an Adi-Dravida and not an Aryan. Then again, Jambavan was a faithful devotee and the commander of the army of Sreeman Narayana. And it was Jambavan that proclaimed to the world, by means of tom tom, the victory of Tiruvickarama, God Narayana, who redeemed the words from the cruel tyrant, Mahabali. Jambavan was also holding the office of a Chief Judge. As it is the custom even now for the crier, to announce the arrival of a judge in the public court, the crier during the days of Jambavan used to announce the arrival of Judge Jambavan by crying out *Mahadigai* which means, the Great is coming. This term *Mahadigai* is now converted into Madiga and signifies a section of the Depressed Classes.

Here, it will be interesting to know something about how the Adi-Dravidas, during those days prior to the advent of the Aryans, managed their country. The head of the administration was a monarch, a hereditary monarch. His power was restricted by five councils known as the Five Great Assemblies and consisting of representatives of the people, priests, physicians, astrologers and astronomers and ministers. The Assembly of the people protected the rights and privileges of the people. The Assembly of the Priests safeguarded the religious ceremonies. The Assembly of the Physicians looked after all matters affecting the health of the king and his subjects and attended to the sanitation of the country. The Assembly of the Astrologers and Astronomers fixed auspicious times for public functions and ceremonies and predicted important events. The Assembly of the Ministers looked after the finance and the administration of justice and also with a keen foresight prevented all that was evil and promoted all that was good for their king and for the people at large. This system of Government was in vogue even in the kingdoms of Pandya, Chola and Chera although they were quite independent of one another.

The chief officers of the State were the High priest, the chief astrologer, the Ministers and the Commanders of the army. There were Judges and Magistrates also who carefully weighed the evidence and interpreted the law without fear or favour. All appeals were finally disposed of by the King. Justice was administered free of charge to the suitors and the punishments were very severe, hence crimes were very rare.

The sources of revenue were chiefly customs, tolls and land-tax.

The King was not only the head of the administration but also the head of the society. He freely mixed with the people and took the lead in every festivity in his capital, above all, he shared the joys and sorrows of the people. When the King came out in public or on state occasions, he was carried in a golden palanquin decorated with tassels of pearls and was clothed in fine white muslin embroidered with purple and gold.

They had their own recreations and amusements. Cock fighting, bull fighting, Rekla racing, driving of horses and of elephants, hunting, swimming, dancing, musical entertainments and religious festivities have been some of the chief amusements of the people during those days. There were gymnasia also, wherein the youths of the country were taught boxing and wrestling and the art of self-defence by means of sticks and swords. Gladiatorial contests between men were also exhibited.

Women had their own amusements, teaching parrots, singing the *Vallai* or *Ammanai*, rocking swings and playing the games of *dhayam, kalanku* or *elangal, pallanguli* and *pandhu*. The game of dhayam was something like the game of dice, the game of the kalanku or elangal was played with seven tiny balls or stones, the game of pallanguli was played with a wooden board on which fourteen holes, in two rows, seven on each row, were scooped out and filled in with a certain number of tamarind seeds.

The science and practice of fine arts were highly developed among the Adi-Dravidas. The bark of trees and cotton cloth served as writing materials, but *cadjan* leaves (Palmyrah leaves) were commonly used. The study of music formed an essential part of a liberal education. The practice of reciting Tamil poems with *ragam* dates from that period. They knew the art of boat and ship building and waving and dyeing and working in gold and other metals. They had attained the highest proficiency in the art of agriculture and irrigation and in pearl fishing. Dancing also was cultivated as a fine art. The Adi-Dravidas acquired proficiency in the art of painting and sculpture.

As regards their religion, they were nature worshippers. They worshipped the sun, the moon, and the five elements. They had even hero-worship but they had no images or idols during those days. These were introduced only after the Aryan conquest.

They were a god-fearing people. Every small village in the rural parts had a temple, the remnant of which can be seen even to-day. In the *Tretayuga*, an Adi-Dravida by name Samvara and his wife Pulini one day came across a *Sivalingam* in the forest. They worshipped it daily by smearing it with ashes from the burial ground. One day there were no ashes. The woman offered to have her body burnt in order to get ashes to be used. The husband did so and performed the puja. After the puja was over, he as usual, forgetting that she was dead turned round to offer the *prasadam* to her. To his great surprise he saw her standing behind him to receive the offering (*prasadam*). God Siva then appeared before them in person and gave them absolution. From this it is evident, that these people were great devotees.

The Adi-Dravidas were a martial race and had a glorious past. They had a regular army with cavalry and elephant corps. They knew the different ways of fighting the enemy by siege and in the open field. They had well constructed fortresses. They were very brave soldiers and they were very humane to the aged and infirm and to women and children. *Purananuru* and *Agananuru* are full of incidents of their sublime heroism. The men delighted in the number of wounds they received in the front part of the body. Heroism was displayed even by women. Virikal (victory stone) was put in honour of the departed heroes. Even the holy Thiruvalluvar has written two chapters in his *Thirukkural* on the excellence of the army and on military spirit. When the Europeans came to India for the first time, it was these people that gave them timely and fraternal assistance and helped them to lay the foundations of the British Empire in India. In the famous siege of Arcot, they were content with gruel and offered the rice to Lord Clive and his assistants. In the Vellore and the Great

Indian Mutiny they stood by the British and fought against people who sought to stir up hostilities by spreading false rumours.

I hope it will not be out of place to refer here to the ancestry of the author. Mr. A.R. Cox, I.C.S. Collector of Madras, said while presenting the Sanad and Badge of Rao Bahadur to Mr. M.C. Rajah, M.L.C., the author on the 15th December 1922 at the Durbar held in the Pachiappas Hall, said as follows –

> You are such a well known public man that it is almost unnecessary for me to say much about you. No doubt you have received this title because of the work you have done for and the esteem in which you are rightly held by the members of your own important community of the Adi-Dravidas. During the labour troubles you did yeoman service in restraining them from violence and in protecting them effectively from law-breakers.
>
> You have represented your community in deputations to the Right Honourable, the Secretary of State and to His Excellence the Viceroy. You are the first Adi-Dravida to enter the Legislative Council and you have the interests of the depressed and poor always at heart.
>
> I understand that your grandfather was an Indian Mutiny Veteran. The courage and endurance which he displayed in times of war are evinced by you in times of peace.
>
> The Government are well aware of the public services you have thus rendered and have therefore conferred on you this title.

In the Great War they offered their services in great numbers, as combatants. Her gracious Majesty the late Queen Victoria having been pleased with the meritorious services rendered by the Sappers and Miners, who were almost all Adi-Dravidas, gave her name to that only regiment and it is now called the Queen's Own Sappers and Miners. As these people were hereditary warriors we find them even to-day in large numbers in the British army doing excellent work. It is a great pity that this ancient martial race is now subjected to all sorts of insults and injuries and is employed in carrying on the most menial work.

Such an ancient independent and important community has been subjected to the most cruel wrongs, wrongs from which thanks to an ever merciful Providence, it is Britain's mission in India to rescue. The Adi-Dravidas are still denied the use of public wells and tanks and at the same time stigmatized as unclean. They are still kept out of schools and colleges maintained from public funds and at the same time despised as ignorant and illiterate. They are still shut out from temples and yet branded as ungodly and unfit to associate with. For access to public roads and even for space to bury the dead, they have to depend very much on the capricious benevolence of their Caste-Hindu neighbours. Such is the enormity of the sins of the Caste Hindus against them. But they are conscious of the fact, that their present condition is certainly, better than what it was before the advent of the British. The British Government in India is the best Government we have ever had. It is the strongest, the most righteous and the best suited to India's diverse population and diverse interests that this country could ever have. The Indian Penal Code makes no difference between the Adi-Dravida and the so-called high caste man.

The Way Out

Have the Caste Hindus given decent burial to Manu's law? Though it is for all practical purposes a dead letter, will it not be reimposed the moment Full Responsible Government is granted to India? During a thousand years of autocratic rule of the Mohammedans and a hundred and eighty years of the benevolent despotism of the British, we have not been able to destroy caste. Caste is still reigning supreme, though it is said that caste is relaxing its hold on the people. Freedom of person will be totally denied to the Depressed Classes by the Caste Hindus, for their law allows it and the courts will support it. Freedom of person is a prerequisite for the development of nationality. Freedom should not be given to the people of India before our social wrongs have been set right. Social equality, social liberty and social fraternity should be enforced among the people who clamour for political equality, political liberty and the political fraternity.

The duty of so-called higher classes to their submerged fellowmen at the present day is at once manifest and insistent. The Caste Hindus ask them. "Why are you not satisfied? What do you want?" The very insolence of these questions is staggering. They reply,

> What do we want? Are we not men like you? What would you want, if you were exploited, if you were intellectually starved, if you were denied the benefits of schools, roads, choultries, wells, temples, etc., if you were lectured, bullied and rebuked day by day? We are not bricks or stones. We have feelings and ambitions and a national pride. We have suffered all sorts of tyranny, exploitation, insult and injury. You have trampled on our national honour and dignity and also heaped outrageous insults on us, added to grave injuries, economic and political. This domineering must go and we must be free.

This is what we want. We want our manhood, our rights as men. We do not want any patronage. We want social emancipation, economic emancipation and political emancipation.

It is a glorious thing to do service to the poor, and the needy. Do not despise the poor, for the poor inherit the Kingdom of Heaven. Lord Jesus was not born in a palace nor was Sri Krishna nor Vamana. Christ was with the oppressed peasants in Gallalie and not in the luxuroious cities of Capernaum and Bethsidea. He preferred the company of publicans and sinners to that of wealthy scribes and Pharisees with their long cloak of self-righteousness. Through tattered clothes small vices appear, robes and furred gowns hide all. The crimes of the wealthy are glossed over with all kinds of soothing explanations. Though the little vices of the outcastes are apparent on the surface yet in their hearts there is ever a fertile soil to receive the good and bear fruit. The safety of India lies in the emancipation of the submerged.

As long as there is such a section as the Depressed Classes in existence, it would be committing the most egregious of blunders either to think of giving Full Responsible Government or of even granting another instalment of Reforms. The very fact of the existence of the Depressed Classes in an unquestionable indication, of the depth of barbarism to which the Indian has sunk, and the enormous resistance that any attempt at their amelioration meets with, is a further sign of how utterly incompetent they are for even an approach towards Self-Government. I am not against Reforms, but I maintain that no greater harm could be done to the country than by the introduction of these Reforms before the country is ripe to receive them.

So long as this great community consisting of more than seven millions of the population remains in bondage, there will be no salvation for South India. The Caste Hindus have sinned long enough against these people. He who did the mischief must undo it. Hasten to make it good even at this the eleventh hour. It is never too late to repent.

Some persons who not very long ago espoused the cause of the Depressed Classes in public meetings, associations, Local Boards and Legislative Councils, both provincial and imperial, are not so willing now to help the work among the Depressed Classes, because these people are beginning to assert themselves and show that they have an individuality of their own. This shows that there is something rotten at the core. I have heard of some elder brothers in charge of their family estates, being unwilling to educate their younger brothers, because they fear that if education is given to these young fellows, they will grow impertinent and disobedient. These elder brothers think that they could reign supreme if their brothers are kept in perpetual darkness. Such families do not endure for many generations. They soon break up and become extinct. If the family heads think that by repressing the healthy growth of self-respect and independence in the junior members of the family they would remain powerful for ever, they are mistaken. Rome, whose greatness was built upon a social substratum of slaves, came to grief and Gibbon could write his famous book on the Decline of the Roman Empire. On the other hand the free nations of the west are able to adjust themselves to changing conditions because they believed in freedom and education permeating every stratum of society. How can any nation be free when a large proportion of its people is kept by the operation of social customs and social prejudices in debt, dirt, drink and darkness, the four evils of social degradation which will consume the body and the soul of even so-called respectable citizens? How can a carriage proceed, if one of its wheels sticks in the mire.

Are not the Adi-Dravidas also children of the soil like the so-called Hindus? Does the fact that they live in miserable huts entitle them to contempt and neglect at the hands of the so-called Caste Hindus? If they are ignorant or dirty, is it not due to the so-called Caste Hindus failing to do their duty by them. If they are too poor, is it not due to the so-called Caste Hindus taking their labour and giving them very little to eat? If they drink, is it not because the so-called Caste Hindus do not set them a good example? If they have no decent houses to live in, is it not because the so-called Caste Hindus live in large houses or houses surrounded by large compounds? One of the most insulting remarks which the Depressed Classes have to endure at the hands of other people, Europeans included, is that they are unclean. In this matter of cleanliness I may point out many a Depressed Class man who is more scrupulously clean than any so-called High Caste man in the country. But if the Depressed Classes are prevented from sharing in the supply of God-given pure water, whose fault is it? The Caste Hindu will not give them water to drink, water to wash themselves with and yet the Caste Hindus have the audacity to say that these people are unclean. As a matter of fact, they rely on insanitary and inadequate drinking water sources the contamination of which is the frequent cause of sickness and epidemics. Great indeed are the sins of omission and commission for which the so-called Caste Hindus are responsible.

When are those disabilities to be removed? There was a time when it was said that once the people of India get power into their hands these disabilities would go. Now are we any nearer to the time, when the Caste Hindus will think with shame of such things having once existed in the country?

I now appeal to the good nature, to the benevolence, to the love of distinction in well doing, if not the patriotism and the religious fervour of the Caste Hindus to make reparation for the age-long wrongs done to these people. It is for them to gird up their loins and hasten to work for the social emancipation, economic uplift and political liberty of the Depressed Classes. Then and then alone the prosperity of India will be assured.

But so long as human nature is what it is, it is futile to expect that the Hindus in the mass will either work wholeheartedly for the uplift of the Adi-Dravidas or even cease to throw obstacles in their way. The achievement of the first Reformed Madras Legislative Council is a sufficient commentary on its zeal for the emancipation of the Depressed Communities.

A few words about the Special Department called the Department of Protector of the Depressed Classes or the Department of Labour Commissioner and how far it received the support of the Caste Hindu Party in power in the Madras Legislative Council will not be out of place here.

Long before the Reforms were dreamt of, this Special Department was created solely for the amelioration of the condition of the Depressed Classes. The following G.O. will explain the conditions which led to the creation of the office:

After a careful consideration of the problem of the Depressed Classes, the Board has come to the conclusion that, however liberal or generous may be the attitude of Government towards them and whatsoever may be the facilities created for the improvement of their condition, the effect desired is not likely to be produced so long as there is no separate agency to carry out the policy of Government in this respect. Proposals for improving the condition of these classes have in the past, from time to time, received the approval of Government, but owing to the lack of special organization of effort, they have failed of effect. There is generally indifference and often hostility to measures calculated to uplift the Depressed Classes and, if the Collector is not keenly interested and has not the force of will to carry such measures through, they become entirely inoperative owing to the passive obstruction or indifferent of his subordinates. It is therefore essential that a special officer, with a suitable staff under him should be appointed as Protector of the Depressed Classes. Such an officer if properly chosen will impart continuity to all the remedial measures which Government have already sanctioned or may sanction in the future and prevent the good intentions of Government from being rendered ineffective by local indifference or opposition. It is only from a long sustained, persistent and well-directed effort that any appreciable result can be expected in elevating these vast masses of the population in view of their apathy, ignorance and helplessness. Further, in view of the rapid steps which are being taken to give India Self-government, it is matter of urgent necessity and mere political justice that, along with the political reforms, social reforms should be pushed more vigorously than before, so that the Depressed Classes may be enabled to make their voicc heard in politics and that they may not be left a helpless prey to the higher classes who at present monopolize education, and, with it, property and power.

It will thus be seen that the Government started this most necessary and useful Department after a most careful consideration. This was the first concerted action of the British Government to improve the lot of the Depressed Classes in the Presidency. In the interests of the civilization and humanity, a full-time officer as Protector of the Depressed Classes and the enlargement and expansion of his functions so as to embrace consideration of the measures to be adopted in each District of the Presidency for the amelioration and elevation of the Depressed Classes are necessary.

The Caste Hindus as soon as they came into power as the result of the Reforms Act set themselves to destroy this very Department. Scarcely a year passes but this Department is threatened with extinction. Soon after the Caste Hindus came into power, in September 1921 Sir P. Thyagaraya Chetty, the redoubtable Knight to Thondiarpet and the head of the Non-Brahman Caste Hindu Party in the Council wrote a most unwise letter to the Government of Madras on the side of Caste Hindu Labourers during the Madras Mill Troubles, protesting against the protection given by the Madras Government to the Adi-Dravidas who were rendered homeless by the incendiaries when they refused to join non-cooperation strikers, and making the most unwarranted statements suggested to Government to deport the Adi-Dravida Labourers out of Madras.

The following extract from my speech on the Budget for the year in the Madras Legislative Council in March 1925 will make it clear that the Madras Labour Strike, referred to above was not a genuine Labour Movement:

This party has a majority in this Council at present; but unless they use this majority with regard for real justice and not merely from an intoxicated sense of power which they wish to retain as long as possible and unless they feel that it is their duty to enlighten and educate and elevate the masses including the depressed classes, that majority will become a thing of past. In this connection I would remind the Caste Hindu that we, the Adi-Dravidas, were the first to denounce non-cooperation in this Presidency. If the example set by us was followed by the non-Brahmin Party in general, the non-Brahmin Hindus would have had timely warning. But what is the use of going to correct wrong notions when the poison has once been injected into the popular mind?

Beside I remember now, soon after Mr. Wadia left Madras, I asked Sir P. Thyagraya Chettiyar and other non-Brahmin leaders to take the leadership of the Labour Union and prevent them for falling into the hands of the non-cooperators.

What did the party in power do then? Was it not because they allowed the non-cooperators to capture labour in Madras that we the Adi-Dravidas felt it a duty we owed not only to ourselves but to the Government and the public at large that we should refuse to join the non-cooperation strikers? And instead of thanking us for refusing to join the non-cooperation strikers the leaders of the non-Brahmin party fell into the trap set by the non-cooperation leaders who, instead of distinguishing between non-cooperation strikers and loyal non-strikers, divided the labourers into Caste-Hindu strikers and Adi-Dravida blacklegs and asked the Caste-Hindu leaders of the non-Brahmin party and worry them to take their side against the loyal non-strikers. And these leaders, partly out of the fright and partly out of flattered vanity and partly in the hope of capturing labour, which had already been captured by the non-cooperators – they might as well capture a peacock by putting butter on its head – played into the hands of non-cooperators by attacking our community and extenuating non-cooperation strikers' acts of incendiarism, etc., against us. If only I had not at that time kept my people from joining the non-cooperation strikers, I leave you, Sir, to imagine what would have been the state of Madras with the non-cooperation Labour Union men in their full strength, when, for instance, the Prince of Wales came to Madras. Even as it was, how did the non-cooperators behave on that day? It was a fine compliment they paid to Sir P. Thyagaraya Chettiyar when they paid a State visit to his house on the 13th January last and made it necessary for the valiant Knight to take shelter in a house in Kappal Bolu Chetty Street so that he could not attend this Council during the Prince's memorable visit to it.

Let me quote an extract from my Presidential Address at the Second South Indian Adi-Dravida Congress held on the 21st and the 22nd July 1925 at Koilpatti, Tinnevelly District, which gives the facts and figures regarding the treatment meted out of the Depressed Classes by the Caste Hindus in Power in the Madras Legislative Council:

Now under the Reform Council consisting as it does of a large majority of the so-called Justice Party what has been done? The council cut down our allotment of money in the very first year of its existence by one lakh of rupees and thus deprived the Department of opportunities of relieving distress among the poor, and in its second year removed all the important and functioning officials of Government. I need hardly remind you how this outrageous procedure crippled all the resources of the Department, and thank God it is not to be in existence much longer than its third year. Their natural animosity towards us was patent even before the labour troubles in Madras the cause and effect of which will be fresh in your minds. I need hardly recount the said circumstances which then necessitated hundreds of our community being driven helpless and homeless. Driven out of our huts and hearths by incendiaries who were so bold and defiant as to try to prevent the police from putting out the consuming fire, we stood helpless before God and man, not knowing where to go. At such a time the Government in the interests of peace and order had to defend and protect us against those who wanted to punish us for no other sin than that we wanted to earn our bread by honest labour against the advice of those who wanted to use us as tools in their camp against constituted authority. It is the fashion for those who want to save their faces and the face of the party which they are supposed to lead from the ministerial office to call us blacklegs in that strike. In the first place the so-called strike of the men in the mills was not a genuine labour movement. Secondly we were not permitted to participate in any organization whose legitimate function is to decide on a strike. To call us therefore 'Blacklegs' is a perversion and an atrocious perversion of truth. Our legs were in no wise specially black but the faces of our tormentors were. I shall not enlarge on this subject especially as anything we might say is likely to be misunderstood by real labour, with the rank and file of which we really have no quarrel now. They were not our real persecutors: they were tools in the hands of political agitators. We harbour no resentment against the Caste Hindu section of labour. They along with us labour under difficulties and disabilities which require urgent and drastic remedy. It is the high handed poisonous action of members of a party who after inflicting all known and unknown injury on our community shed crocodile tears and pose as friends of the Depressed Classes, that we have no room for in our politics. When I am told that the Party in power did several things for the Depressed Classes including making grants for expenditure on our behalf I am filled with amazement at the ingenuity or shall I say the disingenuousness of the political individual responsible for such a statement. Recently one in acting through his mouthpiece (a member of our own community, I am ashamed to confess) collected all the figures from the Government Budget Statement that they represented grants made by the Party in power. Gentlemen, believe me when I say that this is a fair sample of the half-truths and intrigue and unscrupulousness which have brought the Justice (!) Party to power. It is a half-truth to call the figures budgeted for by the Reserved half of Government the figures of sums spent by the Party in power on our amelioration. Rather should we take into account the figures asked for by the Reserved Department and the figures cut down by the Party in power. It is intrigue to set up a member of our community to sing the praises of the Party in power and it is unscrupulous on the part of that party to twist, distort, and misuse facts. As you are aware the procedure in the matter of Budgets is that the Department concerned prepares a programme of work being itself in touch with the needs of the community and ask for the amount of money necessary to redeem its obligations as well as meet the demand of the community. This "Budget estimate" as it is called is placed before the Finance Committee – a Committee in which there is a preponderance of the members of the party in power. The department concerned, manned as it is, by responsible officials prepares a statement only of its minimum demand – the minimum consistently with its deep concern for the deficit in the whole budget of the Presidency. Unless it represented the minimum requirements there is no chance of the figures being accepted by the Hon'ble Member of Government. As I said this very carefully prepared statement of figures has to be approved by the Party in power, first in the Finance Committee and then again in the Legislative Council. In 1921-22 the Department asked for a grant of 6.47 lakhs for Labour and allied departments. This came before the Legislative Council and the grant asked was reduced by one lakh. In 1922-23 the Department budgeted for 12.25 lakhs. After the first sift in the Finance Committee, the amount was cut down to 7.87 lakhs for Labour and allied Department. This amount includes 3.25 lakhs for loans to Co-operative Societies which are to be paid to Government by easy installments. When this amount of 7.87 lakhs came before the Legislative Council it was further reduced by Rs. 21380. The Finance Committee even this year cut down the allotment asked for by the Department by 1.23 lakhs. If you will refer to the proceedings of that committee dated 8.1.23 you will find that no pretence of a reason is even made for this drastic cut.

Our representation in Local Bodies and Municipal Councils is at present in the hands of these so-called popular leaders. And you know what they have done. The scheme for giving us representation in these institutions was not started by this ministry and since their party came into power we have not been assured of even a single seat uniformally in every Local Board and Municipal Council. Perfunctory nominations have been made and when their attention was drawn to deserving candidates or unfilled vacancies the Minister in-charge of the Department referred me to the Presidents of the Boards and would do nothing to justify his presence in the administration. Our nominations were in the hands of the Presidents even before the subject of Local Self-Government was treated as a Transferred Subject. The accession of power has enabled the Minister only to revert to the former position and leave us where we were before. Even the few places given for our members, when they became vacant on account of the death of the holder (as in the case of Thiruvannamalai Municipal Council) or through other causes (as in the case of Chingleput and Cuddalore Taluk Boards) are subsequently filled by members of other Communities especially of the Caste Hindu. Towards the close of last year I suggested in the Legislative Council that a meal at midday might be provided for the poor Adi-Dravida boys in the Government Elementary Schools. You all know in what pitiable state our little boys are and how on account of poverty they have at present to go without a midday meal at their school. My suggestion was, I understood placed before the Finance Committee in which I already said there is a majority of members of the Party in power. The proceedings of the Finance Committee were as follow:

Read – Scheme relating to the provision of midday meal for pupils of the Adi-Dravidas and other Depressed Classes (total expenditure estimated by the Director of Public Instructions is about 67 lakhs per annum). The committee did not recommend the scheme for adoption.

When I read this I could not understand the anticipated cost and suspected that the so-called scheme ought to have been made all-embracing so as to include probably the Communities to which the Hon'ble Ministers themselves belonged. Thereupon I put in a question in the Council on the 27th of February of this year asking for a copy of the scheme drawn up. The answer given by the Education Minister was "No definite scheme relating to the provision of midday meals for pupils of the Adi-Dravidas and other Depressed Classes has yet been drawn up." That my proposal was bound to fail when a gentleman of the type of Rajah of Panagal or Mr. Patro is the Minister in-charge I know, but it was the greatest of surprises to me that a proposal could be allowed to go before the Finance Committee without examination, that the cost of proposal could have been estimated at 67 lakhs without such examination and that a 'scheme' before the Finance Committee could cease to be a scheme before the Legislative Council. The Minister for Local

Government when asked about non-appointment of an Adi-Dravida representative on the Chidambaram Taluk Board said "that the owner of the rented house in which the Taluk Board office is located has objected to the Adi-Dravida representative entering the premises." On this reply I asked the Minister in a series of questions how a public office which according to the Standing Orders of Government should be located in a place to which all castes and communities ought to have access, came to be located under such adverse conditions and the Hon'ble Minister was sympathetic enough to give me the reply (for all my six questions bracketed together). "The Government have no information." These facts constitute the most tragic commentary on the attitude of these Ministers towards our party and on the wasted opportunities that the history of any party, communal or political can afford. It is clear to all those who have eyes to see that beneath the verbiage of some members and beneath the cant of communal representation there is nothing in truth original than the hideous features of the class despotism and caste tyranny.

This year too the usual motions were tabled during the Budget Session in the Madras Legislative Council by the Caste Hindu members for the abolition of this Special Department which is still temporary and continued from year to year. An allotment pertaining to this Department along with others forms one part of the Budget. The demands for the various other Departments were taken up and passed and the time allotted for discussion of demands had run out before the Council reached the provision for the Labour Department. By this very lucky accident, it narrowly escaped the fate, that was awaiting it.

Persistent efforts have been made recently to get the activities of the Department transferred to the control of the Caste Ministry as far as they overlap the Transferred Subjects. This must be resisted stoutly and defeated.

The Special Department must be reinforced and kept entirely in the hands of Englishmen and the Indian Ministers ought not to be allowed to exercise even a semblance of power or influence in this Department. The Special Department should be made a separate Department with a separate Budget working directly under His Excellency the Governor and His Excellency should have an Advisory Board consisting of the Commissioner of Labour and the leading men of the community so that the Governor may consult them whenever necessity arises and His Excellency should not on any account be guided solely by the Indian Members of the Cabinet until it is leavened by the presence of a Depressed Class element.

It has been clearly pointed out that so early in the history of the Reforms in the Southern India, the Non-Brahman Caste Hindu Party in the Local Council, who posed as the guardians of the Depressed Classes has been not only practically arresting the progress of a Community which forms the back-bone of the labouring population, but also has been crushing its hopes and aspirations. This is why, it is very rightly said that the leaders of the people of India could not be safely trusted to look after the welfare and progress of the weak and the Depressed Classes. It is the fashion, to say, of a man, who is not an enthusiastic believer in our immediate fitness for Self-Government, that he is a die-hard; such a thing is easily said and passed on from lip to lip, while it by no means carries them one step nearer so far as fitness for Self-Government is concerned. It is now said, we are all now competent to rule ourselves and the presence of Englishmen is not necessary, and it only impedes our march onwards. And it is proposed to make up for this piece of gross injustice, Indianisation of the different services must be commenced forthwith and completed as soon as possible. I say, woe to India when such a wish is achieved.

The cry for Indianising the Services sounds very patriotic indeed. The agitation for wholesale Indianisation of Services is made only by a handful of educated Indians. It is simply for the purpose of satisfying the ambitions of a few Indians at the top of the services. The Britisher is a foreigner here and he may live for another ten centuries and he will never get to know the Indian as we in the country do. Used as he is to such a thing as public opinion in his own country and in the continent of which his place but forms a part, which comes right down from the bottom and permeates and vivifies the whole mass, he often makes the mistake of supposing that the loud cries of a few politicians in India must also mean much the same thing as it does in Europe, he yields to it and gradually hands over responsible functions of Government to these cocks that crow from their own dung hill. Of these politicians, public men as they are called in the same sense in which we talk of certain women as public women, nobody need have any concern. A sop to the dog will effectually silence it. Can't we recall scores of instances of these politicians in whom an inordinate love of country has suddenly developed and manifested itself in agitations for Home Rule, Self-Government, Non-cooperation, boycotting of the Prince of Wales, boycotting of foreign goods while we have no means of replacing them and in projects comparing almost with those of the great Laputans for the conquest of the world by means of charka, the moment the till then forbidden and hated and despicable fruit of a fine job in Government Service is offered to them, their intense patriotism takes itself to wings and flies away to find a refuge in more congenial regions, and our erstwhile patriot hastens to conform himself to his new surroundings and cuts a somersault to divest himself of his masque and presents himself in his true colour a base, selfish and self interested place-hunter. Little does he think that while begging for votes, he gave an assurance to the voters that he would never commit the flagrant crime of seeking service under the hated foreign bureaucracy.

Indianisation means only inefficiency in the present stage of the country. Indianisation should not on any account mean the Indianising the character of the administration and the diluting of its British character. The British character of the administration must be maintained and that respect for British ideals of Justice. Liberty, Equality and Progress should be a living force in the Government of the country. The Indian is clannish and when Indians occupy high posts of responsibility they are more amenable to influence that leads to inefficiency, than an European Officer who is able to take an impartial and unbiassed view of things in the affairs of the administration. The following extract from my memorandum to the Reforms Enquiry Committee, Delhi, will show the nature of training an European youth generally gets in England.

Let us take, to begin with, the case of the I.C.S. The man who comes out from England has generally been through one of the two famous Universities of England, Oxford and Cambridge. Let us look at the training that such a person receives. He generally goes through one of those remarkable Public Schools of England and by the time he leaves it, he is about 16. And what is the kind of product that these Public Schools turn out? Most of my English friends would not require an answer to this question; but several of my countrymen would be glad to know something about it. Well, to put the matter in a nutshell, they come out with their character fully formed and thoroughly equipped with the necessary material to enable them to fight life's battles with courage tempered by sympathy, justice by mercy, energy by patience; all this is inspired by a very high sense of duty; a high sense of their calling, and a high sense of responsibility. Into the youngster's mind they are very careful to instill courage, courage not of the barbarian variety, but courage always guided by intelligent and cool unruffled thinking; secondly an absolute dependence on self in the last resource, with a readiness to take counsel from anybody if proper and necessary: a mind that will work energetically and actively during emergencies: a sense of organization, i.e. the habit of quickly organizing themselves into an orderly party, cheerfully submitting themselves to irksome discipline and obeying the selected chief to the death irrespective of his social rank; a sense of law, a sense of honour, a sense of justice. Now, this is the equipment with which a Public School boy leaves his school. He enters the University, there he specializes in some branch of study. During the time that he is there, he is no more a youngster: he is a man who has already begun to do the work he is expected to do in the world to some extent, while at the same time he is equipping himself with knowledge of an advanced nature in some special branch. There the students behave to each other as though they were already men; discuss the great problems of the world with the same serious interest that is seen in them when they begin the work of life proper after they leave the University. To their Union meetings come the great men of parliament and join with the students in the discussion of the problems of the day. To them come the great men of letters, leaders of thought, scientists and men who excel in every branch of literature, to pour their treasures at the feet of the *alma mater*. It is in the midst of such surroundings that these students are nurtured, it is in such an atmosphere that these students breathe, move and have their being. Fed upon such thoughts, nurtured in such traditions, equipped with such knowledge they come out here, to serve us in the Civil Service, Education and other services.

The British character can be imparted to Indian administration through personal touch, personal relationship, personal influence and personal example. The process of Indianising the services and of the elimination of the Britishers from the Government should be proceeded with slowly and carefully, with an eye to the progress of the Depressed Classes. As long as there is caste in this country, so long will there be the necessity for British character of the administration through the agency of the British people. Here let me quote an extract from the Farewell Address presented to H.E. Lord Willingdon on 5th April 1925 by the member of the Depressed Classes of the Madras Presidency.

May we humbly request Your Excellency to tell the Britishers in England that we of the Depressed Classes regard the British Government as the trustees of the people in India; that one reason why the British Government should exist in India is to secure just treatment for the Depressed Classes and to stimulate and guide progress among the weaker communities; that so long as caste remains a ruling factor in the lives of the people, and so long as the labouring population is kept in a depressed condition, so long will there be the need for the supervening, controlling and adjusting hands of the benevolent Britisher in India; that the British Government should on no account sacrifice the interests of the Depressed and Minority Communities, out of deference to the wishes and sentiments of a majority community; that the British character of administration through the agency of the British people must be maintained at any cost; that as for Indianisizing the services, it must be a matter of ages and must be proceeded with to keep pace with the actual growth and expansion of mind of the Caste Hindus, who form about 85% of the population; that the howl that is being raised for immediately Indianizing the services, if by misadventure should be needed to, woe to our land we will cease to exist as a class, for we feel confident that the Caste Hindus, though we do count among them some most ardent and sincere friends individually, would take good care to see that such a thing happens, for then their one present eye-sore will for ever be removed from before them.

What the Depressed Classes need most is education – a liberal education which will make them raise their heads and be men. Education is the panacea for all the woes of the community. It is too late in the day to discuss the importance to individuals, communities and to the nation of the Compulsory Education not only for boys but also for girls. It is education that will make the homes of the Depressed Classes brighter, purer and happier and their labour sweeter. The Depressed Classes are anxious to share in the benefit of education, but their extreme poverty stands in their way. Elementary Education ought to be made compulsory and provision should be made in schools for providing the children of these classes with a square meal in the middle of the day, and allotting the parents, who lose the services of their wage-earning children, a compensatory allowance.

The children of the Depressed Classes must have the benefit of Education at any cost. It is not enough to teach the 3 R's to them and let them drift in life without compass or rudder. It is necessary that they should be taught to earn their daily bread by some useful occupation in which both mind and body will be brought into play. A scheme of Vocational training has to be considered as part of the curricula of these schools. The facilities offered by Government at present to these children are inadequate and even as they are, they are the outcome of the sympathy of the British Officials during the Pre-Reform days. In the year 1925 I moved a resolution in the Local Legislative Council asking for an increase in the number of scholarships for the children of the Depressed Classes. The Caste Hindu Minister for Education vehemently opposed the resolution on the ground that poverty was not the monopoly of the Depressed Classes. I spoke out my mind in my Budget Speech in March 1925 in the Legislative Council regarding the attitude of the Minister for education thus:

Regarding scholarships for the Depressed Classes, I must take this opportunity of recording my emphatic protest against the speech of the Education Minister the other day when I asked for an enhancement of their amount in view of the extreme poverty of the boys of my Community. He told us then that poverty was not monopoly of the Depressed Classes and that Brahman boys too were poor. I wonder when and where he discovered these facts, whether before or after he assumed office. If Brahman boys are poor, why did he not press their claims as a Non-Brahman leader, and if the Depressed Classes were not the only classes suffering from the pangs of hunger, why did he and his party make a specialty of the advocacy of their claims. Does he see no difference between the poverty of the Depressed Classes and the poverty of other classes? Does he not know, the poverty of the Depressed Classes is due to age-long oppression by the classes? And is it not bare justice that we ask and when we ask for special encouragement being given to them? If he has forgotten the first lessons of his political school, shall I read to him what the recent Report and G-O No. 239 referred to above says:

"The Committee considered the needs of the special classes and communities and agreed, so far as the Depressed Classes are concerned, that adequate boarding and fee facilities should be granted to them. It was felt that the position at present occupied by the members of these classes was due in large measure more to the peculiar customs and usages of the country than to any inherent defects of the classes themselves. Viewed from this point, the education of the Depressed Classes became a matter of national duty, and public funds should in justice be available to all reasonable extent in serving their interests.

Let me say in conclusion that his speech the other day was the most graceful speech I have ever heard from the lips of a responsible Minister in this House."

The Hon'ble Minister called my attention to the poverty of the so-called backward classes. I find that whenever I press the claims of the Depressed Classes, certain so-called backward classes are brought forward to minimize the claims of my community. I wonder who these backward classes are as distinct from depressed or untouchable classes. I suppose they are all Caste Hindus. Under these classes come communities to which belong at least two of the Ministers.

The Depressed Classes anticipated this kind of attitude on the part of the caste Ministers long before the Reforms came into being. When the Madras Adi-Dravida Mahajana Sabha, the Premier Political Association of the Depressed Classes of the Presidency was asked by the Governemnt to send in their opinion on the Report on Indian Constitutional Reforms in the year 1918, the said Sabha expressed themselves as follows:

> We may indicate, however, in a general way, our attitude towards the Reform Scheme. We are averse in the present condition of public opinion, and in the present stage of social and moral progress, and with the ideas which now rule the social relations of communities, to the establishment of a dual Government in this country. We are therefore opposed to any department of the administration being transferred to popular control. We would particularly protest against education being vested in "Ministers." These Ministers would look after the interest of their particular communities and either neglect us or train us in such a way that we may look upon them for ever as our masters.

As adequate number of scholarships and liberal fee-remissions should be instituted for these children attending recognized Schools and Colleges. There should also be a network of free Hostels established throughout the Presidency for the children of these men.

It is feared in certain quarters that if these children are sent to school, it will become difficult to obtain labour and that the children of the Depressed Classes will become gentlemen. Why should they not? Are they not the sons of the soil and citizens possessing equal rights and privileges with the Caste Hindus?

Why should they remain hewers of wood and drawers of water for ever and the Caste Hindus remain lords over them for ever? The wheel of progress is moving and the wheel must revolve full cycle. Adequate representation should be given to these Classes in the Public Services as an incentive to their education. In a country like this, where, caste has not relaxed its hold on the people and where social culture has been mistaken for and identified with religious tenets the predominance of any particular class in the Public Services is a danger to the country. It is all very well to talk of Hindu-Moslem Unity and it is very easy to blame the Mohammedan for not joining the Hindus. Physician ! heal thyself. When there is no unity among the Hindus themselves, how on earth can one expect to have Hindu-Moslem unity?

So if the scale of justice is to be held evenly in the public administration, it is very necessary that all classes should be represented in the Public Services and especially those classes whose backward condition renders them absolutely inarticulate. The mere fact that a particular class is wealthy and can make itself heard or can win the good graces of those in authority is no reason why it should wield influence which will tilt the balance against the others. Official posts carry with them not only salaries, but also officials and administrative and even political influence. If men belonging to the Depressed Classes are appointed, the grievances of the Community will be attended to more readily and people who wish to ride roughshod over their rights will think twice before they make up their minds to do so.

The holding of Government posts acts like magic upon the public mind in divesting it of stupid notions of touch and distance pollution. It is not Mr. Gandhi's untouchability propaganda that will drive the demon of untouchability and unapproachability. A strong Depressed Classes element alone in the Public Services will raise those classes in the estimation of others as being invested with all the prestige and authority of the Governmental machine.

Sixty-three per cent of the Government appointments, both in the higher and lower grades, have been reserved for non-Brahmins. At least 30 per cent should be reserved for the Depressed Classes and that the minimum qualifications required under the Public Service Notification should be considered sufficient.

As a matter of fact considering the gross injustice that has been meted out to them, it would be but bare justice to allow the Public Services to be entirely recruited from them for at least a quarter of a century to come and perhaps then the bitterness that has been rankling in the minds of these men on account of oppression by other castes through the ages will be softened and the time may come when the Depressed Classes will gladly march hand in hand with the other communities towards the goal of Self-Government. India will then become one happy family with joy radiating from every home and English will then be only too glad to invest her with full Responsible Self-Government.

I must now turn to consider how best to stir the public conscience, combat the apathy and active hostility of caste opinion, arm the Depressed Classes with the necessary amount of self-respect and political leverage and hasten the process of their amelioration. A great deal is now being said on this question all over India. The Depressed are told that they have equality before the Law and are advised to stand on their own legs and assert themselves as member of the Hindu Community. This is merely begging the question. It is possible in the present circumstances for the Depressed communities to assert either their elementary rights or work for their higher aspirations of having their due share in the Councils of the Government. Owing to their economic and social depression they form a negligible factor in the General Hindu Electorate and they have absolutely no chance of influencing, by the exercise of their franchise, the conduct of any representative of a General Constituency. The number of the Depressed Class Voters in the whole Presidency is very small. The problem then, I submit, is to arouse their self-respect and capture the imagination of the other sections of the South Indian population by a bold act of statesmanship on the part of the Government and to arm the members of the Depressed communities with the most elementary of political weapon, the franchise. They must also be assured of an effective voice in the public bodies and the legislatures of the country.

Lord Morley of Blackburn, when he found that Indian discontent had a central core of racial bitterness, appointed Lord Sinha of Raipur, then Mr. S.P. Sinha, to the Viceroy's Executive Council to show to all the world that His Britannic Majesty's Government knew no distinctions of race, colour or creed. The Adi Dravidian problem in South India is similar in origin and results, although intenser in the agony of bitterness that is producing in the hearts of seven millions of people in this Presidency and fifty millions of human beings all over India. The Mohammedan Community numbering less than three millions in the Presidency has rightly asked for and obtained separate Communal Representation in the legislatures and their interest are always safeguarded by the appointment of their co-religionists to high offices in the State. There used to be a Mohammedan judge on the High Court Bench at Madras and there is now a Mohammedan Member of the Governor's Executive Council in the Province. Although I do not suggest that those appointments go merely on racial or communal consideration of equipoise of communal interest have something to do with the origin of the system. The Depressed Classes of the Presidency numbering more than seven millions, out of a total of nearly forty-three millions should have their interests safe-guarded by the inclusion of a number of their community in the Cabinet of the Province.

The question of Adi-Dravida representation on the Legislatures is a more knotty problem. They are economically backward and socially depressed. In the absence of special measures they can never hope to influence in any way the deliberations in the Councils of the country. They should be given the Franchise in sufficiently large numbers. This could be done only on a differential basis of qualification in the General Electorate and this arrangement will be open to very serious objections on grounds of principle. The alternative would be a purely Communal Electorate and any prescribed set of qualifications in such an electorate cannot be constructed as preferential treatment or infringement of the rights of others.

As it is, the Caste Hindus who form the bulk of the population and of the General Electorate know full well that any member of the Depressed Classes has absolutely no chance of being returned to the Council for any General Constituency and it is this conviction that is at the bottom of their attitude towards the communities in the council and the country. The only remedy for this state of things would lie in ensuring the presence of a sufficient number of these classes on the Public Bodies and the Legislative Council that they cannot be ignored by any party would be in power. This can be done either by nomination or election of such members.

The following points respectfully urged by me on behalf of the Madras Adi-Dravida Maha Jana Sabha on 24-9-24 for sympathetic consideration of His Excellency the Governor of Madras, will explain this matter:

Representation in the Local Legislature:

We wish at the outset to make it clear that we require and demand Communal Representation of our community in the Local Legislature on an elective basis. We are entirely opposed to the principle of nomination in the matter for the following reasons:

(a) Representation by nomination is no real representation. It is at best only a makeshift and not the real thing.
(b) The Cabinet in which the Indian members including the ministers are in a majority, have at present the predominant voice in the selection of men for nomination and are therefore in a position to exercise undue influence in the course of their conduct of Council. The political views of the Indian section of the Cabinet and particularly of the member who holds the portfolio of nominations have been or still diametrically opposed to the views of our Political Association and the real interests of our Community. The members selected by them are therefore likely to be of the pliable type who would subserve their interests in opposition to the real interests of our Community.
(c) We would therefore respectfully urge that, so long as the principle of nomination holds the field with regard to our representation on the

Local Legislature, His Excellency the Governor may, in accordance with the letter and spirit of the Instrument of Instructions issued by His Gracious Majesty the King Emperor be pleased to reserve the portfolio of nominations in his own hands and nominate representatives of our Community on the Legislature in consultation with the recognized Political Association of the Community, the Madras Adi-Dravida Mahajana Sabha, which has ever since the Montagu-Chelmsford visit, helped in securing Representation for the Depressed Classes and has been consulted on such questions as the Constitutional Reforms including Franchise and Functions, Rowlatt Bills etc.

(d) We number 7,503,475 out of a total population of 42,794,115 inhabitants of the Presidency. We are mainly engaged in agriculture and suffer from various disabilities, political, social, economic and educational arising from and aggravated by the stigma of untouchability and unapproachability riveted on us by the united force of caste opinion. We are now represented on the Local Legislature by five nominated members. The Mohammedans who number only 2,865,285 in the Presidency are allotted 13 elective seats. The Indian Christians who number only 1,389,672 out of the total population have 5 elective seats and three nomination seats (total 8) secured for them. The Anglo-Indians who number only 23,492 in the Presidency have one elective seat and one nominated seat (total 2) given them. We who number more than one-sixth of the population engaged on the land, the basic industry of the Province and have our undoubted, age-long grievances to redress, are certainly entitled in Equity, Justice and good Conscience to a much greater representation than we have at present. We would therefore respectfully urge for your Excellency's sympathetic consideration that a minimum of twenty seats for our Community on the Legislature is an urgent necessity.

II. We wish to respectfully press our undoubted right as a distinct community to elective representation on the Legislature, in consideration of our separate interests, our numerical strength, our political importance and our undoubted disabilities as "Depressed Classes" with all that the term connotes. The various Conferences and Congresses held the Depressed Classes in different parts of the Presidency and the demands put forward by them during the past decade are sufficient indication of the political consciousness of our Community. The members of the Depressed Classes are not one while less articulate or less conscious of their interests or less responsible than the classes that have been enfranchised under the Reforms. The factors of social, economic, and educational depression in our Community which have been produced and aggravated by the stigma of untouchability rivetted on us by age-long oppression in Pre-British days have resulted in their present economic position which disqualifies them for the franchise under the qualification laid down by the rules framed under the Reform Act of 1919. The only solution of the problem would seem to us to lie in granting to our Community a system of Communal Representation, either by a reservation of an adequate number of seats in the General Electorate and enfranchising a sufficient number of Community on a differential set of qualifications or by direct election through Communal Electorates enfranchised in sufficient numbers. Under either arrangement, we respectfully submit to Your Excellency that our Community is entitled to not less than twenty elective seats on the Legislature in consideration of our numbers, political importance and undoubted disabilities of all possible kinds.

It is only when we submit to Your Excellency that the voice of our representatives will be effectively heard in the Council Chamber and will make it worth the while of any party which would be in power to court our support by conciliation or fear our opposition to continuous caste domination. The history of the amelioration of the condition of the Depressed Classes during the tenure of the First Reformed Councils with a non-Brahmin majority and non-Brahmin Ministry in power tells a sad tale of every conceivable obstruction by the Caste-block in the Council and throws an interesting side-light on this question. We would suggest, as an additional safeguard that there should be a statutory provision that no legislation affecting our communities should go into the Statute Book unless clear two-thirds majority of our communal representatives are in support of the measure and that His Britannic Majesty's Government should in any event reserve to themselves the right to veto any legislation that in their opinion is contrary to the interests of our Community. These provisions, we respectfully submit to Your Excellency, should form an integral part of the Parliamentary Statute when it comes up for revision.

Indian Assembly and Council of State: The same argument apply *mutatis mutandis* to the question of our representation on the Indian Legislative Assembly and the Council of State. We have more pressing and peculiar problems to solve. Social and Labour Legislation affect our Community more intimately.

The Cabinet: We would urge for favourable consideration the feasibility of appointing a qualified member of our Community on His Excellency's Executive Council, on the same basis of qualification as laid down for the members of any other minority community like the Mohammedans.

Separate Department: Finally we request your Excellency to make the interests of the Depressed Classes a special concern of the Governor to be looked after adequately by Separate Department under His Excellency the Governor.

CONCLUSION

Our demands, our wants and our needs are multifarious and numerous. It is needless to repeat over again here what has been said time and again in hundreds of Conferences and Conventions. Briefly, I would say we need at the hands of our fellow countrymen a recognition of the fact that we are men equally with themselves. We are not to be segregated; we are not to be treated like lepers. From being Kings, Emperors and Ministers, for having taken up arms against a foreign invader, the Aryans and then when defeated for refusing to embrace their civilization, the punishment, the like of which is unknown in the history of any other part of the world was imposed on us and that was to be perpetual: not only those that revolted then but their descendants and their descendants' descendants were to suffer for ever and ever. The inquisition, the atrocities committed by barbarians in their inroads to Rome, the sufferings of the heretics in the Netherlands, the enormities of Nero, the cruelties perpetrated by Tamerlain and Chinghiz Khan, these pale before the horrors of caste.

This equality that we claim, they will not accord. Now will the Government do that? How is this to be done? Communal Representation has been acknowledged as a principle and given effect to in practice. We are as much a community as either the non-Brahmins or the Mohammedans for the matter of that. Seats are reserved for the non-Brahmins to protect them from the Brahmins: how much more necessary it is then to reserve adequate number of seats for us, who labour under so many disadvantages. Secondly, why are we not represented in Executive Council? Why should there not be an Adi-Dravida there to represent his community along with others? Is it a *sanctum sanctorum,* not to be polluted by the presence of an untouchable?

The Earl of Winterton, while speaking about Reforms, distinctly said, that so long as there existed a class known by the name of the Depressed Classes, India was utterly unfit for another instalment of Reforms: and he said the mission of England in India was to remove that stigma for her fair name. We earnestly hope he will do what he said, if he should get the opportunity. And let us also hope and pray, fervently, that the Unionists now in power will take a special interest in our community and help to advance our cause during their tenure of office, so that when the time comes for them to make room for next Government they will carry with them along with others the blessings of a whole population that they redeemed from slavery lasting over a period of two thousand years, which noble and glorious work it was reserved for them to accomplish.

"Never for me the lowered banner, never the lost endeavour."

PART II

REPRESENTATIONS TO THE BRITISH GOVERNMENT, SPEECHES AND LETTERS

Memorandum by Rao Bahadur M.C. Rajah, Honorary Secretary, Madras Adi-Dravida Mahajana Sabha*

In reviewing the report of the Royal Commission of the superior service must be borne in mind the very strict condition under which they had to work. They were not a kid to consider whether or not India was fit for Self-Government; but to seek the means of carrying out the promise of 1917 at the earliest possible date. It is a matter of congratulation for the Englishmen that they threw themselves into the cause most heartily, shutting their ears to the reverberations of their own past experience and of the accumulated experience of hundreds of wise men who went before them. It is the fashion, to say of a man, who is not an enthusiastic believer in our immediate fitness for Self-Government, that he is diehard; such a thing is easily said and passed on from lip to lip, while it by no means carries them one step nearer so far fitness for Self-Government is concerned. It is now said, we are all now competent to rule ourselves, and the presence of Englishmen is not necessary, and only impedes our march onward. And it is proposed to make up for this piece of gross injustice, Indianisation of the different services must be commenced and completed as soon as possible. I say, "Woe to India when such a wish is achieved."

Dyarchy they say has proved a failure because of the inherent drawbacks arising from the nature of such a situation. Others say it has proved a glorious success viewing it from whatever standpoint; whether as a success or a failure they agree in asserting that instead of Dyarchy they must have local Self-Government. And, that, they say, is the panacea that will cure all the evils under which we are suffering now. To us it appears, even Dyarchy is a blessing, because, though some of the subjects have been transferred entirely to the hands of the Indians, the momentum of the administration of the rest has carried these forward. Now, this is a fact that is seldom

*Appendix 5, The Report of the Reforms Enquiry Committee, 1924 (Written Evidence), Simla, 1924.

understood; the men in charge of transferred subjects take credit to themselves for administering them successfully. It is easy to delude oneself like it, because one is always happy to think that one is a genius; so one feels, when he is suddenly lifted up from – where shall we say, will the ministers, at least the ministers of Madras know it themselves – to the place of ministers, that there must have been marvelous ability buried deep down in their natures to be suddenly called to life upon their elevation to the ministership to dazzle themselves and the world. But we do hope it has not so blinded them as to think themselves transformed into Gods. If that be so we will not disturb them in their Elysium. Like the fly seated on a spoke of the wheel, their loud cries of successfully driving the machine will impose on none but themselves their wives and their own Government. All this does not look very hopeful to the Indian who seeks Self-Government. If we were going to indulge in rhetoric nothing would be more easy than to shout from every house-top, how the Englishmen came to India, filched our country from us, denationalized us, enervated us, demoralized us and finally rendered us unfit for even ruling ourselves: the cry would be taken up by every idler and mischief-monger, and then it spreads like wild fire among the mob; the inevitable consequences of which are events like the Punjab rebellion, the Moplah rebellion, the boycott of H.R.H. the Prince of Wales, etc. And then, and only then it is interesting to see how these so-called Indian leaders of thought, leaders of parties, leaders of movements would behave. The conflagration is easy to light up; but once it is ablaze it is not so easy to quench it. This our leaders see too late. All this I say, not to belittle, my countrymen; but to face the facts and deal with them rather than with philosophic disquisition and visionary utopias.

Let us take, to begin with, the case of I.C.S. The man who comes out from England has generally been through one of the two famous Universities of England, Oxford and Cambridge. Let us look at the training that such a person receives. He generally goes through one of these remarkable Public Schools of England and by the time he leaves it, he is about 16. And what is the kind of product that these Public Schools turn out most of my English friends would not require an answer to this question; but several of my countrymen would be glad to know something about it. Well, to put the matter in a nutshell, they come out with their character fully formed and thoroughly equipped with the necessary material to enable them to fight life's battles with courage tempered by sympathy, justice by mercy, energy by patience; all this is inspired by a very high sense of duty; high sense of their calling, and a high sense of responsibility. Into the youngsters mind they are very careful to instill courage, courage not of the barbarian variety, but courage always guided by intelligent and cool unruffled thinking. Secondly as absolute dependence on self in the last resource with a readiness to take counsel from anybody if proper and necessary: a mind that will work energetically and actively during emergencies. A sense of organization, i.e. the habit of quickly organizing themselves into an orderly party, cheerfully submitting themselves to irksome discipline and obeying the selected chief to the death irrespective of his social rank; a sense of law, a sense of honour, a sense of justice. Now, this is the equipment with which a public school boy leaves his school. He enters the University, there he specializes in some branch of study. During the time that he is there, he is no more a youngster; he is a man who has already begun to do the work he is expected to do in the world to some extent, while at the same time he is equipping himself with knowledge of an advanced nature in some special branch. There the students behave to each other as though they were already men: discuss the great problems of the world with the same serious interest that is seen in them when they begin the work of life proper after they leave the University. To their Union meetings come the great men of parliament and join with the students in the discussion of the problems of the day. To them come the great men of letters, leaders of thought, scientists and men who excel in every branch of literature, to pour their treasures at the feet of the *alma mater*. It is in the midst of such surroundings that these students are nurtured, it is in such an atmosphere that these students breathe, move and have their training. Fed upon such thoughts, nurtured in such traditions, equipped with such knowledge they come out here, to serve us in the Civil Service, Education and other services. And we say, why should they come; are we not as good as they; how are they better than we? Will my countrymen honestly look at themselves for a minute and then say that they are as good as those? If they do, I am sure there is no salvation to them. A man who honestly believes his is a case that calls for improvement and sets about it, has a chance of improving, however dull he may be; but one who mistakes his dullness for intelligence, and fully believes it, has not got a ghost of a chance to improve, and must grow from bad to worse with the only hope left to him "Oh I am as good as anybody else" till at last he becomes a laughing stock to the world. In the picture that I have given above of the Englishmen do my countrymen recognise any feature familiar to them? No, they can't, but they would see much that they can understand in the negative side of this picture; nor need they be ashamed of it. The traditions in which we have been brought for ages, the training we have received, these go a long way in making us what we are. We have to break through these traditions, we have to receive the training our rulers receive in their country before we can say we are fit for Self-Government. We may cry as long as we please, we may shout as high as we like "oh, are we not fit for Self-Government". It is earnest work, it is earnest preparation that will get us. All this has been forgotten; instead of directing their attention to the education of the people, education that will give us men of the kind that Oxford and Cambridge send down to us, we are vainly crying for the man in the moon. It is a matter of surprise that the committee instead of devoting their attention to these important points has recommended the immediate Indianisation of the several services. I cannot for a moment believe, that the British have become so dead to their sense of responsibility as to allow a predominating Indian element into the administration and vitiate and weaken its character. Until and unless we have schools similar to the Public Schools of England and Universities like those of Oxford and Cambridge, we ought to keep down the Indian elements and prevent it from containing the administration.

A two or three years training in Oxford or Cambridge to an Indian student does not by any means leave such a strong impress on his character as to make up for all the deficiencies arising from a lack of training in one of those Public Schools of England. Beyond the habit he acquires of wearing a hat and a boot, and an affection in the manner of his speech, and the airs he gives himself as though he has been transformed into a supreme being by crossing the sea and stopping within the walls of a college hammering away at his studies, we see nothing in him that calls for praise, though there is much that causes aversion. Above all, to send out a man to Europe for a matter of seven or eight months, at the expense of the people, pretending that he is going to master all the various systems of education; while as a matter of fact, it is only a fraud practised upon the people, to prevent them from seeing the truth, viz., a desire to promote a man, recommended by men in high places: to provide them with a plausible excuse for the step that they have contemplated to take, is a thing that cannot be sufficiently condemned.

I. It is proposed that out of the 60 per cent of Indians in the I.C.S. Service, 20 per cent are to be lifted up from the lower ranks. A more serious blunder cannot be made. A man who has been used to stooping all his life before his immediate superior, and tyrannizing over his immediate inferiors renders himself utterly incompetent to rise into the higher service. Habits of mind and character that reliance on self, that habit of turning to one's own mind and conscience in times of exigencies, that power of rapidly summoning one's own thoughts so as to be able to arrive at a quick decision when time presses these qualities that characterize an Englishman and render him eminently fit for any service, are just as things, the lack of which renders us eminently unfit for any service except as subordinates under them, to carry out orders issued by them, and leaving the whole responsibility in their hands. When such is the case the majority of our countrymen, with what stronger force does it apply to those men, who starting in the subordinate service, having been bending their backs so much that after 15 to 20 years they find it difficult even to stand erect. It would be a sin of life such a man into the higher service and expect that he would do justice to the position he holds. That man if he be really honest, would rather shun the job, than take on himself a responsibility, for which at the bottom of his heart he feels he is unequal.

II. *Indian Police Service* – All that I have said about the I.C.S. apply with equal force to the police service. That is a department that calls for the exercise of qualities that are entirely absent in the majority of Indians. From the bottom to the top, that portion that is manned by the Indian has always been condemned. The report says that at present the best type of Indian is not being obtained. This is not so, the type of man that is required for this service, you don't find in India. Such a type has yet to be created. Education and training alone will bring such a man into being. Meanwhile you have to make the best of the stuff you find. And instead of rushing to equalize the proportion, an effort ought to be made to choose the best men, give them the best training and in course of time create a tradition, which in its turn will re-act upon the members of the corps, and exercise a powerful influence in keeping them honest, vigilant, active and endowing them with a sense of responsibility which, while not courting danger will not shirk it, when necessity arises. It is best to leave the service as it is at present, and not meddle with it in the manner proposed so as to bring ruin and disaster upon the country.

III. *The Indian Forest Service* – As it seems to be agreed that the instruction and training available at the Forest Research Institute and College at Dehra Dun, will not be inferior to that obtainable in other parts of the world, recruitment may be at a higher rate than at present but the proposed rate of 75 per cent is simply preposterous.

IV. *Indian Service of Engineers* – Sub Division no. 1. As suggested the matter may be left entirely in the hands of the local Government. But it must be distinctly understood that the thing will prove calamitous if left in the hands of the Indian Ministers. The principle that guides them is caste, and not ability nor efficiency. So long as this is so, how can it be left in the hands of the Indian Ministers, nor can we expect any thing better so long as Ministers continue to be appointed as at present. How can you expect absolute incompetence and inefficiency to exercise intelligence, and make a good choice of able and honest men for different services. An ass is but an ass, though he might be clad in a lion's skin and the moment he opens his mouth to utter his oracular opinions, the note, the distinctive note, of the bray, in spite of all his attempts to conceal it, show itself unmistakably.

With regards to no. 2, I would suggest 60 per cent of European as against 40 per cent Indians of which five might be raised from the lower ranks.

With regard to no. 3, I would suggest that any Indian recruited in England must be outside 50 per cent which must be reserved entirely to Europeans.

V. *The India Agricultural and Veterinary Services* might be kept in the local Government. Although we do hope the Ministers will not stand in the way of recruiting first class men from England, in preference to mediocres, who happen to belong to their own caste, or to be their own relation.

With regards to the *Educational Service* the less of Indians put in these the better. It is a mockery of mockeries to ask an

Indian to lecture on English literature. The wonder to me is, how the absurdity of it does not appear either to the Indian or to the Englishman. And in formulating educational policies the last person you can trust is the Indian. It may be recalled that while dealing with the I.C.S., I said that until and unless an educational policy is laid out, that will render it possible for schools of the type of the Public Schools of England, the Indian element should be kept down. Now, of all services, the educational service is the most important. Because upon it depends the whole future of the country. If India really wants Self-Government if she means it in dead earnest, the best thing for her to do would be, to stand aside and allow the Englishman to chalk out the course unfettered, and let him guide us to the intended goal. Moreover the education of the Depressed Classes would suffer seriously. Indians that get into the Educational Service, will either be Brahmins or non-Brahmin caste Hindus, who would look after the interests of their particular communities and either neglect us (the Depressed Classes) or train us in such a way to look upon them for ever as our Masters. Again with regard to Medical Service I agree with the suggestions of the Commission.

VI. *Central Services*

(a) *Political Department:* There ought to be no recruitment to this department from the Provincial Civil Services.

(b) *Imperial Customs Service:* I would suggest only one alteration. Instead of not less than half the vacancies, I would say, not more than that half the vacancies are to be filled by appointment in India.

(c) *Superior Wireless and Telegraph Branch:* I would suggest recruitment of 50 per cent in England, and, the balance in India. Since this is the service that is likely to be of the greatest military value in times of war, it is best that 50 per cent of Englishmen are retained, while the balance might be Indians. Perhaps it may be objected that the Indian would be just as efficient, trustworthy, and otherwise competent at such times. But I leave it to my own countrymen to judge and decide honestly whether they would act and conduct themselves, like the Englishmen by the side to lean on in times of emergencies and trouble. What the Indian lacks is a stiff backbone, and without it, he stoops and bends constantly. No doubt he develops a supple back, and this stands him in very good stead in subordinate positions. But when you ask him to assume a position of great responsibility, his incompetency begins to show itself. And then it is that people see the ass under the lion's skin.

(d) *State Railway Engineers:* From a military point of view this service is just as important as, if not more important than, the other services and hence it is extremely necessary that the percentage of Indian element be kept down and the British element be made to predominate to as great an extent as possible. Perhaps it may be asked why it should be so. The answer is not far to seek. It can be easily judged how our great Indian engineering friends behave in times of flood, or, when a bridge is washed away.

I have all this time spoken of the incompetency of my countrymen arising from their inherent weakness of character, and then want of proper education and training. There is another important feature to which I have not adverted till now: because I have reserved it for special mention, since it is of the highest importance. As long as there is such a section as the Depressed Classes in existence, it would be committing the most egregious of blunders, either to think of Indianising the Government or of even admitting a larger proportion of Indians into the Government. The very fact of its existence is an unquestionable indication of the depth of barbarism to which the Indian has sunk, and the enormous resistance that any attempt at their amelioration meets with, is a further sign of how utterly incompetent they are for ever an approach towards Self-Government. No doubt, the caste Hindus to subserve their own selfish interests will hold out large promises to the ear, only to break them the moment their ends are accomplished. Before the reforms were introduced the Depressed Classes were begged by the non-Brahmin Caste Hindus to throw in their lot with them, that together they might fight the Brahmin successfully, and when he has been crushed they might share the spoils together. The most unfair tactics were employed by the caste Hindus. The falsest and barest of imputations were made against the Brahmin and by merely shouting aloud, and in very large numbers they successfully imposed on the British public, who fell an easy prey to the wily caste Hindus. And after having won all their points and crushed the Brahmin they turned their attention to the Depressed Classes. 99 per cent of the Depressed Classes are agriculturists and manage to eke out a living upon very precarious terms from the land. And 99.9 of the men who own these lands are the caste Hindus, and the way they treat the Depressed Classes eludes all attempts at description. A sword is hanging over their heads all the time suspended by a hair, and the men are living in a state of deep anxiety all the time to the end of their lives. This is perpetuated from generation to generation. This has been going on from time immemorial and is going on still. At a moment, if the landlord wills it, he can serve a notice of ejectment on all these men, and they have noting for it but to obey. And such opportunities often arise. These men from the ideas they entertain of their own descent and of their own consequence, regard themselves as so many celestial beings, whom even to approach within a distance of ten yards, is looked on as a serious offence by them, for which they inflect condign punishment. Soon after the non-Brahmin caste Hindus came into power, in September 1921, Sir P. Theagaraya Chetty the redoubtable knight of Toudiarpet and the head of the non-Brahmin caste Hindu party in the Council wrote a most unwise letter to Government taking the side of caste Hindu labourers against the Adi-Dravida labourers and made most unwarrantable statements ill founded on facts and suggested to Government to deport Adi-Dravida labourers out of Madras. To such ravenous and bloodthirsty wolves and vultures, the poor depressed classes men would be handed over in any system of Government, where the services would be largely Indianised. I cannot imagine that the British Government (though at present the Labour Party rules) have become so lost to a sense of moral responsibility, which is their best if not their only title to their presence in India. It is that that makes them afford special protection to the members of the depressed classes against the cruel and relentless persecution of the caste Hindus. Long before the Reforms were even dreamt of, a department had been created whose sole duty it was to ameliorate the conditions of the depressed classes, and, in general to look after their interests. The caste Hindus, as soon as they came to power, as a result of the reforms, or perhaps as a result of the particular manoeuvre of Lord Willingdon (for it is impossible to believe that the measure contemplated the remaining in power of the caste Hindus to all perpetuity, still less that two or three non-entities would hold power and draw the emoluments of office for two successive ministries in spite of the tremendous amount of opposition from among their own people which among others contains few inferior or to them, either in ability, honesty, or character) set themselves to destroy this department, and to considerable extent they were successful. And I understand that an attempt is now being made to bring even the remnant under the power of Indian Ministers. This must be resisted, and battled with and baffled. The special department must be reinforced and kept entirely in the hands of Englishmen, and the Indian ought not to be allowed to exercise even a grain of influence or power in that department. More powers must be given to this department, so as to admit of papers being disposed of quickly without reference to this or of that department, which generally entails interminable delays caused in some cases by negligence, in others by ingrained, unconquerable prejudice, and spite towards the depressed classes. Over and above everything else 15 per cent of all the superior service must be reserved to the members of the depressed classes while a similar percentage must also be reserved in the Provincial and Subordinate Services. My evidence will prejudice my personal relations with my countrymen, besides increasing the obstacles already insurmountable in the way of the progress of my community. The caste Hindus will now offer determined and organized resistance to any efforts that might be made towards softening the hardships and cruelties to which the members of my community are subjected. In spite of this hazardous contingency I feel I am morally bound to speak the truth irrespective of whatever injurious consequences which may entail upon my community.

Note on the Depressed Classes by Rao Bahadur M.C. Rajah, M.L.A.*

The Depressed Classes in India present a definite problem in political and social evolution. They are the resultants of historical forces, religious, economic and social. They are the embodiment of exploded social ideas and the disabilities imposed on them by the original framers of Hindu polity have been aggravated by long centuries of segregation and neglect. The origin of these Classes and the beginning of their woes rightly belong to the domain of historical research but their betterment, economic and educational, is an imperative political problem. Their class consciousness is growing, stimulated partly by the sympathy of the Government and partly by the belated awakening of the Hindu social conscience. Still the new forces are encountering great opposition from the hostility of orthodoxy on the one side and the inertia of ignorance on the other. Every political party admits the existence of the problem and the need for special ameliorative measures.

Difficulties have been raised as to who exactly constitute the "Depressed Classes". The term "Depressed Classes", and "Backward Classes" are bandied together and not infrequently cause confusion. The doubt whether a certain section came under the classification or not has often been brought out as an excuse to show there is nothing like Depressed Classes and that no such problem exists at all. The first attempt to enumerate these classes was made in the census report of 1901 and the next report (1911) showed that the classes (Untouchables) who came under this category numbered 45 millions of the total Hindu population. The existence of the problem itself was recognized much earlier when the Madras Adi-Dravida Jana Sabha, now called the Registered All India Adi-Dravida Mahajana Sabha, was organized by Mr. P.V. Soobramaniam Pillay in December 1892, incorporated under Act XXI of 1860, and began making

*East India (Constitutional Reforms), Report of the Indian Central Committee 1928-29, London, 1929.

periodical recommendations to Government regarding the protection of the interests of Untouchables otherwise known as the Depressed Classes. The question was first raised on the floor of the Legislature when the Hon. Mr. (now Sir) Dadabhai moved a resolution in the Imperial Legislative Council in 1916 asking for a survey of the problem. As a result of the resolution the Government of India circularised all the Provincial Governments and the replies of these Governments for the first time revealed the magnitude and gravity of the problem (vide Government of India Memorandum; The Depressed Classes). Subsequent Government reports, educational and political, have only served to emphasise the importance of the problem. Owing to the extreme backwardness of the communities and the prevalence of untouchability the education of these classes presented special difficulties. In his quinquennial review of education, 1912-17, the Education Commissioner, Sir Henry Sharp, by grouping together those whose educational needs presented difficulties owing to the fact of their being Untouchables arrived at a total of 31½ millions of Hindus. In this classification the aborigines, the Hill tribes and the criminal tribes had been omitted. The figures collected by the Franchise Committee in 1919 appointed in the wake of the Montagu-Chelmsford Report, yielded a total of 42 millions comprising the group "Others" as a third Hindu group, identified by them with the Depressed Classes mentioned in Para 11 of their Report and again these do not include the aborigines or the animists or the Hill Tribes. The Franchise Committee followed these figures in the matter of framing franchise and apportioning representation. There was fresh enumeration again in the census of 1921 and the Commissioner, Mr. J.T. Marten, puts the figure at what he himself calls a "low and conservative minimum of 43 million in British India". "We may," he adds, "confidently place the numbers of these Depressed Classes, all of whom are considered impure, at something between 55 and 60 millions in India proper." This coincides with the figures of Mr. J. Coatman in his book "India in 1926-27". The Reforms Enquiry Committee of 1924 accepted these revised figures in paragraph 64 of their Report and the minority and the majority alike amply recognized the importance and seriousness of the question. On 23rd February 1928, Mr. M.R. Jayakar moved a resolution in the Legislative Assembly recommending the local Governments be instructed to provide special facilities for the education of Depressed

Classes and also for opening all public services to them especially the police; and the late Lala Lajpat Rai moved an amendment thereto recommending the setting apart of a sum of a crore of rupees for affording special educational facilities for these classes. The Government spokesman, Mr. G.S. Bajpai, opposing the amendment, for the first time attempted to lower the figure and belittle the problem. Mr. Bajpai took his figures from the Educational Department, of which he happened to be the Secretary, and represented that the total for British India, excluding Burma and Assam, was only 28½ millions. The accuracy of this figure was challenged and disproved when I sent in an interpellation on 4th September 1928, in answering which the Home Member of the Government of India estimated the total of Depressed Classes at 60 millions for India proper. This coincides with the Census Commissioner Mr. Marten's estimate quoted above. Still the incorrect figure of 28½ millions is persisted in, in the auxiliary Education Committee's Report. But that is so because the Educational Officer, who compiled the figures in respect of Mr. Bajpai's figure also, happens to be the Secretary of the Auxiliary Education Committee. The Secretary of the Indian Central Committee early in January 1929, circularised the various Provincial Governments asking for the latest figures and these yielded 44½ millions. This does not include the aboriginal and criminal tribe's population.

A detailed examination of the figures collected by the Hartog Committee reveals two serious errors. In the case of the United Provinces the figures given by the Government show the Depressed Classes as thirteen millions. But the Hartog Committee erroneously takes them at the lower and incorrect figure. In the case of Assam the error is more serious. The Committee have altogether denied the existence of anything like Depressed Classes in this Province. The figures of the local Government enumerating the various subcastes coming under this category give them a total of 1.55 millions. Again deputations of Depressed Classes waited before the Joint Free Conference in Shillong on 4th January 1929, and detailed their grievances.

As I am writing this I have received intimation that on the 17th August 1929, the Governor of Assam has nominated for the first time a member of the Depressed Classes to the local Legislative Council. In the face of this irrefutable testimony to say that there are no Depressed Classes in Assam is clearly incorrect.

THE POPULATION OF THE DEPRESSED CLASSES (UNTOUCHABLES) IN MILLIONS

Provinces	Franchise Committee's Figures 1919	Census Figures of 1921	Reforms Enquiry Committee's Figures 1924	Hartog Committee's Figures 1928	Indian Central Committee's Figures 1929
	(1)	(2)	(3)	(4)	(5)
Madras	6.4	6.4	6.4	6.53	6.50
Bombay	.6	2.8	2.8	1.46	1.47
Bengal	9.9	9.0	9.0	6.64	11.50
United Provinces	10.1	9.0	9.0	7.89	13.00
Punjab	1.7	2.8	2.8	1.70	2.80
Bihar and Orissa	9.4	8.0	8.0	2.53	5.00
Central Provinces	3.8	3.3	3.3	3.01	2.67
Assam	.3	2.0	2.0	*	1.55
	42.2	43.3	43.3	29.76	44.50

Notes: * It is stated in the Hartog Report that there are practically no Untouchables in Assam (vide p. 218, Table XCI of the Report of the Auxiliary Committee of the Indian Statutory Commission).
Figures under (5) have been taken from the printed list supplied by the Secretary, Indian Central Committee, to the members.

Without even going so far as to debate the accuracy of these figures, one has only to look at the numerous social and civic disabilities (of which typical instances are furnished later) prevailing almost everywhere in India to realize the magnitude of the problem. The records of the Reform Legislative Councils are replete with evidence testifying to the undeniable existence of these hardships and debates on proposed ameliorative measures.

Interpellations covering specific statutory or social disability hampering members of these classes and resolutions and bills recommending removal of general disabilities form a regular feature of every session of every Provincial Council. The rules framed under the Government of India Act make provision for special protection of their interests and enjoin upon heads of local governments the necessity for making provision for adequate representation of these classes in the Legislatures and the various Local Bodies.

1. The Governor of Madras, under Rule 3 of the Madras Electoral Rules, is instructed to nominate "ten to represent the following

communities, namely the Paraiyans, Pallans, Valluvans, Mallas, Madigas, Chakkiliyans, Tottiyans, Cherumans and Holeyas".

2. By virtue of Rule 3 of the United Provinces Electoral Rules, the Governor is instructed to nominate one to represent "classes which, in the opinion of the governor, are Depressed Classes".
3. The Governor of Bombay is instructed to nominate two to represent classes which, "in the opinion of the Governor, are Depressed Classes". (*Vide* Memorandum prepared by the Government of Bombay for submission to the Indian Statutory Commission, 1928, para. 387.)
4. The Government of Bengal nominates a member of the Depressed Classes. (*Vide* Report on the working of the Reformed Constitution in Bengal, 1921-27, para. 178.)
5. The Governor of the Central Provinces nominates members of the Depressed Classes, and "the number of members nominated from the Depressed Classes has been raised from two to four in the third Council. (*Vide* Memorandum on the working of the Reformed Government in the Central Provinces and Berar, vol. I, p. 23.)
6. The Governor of Bihar and Orissa nominates two members "believed to be in sympathy with the class (Depressed Class), though not as a rule actually of that class". (*Vide* Memorandum for the Indian Statutory Commission on the working of the Reforms in Bihar and Orissa, para 154.)

THE REPRESENTATION OF THE
DEPRESSED CLASSES AS IT IS AT PRESENT

Legislatures	Total population	Population of the Depressed Classes	Total number of seats at present	Seats for Depressed Classes
Madras	42 millions	6.50 millions	132	10
Bombay	16 millions	1.47 millions	114	2
Bengal	45 millions	11.50 millions	140	1
United Provinces	47 millions	13.00 millions	123	1
Punjab	20 millions	2.80 millions	94	nil
Bihar and Orissa	33 millions	5.00 millions	103	2
Central Provinces	12 millions	2.67 millions	103	4
Assam	7 millions	1.55 millions	53	nil

These facts alone furnish an overwhelming answer to those witnesses who, speaking on behalf of certain Provincial Governments, sought to make out that the problem was non-existent in their province.

The lines of division which mark off the Depressed Classes from the rest of the Hindus are clear and unmistakable. Roughly, all those Hindus who are outside the pale of the four varnas, or castes, whose touch or proximity carries pollution, and those whose occupations are considered unclean and impure, constitute the Depressed Classes. They have not the right of the King's highway, nor have they the rights for public waterways and springs. They live segregated in the cheris in the Madras Presidency; in bastis in the Punjab; in mohallas or tolis in the United Provinces; and in the pallis and paras of Bengal. Social rights they have none, and of civic and political rights little. The catalogue could be lengthened by adding local grievances in every province. But the idea of carrying pollution by touch or proximity and the denial of entry to temples or Dev Darshan constitute the G.C.M. of the factors which make up Untouchability. This was also the principle of enumeration adopted by the various Census Commissioners. (*Vide* Franchise Committee's Report, dated 22nd February 1919; Statistical Summary footnotes and Census Reports for 1911 and 1921.)

Despite the fact that there has been a steady enlargement of popular control over the present system of Government, the claim of the Depressed Classes have so far not been adequately recognized. In the public bodies they are inadequately represented and in the public services they are not encouraged. In both the spheres the existing handicaps are heavy, and in the present low position of these classes they cannot overcome them unaided. Though popular representatives were admitted into the Legislative Councils as early as 1861, no member of the Depressed Classes ever found an opportunity to serve on these Councils. Though the Morley-Minto Councils were so formed as to enlarge the popular element so as to constitute a non-official majority, still no room was found to have the Depressed Classes represented. It was only in the last year of those councils that Lord Willingdon recognized their claims and nominated one member to his Council in Madras. The Montagu-Chelmsford Reforms for the first time made statutory provisions for the representation of their interests and enjoined upon the Local Governments the necessity to give them a voice in the Legislative Councils. The number of seats allotted varied in each province; but in many it was not more than one or two and in some nil. In the Central Legislature there was no member of the Depressed Classes till I was nominated in 1927. The rightful claims of the Depressed Classes are dealt with later. Here I only indicate the existence of the grievance. In the various Local Boards these Classes get no representation. All this deprives them of making their troubles known and demanding redress. In the public services the grievance is more acute. The educational and economic position of candidates from the Depressed Classes makes it incumbent on the authorities that their claims should be treated preferentially. Not only is there no such preference, but in actual practice their so-called social inferiority is brought up as a bar and results in the anomaly of even higher qualifications being neglected to make room for social prejudice. A question in the Punjab Council; a resolution in the United Provinces Council; the reply of an Inspector-General of Police to an applicant for a Deputy-Superintendent's post in Assam; a District Collector's reply to an applicant for an Honorary Magistrate's post in Bombay; and a recent instance of selection of sub-registrars in Bengal furnish typical instances of the difficulty. The instances are cited from different provinces and furnish unmistakable proof of their universality.

Punjab Council – Question No. 466. Lala Mohan Lal: "Will the Honourable Member for Finance be pleased to state if members of the Depressed Classes are taken in police? If not, does the Government intend to direct that in the matter of recruitment of police constables, the members of the Depressed Classes should also be taken?"

The Honourable Sir Geoffrey de Montmorency – "Members of the Depressed Classes are not enrolled in the police. When there is evidence that the Depressed Classes are treated on an equal footing by all sections of the community, or when Government is satisfied that enrolment of members of these classes will satisfy the requirements of efficiency and be in the best interests of the composition of the service, Government will be quite prepared to throw open recruitment to them, provided they come up to the physical and other standards required of all recruits."

United Provinces Council – On 17 December 1925, a Resolution was moved in the United Provinces Council for the removal of caste restrictions for admission to the police and other public services. (*Vide* Reports on the working of the Reformed Constitution 1927, pp. 226, 227.)

Assam – The following is the reply of the Inspector-General of Police, Assam, to Mr. Sonadher Das, Secretary, Bania (Depressed Class), Samaj. The candidate was a member of the Depressed Classes and a Master of Arts.

From

The Hon'ble Lt. Colonel D. Herbert, I.A., Inspector-General of Police, Assam.

To

The Secretary to the Brittial Bania Community of Assam Proper, Shillong.

Dated Shillong, the 23rd October 1918.

Sir,

With reference to your letter, dated the 4th October 1918, I have the honour to inform you that while I sympathise with the aspiration of the Assam Brittial Bania Community, I regret that so many considerations govern the appointments of Deputy Superintendents of Police at present, e.g. the fact that suitable candidates with war service have preference, that I am unable to give any definite reply. I do not, however, think that in the present conditions of Indian Society a member of a community suffering from social depression, as referred to in the letter under reply, could make a successful Deputy Superintendent of Police. I, therefore, recommend the candidate you refer to press his application for appointment to some other branch of Government Service.

I have the honour to be,
Sir,
Your most obedient servant,
(Signed) D. HERBERT,
Inspector-General of Police, Assam.

Bombay.

The Collector of Khandish District, Bombay Presidency, in his reply dated 25th September 1928, to Mr. Medhi, a member of the Depressed Classes, who applied to him for the post of an Honorary Bench Magistrate, wrote thus:

"The Collector has every sympathy with the aspirations of the Depressed Classes and is glad to recognize and appreciate Mr. Medhi's good work in the various fields of public activities; but in his opinion time has not yet come when a member of the Depressed Classes can be given a seat on the bench of Magistrates, and until Government makes some pronouncement favourable to the aspirations of the Depressed Classes in this Presidency, he must regretfully express his inability to recommend such an appointment." (*Vide* Evidence, Depressed Classes Deputation, Bombay.)

Bengal.

The following is an extract from the evidence of the Depressed Classes Deputation, Bengal, that appeared before the Joint Conference on the 21st January 1929, led by Mr. M.B. Mullick, M.A., B.L., President, All-Bengal Namasudra Association:

"Q. 76. I supposed there are a number of graduates in your community? – A. There are a fair number.
"Q. 77. 400 to 500? – A. Yes.
"Q. 78. There are M.As and B.As? – A. Yes.
"Q. 79. Are there many of them in the public service? – A. Only a few.
"Q. 80. I should like to know whether they find any difficulty in entering the provincial or subordinate services? – A. Yes, they do find difficulty.
"Q. 81. I understand, as recently as January 1928, they recruited some sub-registrars? – A. Yes.
"Q. 82. And for that the Government asked the various Commissioners to send up nominations? – A. Yes.
"Q. 83. The Commissioners in turn asked the various Collectors? – A. Yes.
"Q. 84. That is, qualified candidate for these posts? A. That is so.
"Q. 85. In the Dacca division I understand the Commissioners sent in four nominations? – A Yes.
"Q. 86. Two Hindus and two Mohammedans? – A. Yes, that is so.
"Q. 87. Out of these two Hindus only an M.A. belonged to your community? A. To one of the Depressed Classes.
"Q. 88. And the other was B.A., a Kayastha? – A. Yes.
"Q. 89. Out of other two Muhammadans, one was an M.A. and the other a B.A.? – A. Yes.
"Q. 90. And out of these, two were appointed? – A. Yes.
"Q. 91. Although in the notification it was said that preference would be given to Backward and Depressed Classes? – A. I believe that was the notification.
"Q. 92. In spite of that they thought it fit to offer the appointment to the B.A. Kayastha, overlooking the Depressed Class M.A's claim? – A. Yes, It was published in the last gazette.
"Q. 93. Again, in June 1928, in the Dacca civil court there were a number of vacancies for clerks, but they did not even care to advertise? – A. That was what we knew.
"Q. 94. There were a number of graduates belonging to the Depressed Classes who sent in their application for these clerkships, but the son of an official who was a matriculate was preferred? – A. That we discovered later.
"Q. 95. And a brother-in-law of the head clerk, an undergraduate, was preferred? – A. Yes.
"Q. 96. And the graduate belonging to the Depressed Classes did not get a chance? – A. No.
"Q. 97. And recently, about five months ago, there were some appointments under the Controller of Currency, in Bengal? – A. Yes, and also under the Accountant-General, Bengal.
"Q. 98. There, also, members of the Depressed Classes who were graduates applied for those posts? – A. They did.

"Q. 99. And they did not get them? – A. No although an advertisement was made, and it was said in the advertisement that some appointments would be reserved for them.

"Q. 100. Also as regards sub-registrars in Khulna, Faridpur and Jessore districts, several members of the Depressed Classes, graduates applied for these appointments, but they were not preferred? – A. They were nominated by the Collectors, but I do not know what happened after that."

The Inspector-General of Police, Bombay, when examined by the Commission said that the members of the Depressed Classes are not admitted in the Police service in the Bombay Presidency. The Inspector-General of the Punjab also said that the Depressed Classes are not admitted in the police department in the Punjab.

The superstition attaching to the so-called pollution results in innumerable social and civic disabilities; though these are slowly disappearing, yet they are generally prevalent. The children of the Depressed Classes cannot go to the same school (*Vide* Memorandum submitted by B. Ram Charan, B.A., LL.B., M.L.C. [U.P.]). The members of the Depressed Classes cannot engage in occupations which would bring them into close contact with other Hindus. That bars out all possibilities of social intercourse or economic betterment. The system of forced labour or Begar is still prevalent in the Punjab and the Depressed Classes are daily being harassed by officers throughout the province (*Vide* Memorandum, The Depressed Classes Mission, Lahore, p. 2). A Resolution was also moved in the Central Province Legislative Council for the abolition of Begar. In the lower courts Depressed Class witnesses must stand aloof when they give evidence. (*Vide* Evidence Depressed Classes Deputation, Bombay.) No untouchable can come into any public office for the transaction of business in the villages and minor towns. He cannot enter a post office to buy a stamp or post a letter (*vide* Evidence Depressed Classes Deputation, Bengal). Hospitals maintained out of public funds have no accommodation for him. The right of using public rest-houses is denied to him. (*Vide* Memorandum prepared by the Government of Bombay for submission to the Indian Statutory Commission, p. 527 [9].) I am depicting no imaginary or historical grievances. Caste Hindus of Bombay, led by such an enlightened and progressive leader as Sir Manmohandas Ramji, protested against a resolution passed by the Corporation of Bombay abolishing the practice of compelling the Untouchable children to drink water out of different cups in the Corporation school. The share-brokers of the city took a day off to mark their protest against the corporation Resolution, and my colleague, Mr. Kikabhai Premchend, is an ex-President of the Share Brokers' Association. (*Vide* "Indian Daily Mail", 19 October 1928.) This happened when the Statutory Commission was sitting at Poona. Caste fury assumed a graver aspect when an Untouchable woman was discovered walking in the streets of holy Benares. The offended Hindus belaboured the poor woman most mercilessly. (*Vide* "The Aj", 26 October 1927.) In the recent case in my own province an Untouchable paid with his life for the temerity of polluting a street with his presence. ("Madras Mail", weekly, 1st August 1929.) Even to-day the Madras Council is debating a bill introduced by a private member demanding that all highways be thrown open to the Depressed Classes. In the United Provinces the instance was cited to us by the United Provinces Government (*vide* Report on the working of the System of Government, United Provinces of Agra and Oudh, 1921-28, vol. III, Addendum, p. 50) of Untouchables leaving their pots near public wells in the hope that some charitable Samaritan would fill them. Resolutions were moved in the Madras Council, Bombay Council, Central Provinces Council and Punjab Council, to allow the members of the Depressed Classes to draw water from the public wells maintained by the Local Bodies. The Untouchable children attending common schools are victimised. (Memorandum prepared by the Government of Bombay for submission to the Indian Statutory Commission, p. 528 [21].) In the Punjab there are restrictive laws and customary rules that stand in the way of the advancement of the Depressed Classes. The Depressed Classes are forced to hold the lowest place in society, because of certain customary rules, which are enforceable in Courts of Law, debarring them from purchasing lands in village communities. The attention of the Government was drawn to the matter in the Punjab Legislative Council on 3rd March 1928. The result of the customary rules which have the force of law is that the Depressed Classes are unable to purchase lands or even residential sites in villages. (*Vide* Memorandum submitted by the National Reforms Party, Punjab, p. 22.) The Land Alienation Act of Punjab prevents the Depressed Classes from purchasing lands from the privileged castes notified under the Act as agriculturalists, though the Depressed Classes are themselves agriculturalists. (*Vide* ibid., p. 22.)

The Depressed Classes, though Hindus, cannot participate in common worship, nor can they come into the Temples. They are not even admitted into a public conveyance (Memorandum prepared by the Government of Bombay for submission to the Indian Statutory Commission, p. 528 (19), not to speak of Barbers' Saloon and Indian Restaurants and Refreshment Rooms under the management of so-called caste Hindus. Rigorous segregation and enforced poverty have reduced these communities to nothing more than a physical existence. Aspirations and hopes of progress have been stifled under the load of superstitions and have all but died out. Thought has been fettered and resources crippled, resulting in stagnation and decay. Ninety per cent of India's wealth is reported to be her agricultural produce and 90 per cent of India's tillers of the soil are the Depressed Classes. But of that wealth they get no proper share. Generation after generation they have been forced to live in dirt and squalor and to grow up in ignorance and fear. Ignorant habits and insanitary surroundings make them fall an easy prey to epidemic, and their poverty exposes them to chronic famine.

It is often contended that these disabilities spring from deep rooted social prejudices and that political remedies are of little avail against them. It is asserted that legislation and administration cannot force the pace of social reform, and premature efforts in that direction often retard progress. That was true when States were organized on a limited basis and operated in a limited perspective. But the modern State, organized on democratic basis, embraces every sphere of national and social activity, and as such is the most powerful engine of social reform. It not only embodies and preserves prevalent social ideas, but by its credentials it is authorized to mould and direct social tendencies. Under the more advanced conditions in the Western countries it has taken upon itself the duty of caring for the old and training the young. It acts as an agency in the more equitable distribution of the national dividend. Free education, adult franchise, old age pensions and unemployment insurance bear irrefutable testimony to its solicitude towards those who would otherwise, under the relentless operation of economic laws soon become the Depressed Classes of Europe. The Government in India is progressing towards that ideal, and must sooner than later face this task of levelling up. The history of the last hundred years has shown that education, transport, commerce and political power have acted as solvents of age-long caste prejudices, and it is only by aiding the Depressed Classes to participate in an increasing measure in these activities that the stigma attaching to them could be removed. This is fully recognized in the evidence prepared by the Bombay Government, where they admit

> the problem of Untouchability is not merely a social one. It has an important political aspect. Owing to the prevalence of untouchability a large section of the population is denied the enjoyment of its legitimate civic rights. Untouchability, which is also peculiar to the Hindus, is intimately bound up with the caste system, and has, therefore, in the minds of some people, a religious basis. The untouchable or depressed classes, who form about a thirteenth part of the total population of the Presidency, are denied many of the ordinary civic rights and privileges.
>
> (*Vide* Memorandum prepared by the Government of Bombay for submission to the Indian Statutory Commission, 1928, p. 382.)

The general remedy that suggests itself is immediate and total withdrawal of legal and administrative recognition to the superstition of pollution. The laws as they are administered to-day uphold these superstitions and punish the untouchables who dare to disregard them. Whenever a member of the Depressed Classes attempts to enforce his civic rights, the law steps in under the guise of preserving the peace which, it fears, would otherwise be broken. In practice it amounts to legal protection to the superstition and denial of an elementary right to a member of the community. But, as this aspect is more concerned with internal legal reform and not with the main constitutional re-adjustment, I leave it with a mere indication. In the matter of political power the position of the Depressed Classes has to be safeguarded in (a) Legislatures and (b) Public Services. I have already pointed out that in Legislatures the Depressed Classes never had an opportunity of having their voice heard till Lord Willingdon nominated the first Adi-Dravida member to his council in 1919. Later the number nominated was increased under the Reforms Act, and to-day in most of the councils they have representatives who look after their interests. The suggested reform here is increase in numbers and change in method of representation so as to be more in consonance with democratic practice and better representative of the interests concerned. The change in the method is of more vital importance and demands closer attention. The method hitherto followed was nomination by the Governor, advised by the Executive Councillors, of either untouchables themselves or those in the opinion of the Governor might be expected to look after their interests. The defects of this method are obvious, but it was first welcomed and later tolerated on the principle that the blabberer is preferable to the dumb. Nomination has lived its day of usefulness and has done its part in quickening political life in the community. The preference to-day is for the privilege of direct election. The nominated member, while he did voice the needs of his brethren, bore no representative character and had not the same living touch with those whom he represented as the elected member had. In the Councils he was more prone to follow the lead of those who nominated him. He was not eligible for the Ministry. In a predominantly elected Chamber the nominated members naturally tended to a second place. True, there was no legal difference in status, but their views did not carry the same weight, though their votes did. Nominated representation was welcomed when there was none and was accepted when there was not sufficient date to demand election. But the working of the Reforms during the last ten years has demonstrated the future possibilities, and my demand is fully borne out by the conditions of to-day. There is one more reason why nomination must be abolished in the future, and its validity from the constitutional point of view, I venture to say, could be hardly questioned. In the future councils, according to our recommendations, there is to be no nominated bloc. The Chamber would consist only of elected members. Also the Governor's Executive Council would not be there. The government would be vested in the Governor acting with his Ministers. So any nomination that the Governor would make could only be on the advice of his Ministers. And the easiest way for the Minister would be to get his party adherents nominated; and the constitutional device meant to protect the weaker elements would only serve as a means of co-option for the largest group in the Council to the detriment of the community and Government alike. The privilege of nomination vested in the hands of a political group would be nothing less than a menace. In recommending the system of nomination the statesmen of the day were not blind to its defects. They admitted the existence of these defects but their only plea was that they had no alternative. "In assigning the number of seats in each Council to which non-official representative may be appointed by nomination we have been guided by the existence of the important classes or interests which could not be expected to obtain representation by any practicable system of election. Thus we have been driven to the expedient of nomination for the representation of the Depressed Classes, because in no case did we find it possible to provide an electorate on any satisfactory system of Franchise." (*Vide* para. 24, Franchise Committee Report.)

That was what the Franchise Committee found in 1919. The Joint Parliamentary Committee had the same difficulty. The Depressed Classes appeared before Mr. Montagu, but refused to go before the Franchise Committee, and said:

> We would appear before the Franchise Committee provided the two persons, Messrs. V.S. Sreenivasa Sastriar and Surendra Nath Bannerjee, to whose presence on the Committee we have already objected, are removed from the Committee during appearance before it. We have already stated that Mr. Sreenivasa Sastriar, as a champion and apologist of Brahmin oligarchy in preference to British bureaucracy, and Mr. Bannerjee as one who advised our Sabha and the Community which it represents 'to enlist themselves in the German army fighting against freedom and civilization' because we said in our address to Lord Chelmsford and the Rt. Hon. Mr. Montagu that 'we would fight to the last drop of our blood any attempt to transfer the seat of authority in this country from British hands to the so-called high caste Hindus who had been oppressing us in the past and would do so again but for the British Government,' are unfit to sit in judgment over any representation we may make. If they continue to sit on the Committee, we have no other alternative as self-respecting and loyal citizens of the British Empire, than that of respectfully declining to appear before the aforesaid Committee. (*Vide* Appendix XV, Franchise Committee Report.)

But conditions have improved considerably to-day. The representatives of the Depressed Classes waited in deputations and gave evidence before the Joint Conference at every centre in India and demanded that a definite step in the direction of democracy must be taken. It is suggested as a half-way measure that nomination might be made from a panel of members suggested by Communal Associations or Electoral Colleges, but the suggestion is open to the same objections. Added to them is the danger of mushroom or make-believe associations suggesting their own nominees and creating confusion.

A third alternative would be reservation of seats in Joint Electorates. It undoubtedly marks an advance on the present position but it is not altogether without objectionable features. In the total electorate the proportion of Depressed Classes voters would be small. And the fear is not unnaturally entertained that the candidates who would fill the reserved seats would in reality be the nominees of the majority of the electorate. The constituencies being predominantly caste-Hindu, no one could hope to get elected who did not pander to or at least respect caste prejudices. Against a Depressed Class member elected on the strength of caste Hindu votes would not be beholden to his community. There is thus the danger of the seats being occupied by the dummies of the higher castes. Such a result would largely nullify the power granted to the Depressed Classes in the shape of the franchise. Joint Electorates if they are to work successfully require broadmindedness on the part of the majority community. It is my view that to-day such a favourable atmosphere does not exist.

The following evidence of the Depressed Classes Deputation before the Joint Conference in Bengal on 21st January 1929, will clear the position:

Q. 201. Is it not a fact that there are half-a-dozen Depressed Classes men who are member of the Provincial Council here in Bengal? – A. No, we have one nominated and two elected only, and those two came in with the other people.
Q. 202. Are not those two helping you? – A. No, not in the least.
Q. 203. Why? – A. Because they came in with the caste Hindus.
Q. 204. You mean because they came into the Council with the support of the caste Hindus? – A. Yes.
Q. 205. And therefore they are subservient to the caste Hindus there? – A. Yes.
Q. 206. And they are not in a position to help? – A. Not at all.

The creation of Separate Electorates is the only other means which can ensure direct election and at the same time secure adequate protection. Objections, both theoretical and practical, are raised against the demand for Separate Electorates. But on closer examination they could be found to be not insurmountable and since the demand for it is only for a temporary period even these objections lose their validity. Theoretically it is pointed out that Separate Electorates tend to perpetuate differences and hinder the growth of nationalism. There is weight in the objection but it is more than counterbalanced by the advantages secured under it. Separate Electorates are not new to the Indian constitution. The Muslims, the Sikhs, Indian Christians, Anglo-Indians and Europeans possess them and they have given these communities a sense of security which alone has made all talk of advance possible. The peculiar position of Q. 201. today demands that their interests have to be protected against their Hindu co-religionists. In a common electorate where the voters were actuated by common interests division will follow opinions about the merits of the issues involved. But where conflict of interests is involved the voting will go by interests. When the existence of the conflict is accepted, it is clear that minority interests will never succeed in getting representation. The voter who happened to belong to the minority community would feel that his vote was being thrown away. He would even refuse to exercise his franchise when he is certain that the dice is already loaded against him. The resulting insecurity will not conduce to communal harmony. Where he is afforded the protection of Separate Electorates this danger disappears. He is sure that whoever wins the election has been elected on the community's own votes and not by the votes of the caste Hindus. The vote would thus secure a value in his eye and would give him a sense of security. Political education would then be more rapid and the creation of sufficient self-confidence in the community would soon render the artificial protection unnecessary. The political objections are less weighty. It is said that the creation of Separate Electorates is an impossible task as it is not possible to demarcate the Depressed Classes exactly in each province. This is hardly convincing. The existence of these classes is proved beyond doubt. All that is necessary is that the Provincial Governments should prepare the complete list of classes who according to local custom and usage come under the category of Untouchables and carve out constituencies for them. Such lists have already been prepared by the Government in furnishing the information asked for by the late Lala Lajpat Rai. A suggestion was made that if it was known that the Depressed Classes were being given special representation then there would be a scramble among some of the higher classes to get listed under the term "Depressed". This can hardly be so. It is inconceivable that for the sake of a vote any caste Hindu will be anxious to enroll himself in the Depressed Classes Register. Untouchables live apart from others and there is no possibility of missing the Untouchable and the Touchable. The next objection is that there are not sufficient voters, and that even the small number is so scattered as to make the task of carving out constituencies well-nigh impossible. Full data concerning the voters and how they are scattered has not been made available by all the Governments. The Madras Government, however, have given the whole data and an examination of the same shows that the difficulty is only imaginary.

Under the present electoral qualifications the Depressed Classes in the Madras Presidency have 56,756 votes; the Mohammedans in Madras Presidency have 63,626 votes; Indian Christians have 27,860 votes; and Anglo-Indians have 2,816 votes. Constituencies have been carved out for the Mohammedans, Indian Christians and Anglo-

Indians in the Madras Presidency; and they secure representation by election. The Mohammedans with a voting strength of 63,626, elect 13; the Indian Christians with 27,860 votes, elect 7; the Anglo-Indians, with 2,816 votes, elect one. On the other hand, though the Depressed Classes have a voting strength of 56,756 this privilege is denied to them and their representation is secured by nomination.

The Reforms Officer of the Madras Government has supplied the Indian Statutory Commission with a statement showing the total number of Depressed Classes voters in each District of the Madras Presidency (*vide* his letter of 25/28th February 1929). From this statement we find the voting strength of the Depressed Classes in Cuddapah, South Kanara, Malabar and Nilgiris is under 500; in Bellary, Coimbatore, Kurnool and Madras it is between 500 and 1,000; in Anantapore, North Arcot, Chittoor, Godavari West, Ramnad, Salem, Tanjore and Trichinopoly it is between 1,000 and 2,000; in South Arcot, Chingleput, Ganjam, Guntur, Krishna, Nellore and Tinnevelly it is between 2,000 and 3,000; in Madura it is between 3,000 and 4,000; in Godavari East it is between 4,000 and 5,000; and in Vizagapatam it is over 15,000. The total for the 26 districts is 56,756. This is with reference to the presented restricted franchise. If the present franchise is enlarged, then there would be a rise in their voting strength.

From the above fact and figures it is very clear that the Government of Madras would experience no greater administrative difficulty in forming constituencies for the Depressed Classes than is experienced in making similar arrangements for the Mohammedans, Indian Christians, and Anglo-Indians. So even if the present franchise is maintained, it would certainly be possible to provide separate constituencies for the Depressed Classes in the Madras Presidency. . . .

In this connection let me quote what the Minority Report of the Reforms Enquiry Committee signed by Sir Tej Bahadur Sapru, Sir P.S. Sivasawamy Iyer, Mr. M.A. Jinnah and Dr. R.P. Paranjpye says on this question. It says:

> As regards the representation of the Depressed and working classes, we are of the opinion that the correct principle to follow would be to lower the franchise so as to give them a chance, through the open door of election in general electorates; but where practical considerations point to a different conclusion, we would suggest that for the next few years only special constituencies might be formed for them. (Report of the Reforms Enquiry Committee – p. 180 [c].)

In finally deciding the question, our Committee have recommended Separate Electorates in the Madras Presidency for ten years and Reservation of seats in Joint Electorates in the other provinces. I wanted Separate Electorates for ten years in all provinces. My colleagues were more impressed with the objections against the proposal but in the case of Madras three reasons seem to have induced them to give in. The Government of Madras themselves had admitted that separate constituencies were possible in certain instances; there is a sufficiently large number of voters and the carving out of the necessary constituencies also has been shown to be possible. Finally, they were agreed that the caste differences were most acute in the Southern Presidency and that some protection (as is afforded by separate electorates) was necessary. There can be little doubt that a common electoral roll should be the ideal and that it must be reached as early as possible. I hold that Separate Electorates for a limited period will give the necessary political education and self-confidence to enable the weaker elements to come into the common roll of their own consent. It is not the aim of the Depressed Classes to develop separateness of interests; on the other hand, they wish to lose their sense of separateness. It is really in the hands of the caste Hindu electors as to how long the Depressed Classes would wish to claim protection. If the working of Joint Electorates in other provinces shows that they in no way jeopardize the interests of the Depressed Classes that would quicken the abandonment of Separate Electorates. If, on the other hand, the fear that the Untouchables would be swamped proves true, then the protection afforded to them in Madras would have to be extended to the other provinces.

THE REPRESENTATION OF THE DEPRESSED CLASSES AS RECOMMENDED BY THE INDIAN CENTRAL COMMITTEE

No. 1/11	Legislatures	Total Population	Population of Depressed Classes	Total Number of Seats Allotted	Total Number of Seats for the Depressed Classes
1.	Madras	42 millions	6½ millions	150	14
2.	Bombay	16 millions	1½ millions	114	8*
3.	Bengal	45 millions	11½ millions	200	8
4.	United Provinces U.P. Second Chamber	47 millions	13 millions	182	10

5.	Punjab	20 millions	2½ millions	50	2
6.	Bihar and Orissa	33 millions	5 millions	150	6
7.	Central Provinces	12 millions	2½ millions	150	6
8.	Assam	7 millions	1½ millions	120	8
9.	Burma	–	–	75	9+
10.	N.W. Frontier	–	–	–	–
11.	Central Legislative Assembly	246 millions	44½ millions	300	12

Notes: * Calculated on the population basis.
+ Includes seats for the backward classes and the indigenous primitive races.

Next to the question of electorates is the question of franchise. Owing to their low economic condition and their illiteracy the voting ratio of the Depressed Classes is extremely small in proportion to their population ratio. In the province of Madras their population is six and a half millions and the number of voters is 56,756.

There is no reason to believe that the position of the Depressed Classes in the other provinces is above that in Madras and on that assumption we could see how little political power they possess. The need therefore is to lower the franchise. The lowering of the franchise would not only add to the number of votes but also increase the voting ratio. The Committee has at present recommended doubling the electorate but the process of enlarging the electorate must be carried on till it embraces the whole adult population in the country both male and female.

The position in regard to the Public Services also calls for immediate remedies. The real nature of the grievances which the Depressed Classes candidates suffer from I have already indicated. While their present position entitles them to preferential treatment their actual experience has been the other way. Even when possessing the necessary qualifications their claims have been overlooked because of the superstition of Untouchability. Under the guise of administrative convenience, departmental heads in the various provinces have not hesitated to nullify section 96 of the Government of India Act, 1919, that "no native of British India nor any subject of His Majesty resident therein shall, by reason only of his religion, place of birth, descent, colour, or any of them, be disabled from holding any office under the Crown in India" and the assurance contained in the Queen's proclamation that no person shall be disqualified from any post by reason of his birth. This should not be permitted to continue any longer and I trust that the Fundamental Rights declaration we are recommending shall be fully observed and guarantee the members of the Depressed Classes the enjoyment of their legitimate civic and political rights. The fact that social prejudice exists should not serve as an excuse to brush aside their claims. Efficiency cannot be overlooked but to admit the claims of social prejudice is downright reactionarism. Government service in India carries a dignity unknown in the West and authority invests it with a prestige which acts as a powerful antidote against social prejudice. A Depressed Class lawyer or doctor could be boycotted and drived out of the profession by a concerted campaign but a Depressed Class Deputy Collector or Police Superintendent cannot be got rid of so easily. His position and opportunities of service will largely contribute to the disappearance of untouchability in the circle in which he moves. In the general campaign against this evil this aid cannot be overlooked. The Pubic Services Commission with the Central Government, as also with the various Provincial governments, must take these factors into consideration in their task of recruitment for the services. The Commissions themselves must contain members of the Depressed Classes, who could see the claims of the community were properly safeguarded. By way of administrative measures Government could carry through much ameliorative work. In the matter of education, sanitation and medical relief, facilities should be provided in the shape of scholarships and special grants. Government should sternly discourage the idea of segregation in schools and should withdraw recognition from such schools as recognize Untouchability. Village Cooperative Societies and Panchayats as well as the various Local Boards and Muncipal Councils must be compelled to make adequate provision for the representation of the Depressed Classes. Remembering that the Depressed Classes are mostly identified with agriculture, steps must be taken to ensure them fair economic conditions. Fixity of tenure and a fair living wage must be guaranteed by law and the necessary legislation should be taken in hand without delay in the various provinces. Many of these Classes contain fine material for the Army, and a liberal recruitment from them would considerably enhance the prestige of the community and also relieve the pressure on agricultural labour. Finally I would urge that in every future investigation, political or economic, the Depressed Classes should be properly represented. In the past their claims have been persistently overlooked. The various Commissions and Committees in recent years did not number any Untouchable among their members. But when the present Statutory Commission was constituted Lord Birkenhead, the then Secretary of State for India, explaining the difficulties in the way of appointing Indians on the Commission pointed out the various interests that had to be represented and mentioned specially the Depressed Classes when he said,

> Let me take another case of the depressed classes. There is in India a vast population, even in relation to the number with which we are dealing, a population of 60,000,000 people in India, of the depressed classes. Their condition is not quite as terrible, not quite as poignant as it has been in the past, but it is still terrible and poignant. They are repelled from all social intercourse. If they come between the gracious light of the sun and one who despises them, the sun is disfigured for that man for they cannot drink at the public water supply, they must make diversions of miles in order to satisfy their thirst, and they are tragically known, and they have been known for generations, as 'Untouchables'. There are 60,000,000 of them in India. Am I to have a representative of them upon this Commission? Never, never would I form a Commission, nor would any one in a democratic country, nor would my friends opposite recommend it, from which you excluded a member of this class which, more than any other, requires representation, if you are indeed to put the matter to a mixed jury of the kind which I am indicating. (Speech in the House of Lords on the 24th November 1927.)

The thanks of the community are due to His Excellency Lord Irwin for the watchful interest he has shown in getting them representation in the present committee. The value of representation on such investigatory Committees could hardly be over-rated. My own personal experience on the Committee has shown that I have only to make known the facts and state my view to secure sympathetic recognition at the hands of most of my colleagues. The presence of a minority representative on a committee, even where it does not succeed in securing claims, prevents much unintentional injustice being done, by making known the true position. The question of communal harmony in a country like India which is so sharply divided is so important that I think that every effort must be concentrated in securing it. I should even venture to recommend that one of the Ministers of the future must make it his special concern and devote his activities to ensure communal justice.

The peaceful progress of the Untouchable Classes is a *sine qua non* of the orderly development of Indian Nationalism. Paradoxically as it may sound the aim of the Depressed Classes and those working for their future, should be their abolition. They are an excretion of Hindu Society and they must aim at becoming one with it. The deal should be to become not merely an integral part of it but to become an indistinguishable part. Indeed the restoration of civic and political rights in a measure is vouchsafed to them by alien religious (European) missionaries, but conversion can never be and never ought to be a matter of politics. Recent research has indicated that Untouchability has but shadowy support in ancient Hindu scriptures and that its strength lies in observance and the latter day smritis. Now that the recognition has come that Untouchability is a blot on Hinduism it must be the work of every one concerned in the welfare of the Depressed Classes to spread and strengthen the idea. Whatever could be done by legislation or administrative measure to remove the false idea about the sanctity of the custom will help in the regeneration of these Classes. First attempts at reclamation of the Depressed Classes were made by the European Christian Missionaries. Though Untouchability is as old as Hinduism no Protestants ever arose in that fold to denounce its evil effects. A faint attempt seems to have been made when the Vaishnavite reformer, Sri Ramanuja, sought to recruit his disciples from these Classes also but the attempt died with him. The majority of Hindus realized the enormity of the custom only when they saw what a handicap the existence of the Classes was in the path of democratic self-government. British administrators have all along been struck with the peculiar disabilities of these Untouchables and had been doing their best to ameliorate their sufferings. But Governments have always to look to the preservation of peace, and no great measure of reform could be enforced since caste prejudices were strong. More and more as democracy was accepted as the political ideal the various political parties in the country began to display an active interest in the amelioration of the Depressed Classes. Individual social reformers had been ploughing their lonely furrows but it was only with the growing interest taken by the political parties, desire for reform became general. When the non-Brahmin Party was started in 1917, Dr. T.M. Nair placed the removal of Untouchability in the forefront of his political programme. Later, under the inspiration of Mahatma Gandhi, the Congress took up the question, and though there has been little in the shape of practical achievement there is no doubt the propaganda carried on has made progress in the future easier. A most hopeful sign is the practical unanimity with which educated Hindu India has come to condemn the practice. Hindu leaders like the late Lala Lajpat Rai and Pandit Madan Mohan Malaviya have thrown their weight on the side of reform. Pandit Motilal Nehru recognizes in his All Parties Conference Report "that the Hindus are chiefly responsible for this suppression of a large class". And Sir Tej Bahadur Sapru once aptly remarked,

> I do say what is my most sincere conviction, that unless you are able to solve your own social problems about the Depressed Classes and Untouchables, I do not see any real prospect for real genuine constitutional advance, and any constitution that you may get will certainly not arouse any interest in me, because I do feel, howsoever good, howsoever perfect, howsoever ideal your constitution may be, unless you have got the support of the minorities and unless you command the confidence of those whom in your vanity you may describe as Depressed Classes, your constitution will not be worth a day's purchase.

The following resolutions passed by the Hindu Maha Sabha at its session in Jubbulpore in April 1928, are a clear indication of the awakening of the Hindu social conscience:

> This Hindu Maha Sabha declares that the so-called Untouchables have equal rights with other Hindus to study in public schools, to take water from public wells and other sources of drinking water, to sit with others in public meetings and to walk on public roads. The Maha Sabha calls upon all Hindus to remove such restrictions as may be existing anywhere at present in the way of so-called Untouchable Hindus exercising these rights.
>
> 2. This Maha Sabha declares that the so-called Untouchables are fully entitled to have Dev Darshan, and the Maha Sabha calls upon all Hindus in general and all Hindu Sabhas in particular to provide the same facilities for Dev Darshan, to them as are enjoyed at present by other Hindus.
>
> 3. This Maha Sabha calls upon Purohits (Priests), barbers and washermen to offer their services to so-called Untouchables also.
>
> 4. This Hindu Maha Sabha is of opinion that every Hindu to whatever caste he may belong has equal social and political rights.
>
> 5. This Maha Sabha appeals to all Municipal Boards to provide healthy quarters to the so-called Untouchables, especially the sweepers, and directs the local branches of the Hindu Maha Sabha to draw special attention of their Local Boards towards this matter.
>
> 6. This Maha Sabha looks upon the practice of nomination of the representatives of the Depressed Classes by the Government to the Local Bodies, Provincial Councils and the Assembly as most harmful and injurious to the true interests of the country and considers that this practice will become a source of creating a great gulf in the near future between Hindus and so-called Untouchable Classes. In the opinion of the Maha Sabha the

right course to stop this practice is to put forward and back proper candidates belonging to the so-called Untouchables Classes to the elected bodies named above.

But no amount of outside help or sympathy can help the Depressed Classes if they did not possess within themselves the requisites for development. The necessary requisites they do possess and their recent activities show that the spirit of progress though crippled is not crushed out of them. Wherever given opportunity representatives of the Depressed Classes have always acquitted themselves with credit and have proved worthy champions of their community's progress. "During my long service I have seen a great advance among the Depressed Classes, an advance to my mind greater than has been made by any other community within the same period. . . . Your education is increasing rapidly," said Sir F. Sly, the Governor of Central Provinces to the Depressed Classes Deputation in 1924. The masses themselves are neither inert nor incapable of progress. It is true they are not educated in the conventional sense and are not literate. But within the limits afforded to them they display wonderful native shrewdness and capacity for culture. India has not yet entered the era of industrialized agriculture, but observers have always noted the unlettered Indian peasants' (Depressed Classes) cleverness in the science of the seed, soil and season. Proper opportunities for education and acquaintance with modern machinery will improve the peasant's usefulness and ensure their prosperity. Nor is theirs a tradition of illiteracy from times immemorial. Great poets and Saints have sprung from among them and enriched our literature and our heritage of song. In the foremost rank of Tamil poets stand Valluvar, Kapilar and the poetess Auvvai – all born among Untouchables. Saint Nandanar and Tiruppanazavar and with them many others adorn the galaxy of devotees generally known as the Alwars and Nayanars, while Ravidas of Oudh, Chokha Mela of Maharashtra and Thakur of Bengal represent the tradition of devotion and learning in the North. In the limited sphere made possible to them the young men of these communities have acquired literary education, and to-day there is a virile body of educated young men all over the country who form the nucleus of future progress. While the possibilities of orderly future development are indeed immense, at the same time the danger of obstructing their progress cannot be overlooked. The Depressed Classes of India constitute what in modern political parlance is called the "proletariat", the class which labours without enjoying the fruits of its toil. Everywhere in India the Untouchable ploughs, sows and reaps, but only to hand over the produce to his landlord. The Iron Law of wages has not yet gone out of vogue in India, and what the tiller gets is just what would keep the soul in the body. The questions which the poet addressed to the workers, "Wherefore do you plough? Wherefore do you sow?" Can be addressed and addressed with deadly effect to the Depressed Classes in India. Denied fair living wage, denied legitimate opportunities of development, denied hopes of progress, those questions would arise among them naturally and no one should be surprised if they in their ignorance seek answer in violent revolution and in the wiping out of the *ancient regime*. By instinct and tradition the Depressed Classes are bound to peaceful pursuits. Hope has been reborn into them to-day and they have acquired new ambitions. Political and social conditions must be readjusted to accommodate their legitimate aspirations. And it is the task of the statesmen of the future to guarantee them ways and means of peaceful uplift.

Speech of M.C. Rajah at the All India Depressed Classes' Conference, 31 October 1931*

The following is the text of the presidential address delivered by Rao Bahadur M.C. Rajah at the 9th session of the All India Depressed Classes conference held at Gurgaon, Punjab on the 31st October 1931:

I thank you heartily for the honour you have done me in asking me to preside over the deliberations of the 9th All India Depressed Classes Conference. I am glad to be in your midst once again and words fail me to express adequately my gratitude and appreciation of the great welcome you have given me to-day. At the same time I should confess I do not regard it as merely an honour. I regard it also as a duty. When your invitation came to me to preside over this conference, I felt it was my bounden duty to accept the invitation and to use the opportunity for rendering some service to the community to which we all belong. To-day I propose to discuss some of the important problems which are engaging the attention of our people, the Round Table Conference, Dominion Status, the System of Representation, the Franchise and the Service.

Our first duty to-day is to offer our most cordial and respectful welcome to Their Excellencies Lord and Lady Willingdon. Though His Excellency Lord Willingdon assumed charge of the responsibilities of his high office at a most critical juncture, yet we the Depressed Classes of India wish his Excellency a most successful and a happy career in India, and as loyal and law-abiding citizens assure his Excellency our hearty and unreserved cooperation in his arduous task to make his administration a glorious success. His Excellency Lord Willingdon has been a true friend of the Depressed Classes. His Excellency was the first to appoint a member of the Depressed Classes to a Provincial Legislature. His Excellency was the first to create a Special Department in the Presidency of Madras for the protection of the interests of the Depressed Classes. In Lord Willingdon we

* *The Indian Annual Register*, July-December 1931, rpt., Delhi, 2000.

have a sympathetic Viceroy who knows only too well how real our grievances are and if only we represent our case to him, I am sure His Excellency will see that our interests are not ignored or sacrificed in the disposition and distribution of powers coming in the wake of reconstituted Government of India. We the Depressed Classes of India hope and trust that during His Excellency Lord Willingdon's term of office our claims will be fully recognized, our demands will be readily met and our wrongs will be promptly righted.

The most important topic of the day is the round Table Conference. We wish the Conference all success. In this most important Conference, I am sorry to say that in spite of repeated representations to the government, the government thought it wise to give us only two seats out of about 80 Indian Delegates. Out of a population of (as per census of 1921) 245 millions, the Hindus number 163, Muslims 59, Sikh 2 and Indian Christians 2 millions. Out of the Hindu population of 163 millions, the Depressed Classes number about 50 millions. Thus the Depressed Classes comprise 20 % of the population of British India and 30 % of the Hindu population. The Representation given to us on the R.T.C. is only 2 out of about 80, in the words of Sir Isaac Foot, M.P. "there are only two representatives for the great mass of people who form the Depressed Classes". I do not know what the guiding policy of our Government is with regard to those nominations. With due respect, I say that Government must change their policy in order to inspire confidence in the Depressed Classes. Unless Government changes their policy towards the Depressed Classes, and try to meet their legitimate aspirations, I am afraid they will alienate the regard and respect of a very large section of the population of the country and drive a loyal and law-abiding section into the channel of discontent with results detrimental both to themselves and to the Government. I sincerely hope the Government will become wiser and more responsible to our demands, the demands of those who have been with them through thick and thin and that they will at least from now try to translate their sympathy towards us into action. The representation given to us on the R.T.C. is most inadequate and requires the attention of the Government immediately.

Coming to the question of constitutional changes let me tell our friends that we are not in any way opposed to Constitutional advance for our Country. We are for Responsible Self-Government. We are for Dominion Status. We are also for Federal System of Government for India. But certainly we are not for that kind of Government which if given will only benefit the intelligentsia and will not enable the Depressed Classes who form one-fifth of the population of the country to participate in it with equal benefit.

Let me tell you that political development is only a vehicle for human life and human progress and its function is to provide a nation with means for bringing new hope and for increasing the happiness of the people; for, liberty, unless human brotherhood follows in its steps, may easily become an intolerable tyranny. We have had enough of tyranny exercised under the influence of class-pride and organized economic selfishness and with the sanction of hoary custom and of hereditary religious authority. Let us not have one more tyranny exercised through statute and politics added to the list.

Need I say that the so-called High Caste Indians have been very often profuse in their lip sympathy for us. We have heard them say "Are not these Untouchables our countrymen, bone of our bone and flesh of our flesh." Beyond this they have not raised their little finger to remove this blot of Untouchability on Hinduism but at the same time they have been treating us as worse than beasts. You know that even to this day the Depressed Classes are not allowed access into the king's highway; they are not allowed to educate their children in public schools; they are not allowed to take rest in public rest houses or choultries, they are not allowed into Hindu temples even for worship; they are not allowed to take part in Hindu ceremonies; they are not allowed to read the Hindu Scriptures; they are not allowed to bury the dead in the Hindu cemetery and it is said that they have no place in the Hindu heaven. Still the Depressed Classes are termed as Hindus and they are labeled as such. We are a separate community though we are labeled as Hindus.

We see lot of misrepresentation being carried on in London, Mr. Gandhi is reported to have said at the Round Table Conference that the Congress has been taking care of the Untouchables from the beginning and "the Congress had always stood and still stood for the removal of Untouchability", and "that the Congress has always championed the cause of the Untouchables". I now say that these statements are all untrue.

The Indian National Congress had been functioning for over 46 years. About ten years ago they adopted a resolution for the removal of Untouchability and a few years later Mr. Gandhi included the item of the Removal of Untouchability in the programme of the Congress along with Prohibition and Khaddar. I would like to ask Mr. Gandhi if he and his followers have devoted one hundredth as much attention to the removal of Untouchability as to the promotion of Khaddar though many of them know that Khaddar is a poor economic proposition by the side of mill made cloth. Khaddar is no doubt immediately useful for wresting power from the British people, whereas the removal of Untouchability is not useful for such a purpose, though it is even more useful and more permanently useful for establishing Self-Government in this Country.

If Mr. Gandhi really cared more for Swaraj than for power being transferred to the hands of favoured classes in the Country, he would have placed the Removal of Untouchability in the fore-front not merely of the programme of the Congress but of the activities of the Congress Committees and workers, for Mr. Gandhi himself had said on more than one occasion that "sooner this ban Untouchability is removed, the nearer will India be to the goal of complete 'Dominion Government' and without this removal India will gain Swaraj only to lose it the next month and it is a Reform not to follow Swaraj but to precede it". For Khaddar, you all know there is the All India Spinners' Association with its endless funds and numerous workers and roaring business but where are the workers for Removal of Untouchability? Where are the Congress Missionaries of Social Equality and Social Justice? Might I ask, has the Congress any Social Reform programme? These are all a shop window presentation of Hindu Society to impress foreign observers. But actually there is nothing said and nothing done for laying the social foundation for Swaraj.

Why does not Mr. Gandhi direct his energies to remove the oppressive features in our social structure, and in particular to remove the canker of Untouchability before he makes any further attempt for Swaraj, since he himself had wisely admitted on more than one occasion that this reform should precede Swaraj.

I have often wondered what mighty results would have been achieved if a man of the character and power of Mr. Gandhi had undertaken a real crusade against Untouchability. You are all aware of his memorable march on Dandi by which he started his Salt Satyagraha. Just imagine that same leader of men commencing in that same heroic manner a march on some of these Ancient Temples where the Untouchables are kept from the worship of God by threat of prosecution. I regret that such an idea had never dawned upon him. Some of those who begin to seek for causes and reasons may say that such a crusade would have lacked the theatricality of the march on Dandi or that for actual results it would have been a task marked for failure. But even as a failure it would have been one such failure that would have loved to treasure. But with such a man and for such a cause I would not foresee failure or could it be that even as common mortals "Mahatma" did not want to espouse a cause which would have ensured for him the scorn and hatred of the orthodox Hindu race which would have even lead him to a martyr's death. But the nobility of the cause would deserve the sacrifice.

As I have said on more than one occasion, we welcome Constitutional Reforms which will enlarge the powers of the Councils and give the people greater voice in the Government of the Country. But before such powers are given we must be sure that they will not be used to strengthen the hands of our oppressors, so that they may oppress us more and that we are not placed in a position of helpless impotency from which there is no escape except in revolt and rebellion. It is all very well to say "let us get Swaraj or Dominion Status first and then we shall settle our differences and redress the wrongs of the Depressed Classes". This is the language of the Bania or Bazaar-man who sells mangoes and says that his mangoes are very sweet and if the buyer finds them sour on eating then he will pay back the money. I tell you money once parted with never comes back and Swaraj once obtained is never withdrawn and the poor people who suffer under Swaraj will have to put up with their lot and bite their lips for not having foreseen the consequences and for having been silent and passive before Swaraj was granted.

Mr. Gandhi was always demanding a change of heart in the British government. Is it not our duty now to seek for some sign of change of heart in the Hindu Majority Community towards the Depressed Classes? I see no sign of such change of heart.

Mr. Gandhi only thinks of the Muslims and the Sikhs. He thinks that if the Hindu-Muslim problem is settled everything is over. I say he is entirely mistaken. Does he think that the cause of the Depressed Classes is less just than that of the Muslims and Sikhs? By all means let the Hindus and Muslims come to an amicable settlement. But what about the tyrannies practiced by the Hindus on the Depressed Classes?

The grievances of the Depressed Classes are more real than the grievances of the Muslims and Sikhs can ever be and yet I am sorry to say Mr. Gandhi is contented to leave the wrongs of the Depressed Classes unredressed. The Hindu-Muslim problem, as you all know, belongs only to the Punjab and Bengal, whereas the Depressed Classes problem exists throughout India. The Sikh problem is a problem confined only to the Punjab whereas the problem of the Depressed Classes is an all India problem. The population of the Sikhs is only about 2 millions. The population of the Muslims is about 60 millions and the population of the Depressed Classes is about 50 millions, second large Minority Community next to Muslims. Moreover, the Muslims and the Sikhs do not suffer from any civic disability, whereas we do. Our problem is graver than any other Minority Community in India. If, at all, any community deserves safeguards it is we. The Depressed Classes require greater and stronger safeguards. Yet Mr. Gandhi, who is believed to be an all-round reformer, I am pained to say, is reported to have said at the Round Table Conference that he would resist at the risk of his life any Special Representation being granted to the Depressed Classes. But he would be willing to give Special Representation to the Muslims and the Sikhs. Mr. Gandhi would not give us what we want. We want Separate Electorates for our community as a temporary measure. But he wants to force into our unwilling throats Joint Electorates. Mr. Gandhi evidently does not know our woes, "the toad beneath the harrow knows where each tooth point picks".

As a man, Mr. Gandhi is a gentleman, a good, kind-hearted, sympathetic man. As a man, he has very few rivals, a great man indeed. At present he is a man honoured by the whole world, by all classes and communities. I have a great regard for him. As a politician, we should view him in a quite different light. As a politician, he cannot be a friend of the Depressed Classes. In the Round Table Conference, he is there as Mr. Gandhi the politician, head of the political party the Indian National Congress. He is there as the Advocate of the Congress, and not as the Advocate of the Indians. As a member of the Working Committee of the Congress, his hands are tied and he dare not go against the decisions of the Committee, though as a man he may rightly differ from the Congress in its *laissez faire* attitude towards the Removal of Untouchability. All I wish to say to-day is, beware of Mr. Gandhi the politician.

I have absolutely no quarrel with Mr. Gandhi and I implore you not to have anything to do with Mr. Gandhi. Leave Mr. Gandhi alone. In this connection I wish to congratulate my friend Dr.

Ambedkar on his bold stand at the Round Table Conference when he demanded Separate Electorates for the Depressed Classes. Though Dr. Ambedkar is individually wedded to the system of Joint Electorates with Reservation of seats coupled with Adult Franchise, he in obedience to the demands of the Depressed Classes advocated in unequivocal language the system at Separate Electorates for them. I also take this occasion to thank all those Depressed Classes Associations throughout India that sent cables to London strengthening the hands of Dr. Ambedkar as against Mr. Gandhi. There were also a few cables one from Benares, one from Delhi, one from Ahmedabad and two from Bombay repudiating the representative character of Dr. Ambedkar to represent the Depressed Classes and supporting Mr. Gandhi. We all know what the cables are and how they are manufactured. These cables remind me of that bogus telegram manufactured by the Madras Congress Leaders during the Statutory Commission debate in the Indian Legislative Assembly on the 18th of February 1928 repudiating my representative character to represent the Depressed Classes of the Madras Presidency in the Legislative Assembly. The Madras Congress Leaders in the Assembly then made my esteemed friend Pandit Madan Mohan Malaviya a tool in their hands and made him to read that telegram during the debate. Poor Mr. Malaviya mistaking it as a genuine one read it during the debate. When he came to know of the bogus nature of the telegram he came and apologized to me. Whatever his political views are, I have very great regard for him, for he is a perfect gentleman. So much for that.

In consideration of our separate Interest, our Numerical Strength, our Political Importance and our Undoubted Disabilities, we press our right as a distinct community to Elective Representation on the Legislatures, by means of Separate Electorates. We need hardly say that we want Separate Electorates for our Community. Our men elected directly by us can alone communicate faithfully to Government our thoughts and feelings, our grievances and suggestions for our improvement.

Our sorrows are too deep-seated to be expressed by others. Besides Separate Electorates are Political Schools for educating the Community in the effective exercise of the franchise and effective criticism of the actions of its representatives. The peculiar position of the Depressed Classes to-day demands that their interests have to be protected against the Hindu co-religionists. In a Joint Electorate where the voters were actuated by common interests division will follow opinions about the merits of the issues involved; and where conflict of interests is involved the voting will go by interests, and it is clear that minority interests will never succeed in getting representation. In the Joint Electorates the proportion of Depressed Class voters would be small and the candidates who would fill the Reserved Seats would in reality be the nominees of the majority of the Electors. The constituencies being predominantly Caste-Hindu no one could hope to get elected who did not pander to or at least respect Caste prejudices. A Depressed Class member elected on the strength of the Caste-Hindu votes would not be beholden to his community. There is thus the danger of the seat being occupied by the dummies of the so-called higher castes. Where he is afforded the protection of Separate Electorate this danger disappears.

For the successful working of responsible Self-Government the contentment of all classes is very essential. It would be only wise to grant the community its desire, without forcing into its throats what it does not want. The moment our confidence in the sense of equity, justice and fairplay on the part of the Caste-Hindus grows and our suspicions of majority manipulation vanishes to such an extent as would render Separate Electorates unnecessary we will not hesitate to go in for Joint Electorates with Reservation of seats. The representatives of the Depressed Classes waited in deputations and gave evidence before the Indian Statutory Commission. Out of the 37 associations that placed before the Commission their considered opinion, 35 demanded Separate Electorates, one favoured Joint Electorates with Adult Suffrage and Reservation of seats and the other wanted Nominations.

It will not be out of place for me to mention here that in the Minority Report of the Reforms Enquiry Committee signed by Sir Tej Bahadur Sapru, Sir P.S. Sivaswamy Iyer, Mr. M.A. Jinnah and Dr. R.P. Paranjpye, these members suggest, "that for the next few years Special Constituencies might be formed for them" (Depressed Classes), and in the Nehru Report the authors while admitting that "the Hindus are chiefly responsible for this suppression of a large class" admit also that the only way to secure representation to the Depressed Classes is either by Nomination or by Separate Electorates, and after admitting this and rejecting nomination they deliberately refused to accept Separate Electorates. If there are only two alternatives open statesmanship demands to choose the lesser evil but rejecting both is ignoring the problem and not solving it. Might I add here that the President of the Tamil Nadu Congress also is in favour of Separate Electorates for us?

It may be taken for granted that hereafter the door of Nomination for entering Councils will be closed and closed for ever. It is best that it should be so. The next stage in the evolution of the political consciousness of our community can be reached only through Separate Electorates. I am glad that over this point the Depressed Classes throughout the length and breath of the country are of one mind.

Now what should be our action? It will not do for us to stand aloof and look at the controversy between the Hindus and the Muslims as it did not concern us. We should join hands with other communities like the Muslims, Anglo-Indians and Indian Christians and lodge our protest against a Joint Electorate which while it sooths dreams of a National Unity where no unity exists, is sure to be used by a Communally Minded but Nationally Speaking Hindu Majority for securing political power with which they could oppress weak and backward minorities.

In this connection, on behalf of the Depressed Classes, I wish to offer our thanks to Sir Tej Bahadur Sapru, Dr. B.S. Moonjee, Sir A.P. Patro, Sir Henry Gidney, Dewan Bahadur A. Ramaswamy Mudaliar, Dewan Bahadur M. Ramachandra Rao and Rao Bahadur A.T. Pannirselvam for supporting Dr. Ambedkar in his demands for Separate Electorates for us.

As for the number of representatives in the Councils, the least that should in justice to the community be granted is Representation Proportionate to our population. I would even suggest that we should demand a little more than this so that we may have a sufficient number in the Councils to protect our interests.

We should also urge that the Depressed Classes should have their interests safeguarded by the inclusion of a member of the Community in the Cabinet of the Provinces, as well as in the Viceroy's Executive Council, on the same basis of qualifications as laid down for members of any other Minority Community like the Muslims.

Coming to the question of Franchise, let me tell you that we are for adult franchise as the ultimate goal. But we are conscious of the fact that it is not practicable at the present day. I see Mr. Gandhi too is of the same opinion, yet he opposes the grant of Separate Electorates to us. In our opinion, the present franchise qualifications should be lowered and the present Electorates should be doubled immediately. The process of enlarging the Electorates must be carried on from time to time till it ultimately embraces the whole Adult population both males and females. In such enlargement where property qualification is introduced however low it may be, we should insist so as to bring on the Elector's list, not only those who possess property qualification, whose number in our poverty-stricken community must necessarily be limited, but also persons who may not possess property but may possess education of some sort (Primary School Leaving Certificate). In this connection I am in agreement with the proposal of the Indian Statutory Commission that instruction should be given to the Franchise Commission to devise such qualification as would secure the same proportion of voters to the population in different communities.

It is of utmost importance that there should be at least a member of the Depressed Classes on the Franchise Commission which is to be constituted.

The position of our Community in regard to Public Services calls for immediate remedies. In spite of Section 96 of the Government of India Act that no person shall be disabled from holding any office under the Crown by reason of his religion, birth, descent, colour or any of them the claims of the Depressed Classes have been completely ignored by the Government in regard to Public Services, though the Government concede the policy of Minority Representation in Public Services. Efficiency no doubt cannot be overlooked. But to admit the claims of Social prejudice is down right reactionism. In this connection I should like to invite the attention of the Government to the evidence recorded by the Simon Commission contained in the Indian Statutory Commission Report, vols. 15, 16 and 17 wherein they will find that in the Provinces of Bombay, Punjab, Bengal, United Provinces and Assam the members of the Depressed Classes are not taken into the Police Department on account of Untouchability. Adequate percentage of Government appointments both in the Superior and Subordinate grades should be reserved for the members of the community and that the minimum qualification required under the Public Services Notifications should be considered sufficient. While our present position entitles us in the interests of the country to preferential treatment, even when possessing the necessary qualifications our claims have been overlooked because of the superstition of Untouchability. The fact that Social prejudice exists should not serve as an excuse for brushing aside our claims. Efficiency is no doubt necessary but to admit the operations of Social prejudice in recognizing efficiency is unjust and unrighteous. I hope the Government will not commit this wrong any longer but would see as a matter of policy and justice, to the recruitment of Depressed Classes in all branches of Administration both in the Superior and Subordinate grades.

The Public Services Commission with the Central Government as also with the various Provincial Governments must take these factors into consideration in their task of recruiting to the various Services. The Public Services Commission themselves must contain members of the Depressed Classes who could see that the claims of the community are properly safe-guarded.

Above all it is of utmost importance that there should be declaration of Fundamental Rights embodied in the Constitution of India for giving the Depressed Classes equal citizen rights.

Whatever may happen, it is our duty to be awake and to be up and doing. It has been said that external vigilance is the price of liberty. It may be added that external activity is a condition of progress. People may say we are reactionaries. We are not. We are fighting for freedom. There are two kinds of freedom, freedom from external trammels and freedom from internal restrictions which say, "thus far shall thou go and no further" and this is what the political leaders say. We are not going to be frightened. We should stand up for our rights and obtain internal freedom for our country. In fighting our cause we are fighting the cause of all Minority Communities. If other communities are wise they will not only support our cause at this juncture but join hands with us, recognizing with us their rise or fall.

In conclusion I thank you for the patient hearing you gave me and wish the conference all success. Though things are bad enough at present, it should be remembered they were worse some time ago. That they have improved somewhat is due to the awakened consciousness on our part. That they are not better is due to want of union amongst us. If you want them to be better in the future, you should be awake and united. Let not jealousies divide us into parties and sections and make us an easy prey to those who would like us to sleep as we have been sleeping for ages and to be under their control. Let us become alive to the dangers of the situation and act wisely and unselfishly in the interests of the community. In doing so, we shall not go against the interests of the country as a whole.

The Depressed Classes Deputation Led by M.C. Rajah to the Viceroy at New Delhi on 29 March 1933*

The text of the representation as follows:

On behalf of the Depressed Classes of India who are treated as Untouchables by reason of a cruel superstition prevailing among the Hindus, superstition totally opposed to the principles of the Hindu religion, but yet mixed up with and looked upon as a part of religious practice, we seek the guidance and assistance of Your Excellency's Government in removing the disabilities they suffer under.

Your Excellency was the first to nominate a member of the Depressed Classes to a Provincial Legislature in India. Your Excellency was the first to create a Special Department in the Presidency of Madras for the protection of the interests of the Depressed Classes.

We, the Depressed Classes of India, hope and trust that during Your Excellency's term of office our claims will be fully organized, our demands will be readily met and our wrongs will be promptly righted.

The people, on whose behalf we approach Your Excellency, are not treated as outcastes by Hindus alone. The social bar that has been put upon them in the Hindu society affects the psychology of other communities also, except in the cities and urban areas. Our peoples are treated as unclean by birth and unfit for close association even by the Mussalmans, Christians and other communities among whom they live. The removal of our disabilities is therefore not merely a Hindu question, but a national question.

A superstitious practice that inflicts suffering and unmerited degradation on 46 million souls cannot be treated by the State as a matter in which it can take up an attitude of neutrality. We look to the Government for active assistance in the measures required for our emancipation. We have all along felt that one of the justifications of the British rule is the rendering of justice to and the liberation of

* *The Indian Annual Register*, January-June 1933, rpt., Delhi, 2000.

our oppressed community. We should be deeply disappointed if the Government takes up an attitude of indifference or leaves things to take their own course.

We venture to say the above in view of the awakening of the Hindu conscience that has been noticed in regard to our condition and status, and the reasonableness of public desire for active assistance of the Government to make the movement more successful.

We certainly desire the improvement of our material condition and this is our foremost concern. But the poverty and illiteracy of our people cannot be materially remedied by non-official efforts. They can only be solved by State action and a thorough overhauling of administrative, economic and social outlook. We fear also that the poverty and illiteracy of the vast population of India are such that our difficulties can hardly be solved independently. The one root cause that puts our community in a worse position than other sections of the Hindus is the superstition that makes our people an Untouchable class. Trades, professions and facilities and opportunities open to others are not open to our people on account of their being looked upon as congenitally unclean. The degradation becomes all the worse by the hypnotism that makes our people submit to this superstition. This can be remedied only by a change in our social, religious and legal status.

We therefore welcome the movement in the Hindu community to reform its religious practice in respect of the treatment and status accorded to our people. The opening of temples to our people along with other Hindu castes is a matter of the greatest importance for our social emancipation. We quite realize that we cannot hope for a permanent emancipation and betterment unless our status in the Hindu religion is improved. We, therefore, hope Your Excellency's Government will assist the passage into Law of the Temple Entry and Anti-Untouchability Bills. The *raison d'être* of British rule in India is to secure just treatment for the Depressed Classes and to stimulate and guide progress among weaker communities. The British Government, we submit, should not be afraid of doing a just thing on behalf of the Depressed Classes out of deference to the wishes of the Caste-Hindu community.

The courts in India are now assisting the enforcement of the superstition of Untouchability. British law has not left the superstition to its own resources but has placed the machinery of the courts and the state at the disposal of the Caste-Hindus in the maintenance of those superstitious practices. Even if the Government cannot interfere in the religious practices of the Hindus it should at least refrain from assisting in the enforcement of such practices when they are opposed to humanity and public welfare as in the case of treatment accorded to us. The Bill for the abolition of Untouchability, sought to be introduced in the Assembly, puts an end to this anomaly and does not interfere with the religion of any person or community.

THE TEMPLE ENTRY BILL

The Temple Entry Bill for which we seek Your Excellency's support is drafted so as to provide a legal machinery for peaceful and gradual evolution of reform with the consent of the people concerned. Each locality will be enabled to work out a suitable compromise for solving the question of our status. We beg your Excellency to help in the achievement of a peaceful solution of this question that so fundamentally affects the dignity and the daily life of a community of forty-six million souls who cling to the ancient Hindu religion to which they belong, and who wish to find an honourable place in it without causing turmoil or disturbance.

We submit that there is no substance in the argument generally advanced that the proposed legislation would be an infringement of trust and property rights. There is no attempt in either of the Bills to divert property from their original purpose or ownership. The mode, the manner and the place from which worship is offered, may be changed from time to time. This does not mean that the property of any person is sought to be confiscated any more than the use of public roads being extended to our people, could be interpreted to mean an interference with the rights of others. A narrow interpretation of the law to prevent our emancipation, we hope, will not be tolerated by Your Excellency's Government. Eminent lawyers have assured us that in spite of the phrases employed by the opponents of reform, it is within the competence of the legislature to pass the Bills under consideration.

The special privileges that the Depressed Classes enjoy even to this day point to their former greatness. At the annual festival of the goddess of George Town in the premier city of Madras, the Thali or marriage badge is tied round the goddess by a member of the Depressed Classes in the name of the entire community. A member of the Depressed Classes officiates as priest at the bull games at

Dindigul; during the great Hindu annual festivals at Conjeevaram, Srivilliputtur, Kumbakonam, Trivottyur and other places in the South, the members of the Depressed Classes are allowed to pull the ropes of the huge cars containing the idols. During the festival of Siva at Tiruvalore in the Tanjore District, the headman of the Depressed Classes is specially honoured by being placed on the temple elephant along with the God and made to carry the Chowry in his hand for fanning the idol. In the famous temple of Krishna in Melkote, in the Mysore State, members of the Depressed Classes are accorded special privileges. Melkote is the chief seat of the Sri Vaishnavite Brahmins and the place where Sri Ramanuj lived in the 12th century. They enjoy a similar privilege at Sriperambadur in Chingleput District. In the case of a number of temples there is a periodical admission of the Depressed Classes even under the present practice.

The Valluvars, a section of the Depressed Classes, were priests to the Pallava kings, before the advent of the Brahmins and even for some time after. Sir Harold Steward in the Census Report of 1891 quotes an unpublished Vattelutta of the 9th century which says that Sri Valluvar, the temple minister, will employ six men daily and do the temple service.

Further, Dr. Gustav Oppert in his book, "The Original Inhabitants of Bharatvarsha or India", says, "Valli is a well-known female name common among the Pariahs and Pallars."

"Subramanya, the South Indian representative of Kartikeya, the son of Siva, . . . is credited with having chosen a South Indian girl called Valli as his wife."

"The Subramanya's wife, Valli, was a low-caste South Indian woman."

"Parvati, the wife of Siva and daughter of the mountain Himalaya, is even worshipped as a Pariah woman in her disguise as Matangi".

Among the twelve Alwars or Vaishnavite Saints who are now being worshipped as gods in Vaishnavite temples, the famous Tirupan Alwar and Nambaduwan and Maraneri Nambi belong to the so-called Untouchable Community. The famous work of Tirupan Alwar, *Amaran Adiparan* is chanted in all Vaishnavite temples even to this day. It is accepted by all, Brahmins included, that Tirupan Alwar has become one with God Shree Ranganadha at Srirangam. Among the 63 Nainars of Saivite Saints, the well-known Nanda and the holy Shiruvalluvar, who are now being worshipped as Gods in Saivite Temples, belong to the same Community. Ravi Das of Oudh, Chokha

Mela of Maharashtra and Haridas of Bengal, these notable saints also spring up from the Untouchable Classes of India. In *Bakthavijayam* we find Chokha Mela was accepted as a guru by the learned Brahmins of Pandaripur. It is said in the sacred work *Manushya Panchakam* of Jagat Guru Sree Sankaracharya, the founder of the four Sankara Pedams, that he accepted one Vishwanadham, a member of the Depressed Classes, as his guru and received initiation from him. Arundhati, the wife of Vasistha, the Brahmarishi, who is famous for her chastity, belonged to the Untouchable Community. Jambavan, the custodian of all ancient learning and a mighty warrior, who was the commander of the army of Sri Ram Chandra, also belonged to the same community.

These facts show that the so-called Untouchables were intimately connected with the important Hindu temples in India and that these temples originally belonged to them.

We beg to point out to Your Excellency that non-official Bills can hardly emerge as law without the assistance of the Government. The freedom of debate and discussion that is given under law will be abused for the purposes of obstruction and impediment unless the Government helps to facilitate the passage of the Bills. We fear that if the present opportunity is let slip history will have a very poor opinion of the wisdom of the present generation.

We beg to assure Your Excellency that at no time in the history of reform in India was there so favourable an atmosphere for the removal of our disabilities in a peaceful manner as to-day and we trust Your Excellency will help us to take advantage of this great occasion in the history of progress in India. We have no doubt that Your Excellency who has already earned our everlasting gratitude will put a coping stone to the work undertaken in Madras and now ripe for final and decisive action. In conclusion we express our most grateful thanks to your Excellency for giving us a patient hearing.

Rao Bahadur M.C. Rajah's Statement on Change of Religion*

Rao Bahadur M.C. Rajah M.L.A. President, All-India Depressed Classes Association and representative of the Depressed Classes in the Assembly, issued the following considered statement on the 12th November 1935 with reference to the controversy regarding the change of religion raised by Dr. Ambedkar. He said:

I have received letters from all over the country asking me to express my views on the recent controversy as regards the Depressed Classes renouncing Hinduism.

First of all I should like to make my position very clear. I have regard and reverence for all religions. I have been educated in Christian institutions – Wesley College and the Christian College, Madras. I served for many years in Christian institutions, namely Voorhees College and Wesley College. I have never changed my religion, though I have imbibed many of the Christian ideals. People are at liberty to seek and embrace whatever religion they wish in the interests of their spiritual welfare.

I have not read the full speech of the president of the Depressed Classes Conference held at Yeola on 13 October, for nowhere have I seen it published in full. It is said that a resolution was passed at this conference asking the community to sever itself from Hinduism and embrace any other religion which would guarantee them equal status with other members of that faith. It should be noted that this conference is only a district conference and it is very significant that the president, who made this bold suggestion to his admiring audience, did not recommend any particular religion for them to adopt.

So far Mr. Balu, the famous cricketer, who is the leader of a large section of the Depressed Classes of the Bombay Presidency, has clean bowled out the president of this conference with his well-weighed and weighty statement. Other leading members of the community all over India, Rao Bahadur R. Srinivasan, M.L.C., Rao Sahib V.L.

* *The Indian Annual Register*, July-December 1935, rpt., Delhi, 2000.

Munuswami, M.L.C., Rao Sahib L.C. Guruswami, Ex-M.L.C., Dr. Ram Prasad, Dr. Solonki, M.L.C., Messrs. R.B. Biswas, P.K. Rajbhoj, N.S. Kajrolker and Swami A.S. Sahajanandan, M.L.C., and others have rightly expressed strong disapproval of this resolution.

While I fully share in the resentment which many of our men feel at the treatment meted out to our people in many parts of the country by the so-called high caste Hindus, I would at the same time request them to compare conditions existing now with what they were, say 15 years ago. Conditions have improved considerably today. A large section of educated Hindu India has come to condemn the practice of Untouchability and has thrown its weight on the side of the reform. I venture to say that in view of the awakening of the Hindu conscience that has been noticed in regard to our conditions and status, the days of Untouchability as practiced towards our community are now numbered. It should be remembered that in the course of a decade things have changed considerably in favour of the Depressed Classes and there is also a very strong awakening among the Depressed Classes themselves.

The Congress under the inspiration of Mahatma Gandhi has taken up the question of removal of Untouchability and the Hindu Mahasabha has followed suit. It is our duty to help them in their endeavour and not to throw obstacles in their way.

In the last Legislative Assembly two Bills were introduced and discussed – The Temple Entry Bill and the Untouchability Abolition Bill. Both these Bills were intended to give equal status to the Depressed Classes with the other Hindus and to remove obstacles in the way of such equality. What part did the organizers of this Yeola Conference play then in regard to these measures? Did not some of them help the opponents to these measures to strangle the Bills? Did not the chief opposer to these Bills and the stout champion of Sanatana Dharma, Raja Bahadur G. Krishnamachariar, call to his aid the president of the conference and that he did not want temple entry and quote him as saying that the dispute was not between the Caste Hindus and the Depressed Classes but between the Caste Hindus and Mr. Gandhi? The Depressed Classes have every right to ask him when he ever set any value on religion as a means of social uplift? Is it not a fact that he opposed Mahatma Gandhi when he placed the religious reforms before the economic? There is Mr. C.F. Andrews testifying to this fact in an interview granted to the *Manchester Guardian*.

The Depressed Classes have every right to ask him whether he had ever before taken any interest in their religious life and given any hint that Hinduism as a whole was to blame for the social and economic depression of these classes? Did he ever take any part in social and religious reform movements in Hindu society before coming to the conclusion that Hinduism is unreformable, before taking upon himself the responsibility of advising 70 millions of people to change their religion?

It is to be noted that while he gives the negative counsel that they should renounce Hinduism, as if it could be done in a moment – the moment the word is spoken by a single man – he does not say in what direction they should move and what religion they should embrace in place of the one they are called upon to renounce. What is the use of such destructive advice without a constructive proposal? Whither does he want to lead the people? Does he want to play the Moses in the Bible or of Zebek Dorshi – the less said about him the better. One has only to read De Quincy's classical story to realize the untold miseries resulting in extinction to which he subjected his people and all for giving vent to his spirit or ambition and vengeance.

Even now it is not too late for the president of the Nasik Conference to say what religion he has in view – Christianity, Zoroastrianism or Islam?

The immediate remedy that suggests itself to me is the total withdrawal of the legal and administrative recognition to the superstition of pollution. The laws as they are administered to-day uphold these superstitions under the guise of preserving peace and punish the Untouchables who attempt to enforce their civic rights. On September 26, last I introduced in the Legislative Assembly a Bill called the Removal of Social Disabilities among certain classes of Hindus. Bills like this, if passed into Act, will go a long way to remove civic secular disabilities from which the depressed classes are suffering under the existing laws. This Bill will also remove the obstacles created by the British India courts giving legal recognition to certain social customs and usages which enlightened public opinion regard as unjust, anti-social and irreligious.

If we do not achieve social and religious equality in Hindu society it is not only the fault of the Caste Hindus but it is also our fault. Are we united? It must be acknowledged that the lack of unity among those who speak in the name of the community has had adverse effects on the rise of the community and has seriously jeopardized the work on its behalf; and without unity among ourselves the interests of the people are bound to suffer. I appeal to my people to consolidate the community and stand united and work with patience and determination. If this is done our success is assured.

I now appeal to my people not to be led away by the speeches of people who do not really understand the inwardness of things.

I appeal to them not to lend their support to men who for reasons of their own seek to undermine the solidarity of the community and to defeat the endeavours towards uplift by setting up rival organizations and thus becoming rival leaders whose only business nowadays seems to be to sow seeds of dissatisfaction, distrust and class hatred in the hearts of our poor and innocent people. I am not at all perturbed by the speeches of such impulsive and vehement politicians.

Those who are in actual touch with the Depressed Classes will see that they are now passing through a stage in their history, when they began to adopt and adapt such Hindu customs, ceremonies and worship as are suited to their social and religious needs and that every Cheri, Mohalla and Basti has a temple; where hitherto there have been no temples and all worship was neglected, there is a tendency for religious revival. People bath, dress cleanly and wear marks of religious devotion and this is due to the influence of reformed Hinduism.

Hinduism is our religion and it is sacred to us. It is our duty to preserve it and purify it. We do not want to cut away from the Hindu-fold. We want a better recognition – recognition of the fact that we are men equally with themselves, the caste Hindus. Our goal is the removal of Untouchability and our aim is to become an unsegregated and unquarantined part of the Hindu society.

M.C. Rajah's Reply to the Letter Written by B.S. Moonje on 30 June 1936*

Dear Dr. Moonje,

You will excuse my saying that you view the whole problem of the Depressed Classes, in view of Dr. Ambedkar's proposal, as one of the communal migration and not as a religious problem. One would expcct the President of the Hindu Mahasabha to view it as a social and economic problem. One can understand your concern if as President of the Hindu Mahasabha you placed the spiritual welfare of the Depressed Classes first and foremost and thought of the social and economic welfare next and lastly thought of them as a political factor. Your solicitude for the place of the Depressed Classes in the political scheme not only exposes the interested nature of your concern for these classes, but is like placing the cart before the horse. One would expect you as President of the Hindu Mahasabha to ameliorate the social condition of the Depressed Classes by removing civic and social disabilities of these classes, not to speak of securing for them the right of worship in Hindu temples on an equal footing with other worshippers, and to further the Harijan movement started by Gandhiji all over the country. Instead of doing this, what is it that you are doing? You are dissecting the Depressed Classes and affiliating them religiously to the Sikhs while retaining them politically as Hindus.

The whole thing seems to me not to be conceived in the interest of the Depressed Classes, but on the other hand to be planned in the communal interests of the Hindus and the Sikhs. We are no sheep and cattle to be bartered away in this fashion driven from one political fold to another as a result of a bargain between the leaders of different communities. We want to remain as solid community moving of our own accord in the direction of progress and this we can best do by not throwing away our birth rights as Hindus but by remaining within Hinduism and changing it so as to make it more comfortable not only to our community but to other Hindu communities which are

* *The Indian Annual Register*, July-December 1936, rpt., Delhi, 2000.

suffering from similar liabilities though our hardships are greater and more palpable. It is not our purpose to weaken the Hindu community but to strengthen it by reforming it from within. We do not wish to be pawns in the game of communal conflicts and competition.

Your proposal involves of electoral fortunes of Hindus, Sikhs and Muslims. If you want us to shift religion from the Hindu fold, we shall have to choose religion between the Sikhs and the Muslims, who are the bidders for our communal migration, wrongly called conversion. Why should we antagonize and stand arrayed against Muslims? They are our brothers as much as the Sikhs and the Hindus. If the Depressed Classes are all to become Sikhs and call themselves Neo-Sikhs, it will create all over India a Sikh Hindu Moslem problem as in the Punjab made more complicated by the fact that the so-called Neo-Sikh belongs to the Depressed Class even among Sikhs. This question of conversion or the communal migration as a move of the political chess-board does not disturb us much in South India. We are content to work under the Poona Pact, partly as a Separate Electorate and partly with a Joint Electorate preserving our status with the Hindus both religiously and politically. I would therefore be no party even to the political manipulations which are proposed in your letter. I would urge the Hindu Mahasabha to address itself to the task of making it easy for the Depressed Classes to stay within Hinduism and Hindu society instead of arranging for the ticket for entertaining them to some far off destination. As the question you raise is likely to rouse a lot of discussion I reserve to myself the right to publish my reply when the occasion arises.

M.C. Rajah's Correspondence with Gandhi*

29 NOVEMBER 1936

My Dear Mahatmaji,

I thank you for your kind letter. I have since had talks with Dewan Bahadur R. Srinivasan and other leaders of my community. Mr. Satyamurthi has also sent me a copy of your letter to him dated the 19th November. Yesterday I had a (communication) from Mr. Satyamurthi and Mr. Bhakthavatsalam, one of the local Congress Secretaries. They offered certain terms and asked us to join the Congress and stand for election on the Congress ticket. They have since sent those terms in writing, copy of which I herein enclose.

We cherish your advice (which I for one regard as divinely inspired) that we should not identify ourselves with any party, not even with the most advanced party. The reason you gave for this advice shows how deeply you understand and sympathise with our difficulties, namely that in present condition we require the help of all parties, including the British Government.

Our present difficulty lies in this, I am speaking for all members of our party, that we wish to see the present Constitution worked for all it is worth, with a view to broadening the basis of freedom for our country, and we are not in favour of wrecking it. Our position is the logical outcome of our cooperation with all the committee and conferences through which it has been evolved. To ask us now to change our attitude and to join a party which makes no secret of its desire to wreck it, is something like asking us to abjure the faith in which we have grown up and to adopt on the eve of Elections a time-serving policy which is quite contrary to all our sincere endeavours in the past.

We are thankful to you for having brought up the subject of Untouchability and advanced it so far, and we are confident that under your guidance the Congress will have the uplift of the Harijans as an integral part of its programme (though it may not follow you

*M.C. Rajah Papers, Nehru Memorial Museum & Library, New Delhi.

in trying to remove all the social discriminations implied in Caste). We are therefore, as you suggest, naturally drawn towards the Congress. We would therefore earnestly and gratefully cooperate with the Congress in its social and constructive programme. But whether we could go further in our present condition and in the present circumstances and join the Congress party in wrecking the constitution is a matter which require serious thinking and one which I crave your counsel and guidance.

I fully understand the need for Harijan candidates securing the support of other parties not only for minimizing or avoiding the cost of elections but also in other respects. This naturally necessitates a certain measure of cooperation on their part with other parties.

In our Scheduled Castes Party, there are men of different shades of opinion and different political leanings. But so far as Congress is concerned, I feel there is a certain amount of mutual obligation between our people and the Congress.

The Madras Government have fixed the 8th December as the date for filling nominations for the Panel elections.

With kind regards,

Yours sincerely,
M.C. Rajah.

12 MARCH 1937

My Dear Mahatmaji,

I feel very much encouraged by the words you spoke to me when I called on you at Seagoan on my way from Delhi to Madras.

Especially your saying that you still hold by the advice you gave me at the outset that I should remain a Scheduled Castes representative without joining any party has dispelled doubts and fears which came into my mind about my position in the Assembly.

My cooperation with you with regard to the position of the Depressed Classes in Hindu Society and in the body politic began when I advocated the inclusion of my people in the Joint Electorate instead of their being segregated in a Separate Electorate and our Congress leaders are aware how deeply I shared in their anxiety and how unsparingly I cooperated with them in persuading the representatives of my community in spite of opposition from a certain section to agree to the terms of the Poona Pact. Perhaps not all of them know how much pressure was brought to bear upon me by high Government authorities including the Viceroy, the Home Member and the Indian Law Member at the time of the 'Epic Fast' to prevent me from advocating and inducing my people to accept a Joint Electorate upon which your heart was set and without which life was not worth living for you. Others also know how effectively I can cooperate with them in practical administrative measures making for the good of all classes including the uplift of my people. I have also endeavoured to prevent my people from identifying themselves with the reactionary party in this presidency. When I was in the Madras Legislative Council (1919-26), before coming to the Indian Legislative Assembly, I incurred on several occasions, in spite of my being a nominated member, the displeasure of the party in power for opposing measures which I thought were not in the public interest. While I am thankful to say that my endeavours met with not a little success, I have always had to fight against some representatives of my community who were not able to resist the inducements offered by the Party in power, and this party knew this very well, and their vengeance was wrecked on me at the recent election by their setting up and supporting a candidate against me, whom I am happy to say I have defeated. I must here acknowledge that the Madras Congress Committee were so deeply convinced of my attachment and loyalty to the objects of the Congress that they deliberately refrained from setting up a rival candidate against me, and it is well known that in my Constituency I not only defeated the candidates set up against me by the Justice Party but cooperated with the Congress candidate (Mr. K. Bashayam Iyengar) in defeating his rival of the Justice Party. Some of my community men who were basking in the sunshine of the Justice Party, thought it wise on the eve of the elections – one of them in particular just two days before filing nomination papers on the 8th December 1936 – to join the Congress in order to avoid Congress opposition and secure the support of the general electorate which they could not otherwise obtain. I am wondering whether all my labours extending over so many years to keep the national aim before my people without sacrificing it to immediate temporary advantages will be counted for nothing before a sort of overnight conversion to Congress party resembling the nominal conversions secured by Christian Missionaries from among the distressed members of my community.

I wish on the top of all this, to call attention to the fact that I so completely and unhesitatingly identified myself with the aims and activities of the Harijan Seva Sangh from its very inception, that when the Executive Committee of the All India Harijan Seva Sangh was constituted I was placed on it as a leading representative of the community. I have served all along on the Provincial Seva Sangh; and in which connection I toured through the Southern Districts of Tamil Nadu in company with Dewan Bahadur Bashayam Iyengar and Dr. T.S.S. Rajan with the object of bringing about amicable relations between the Harijans and the Nattars of that area. I may add that though we did not succeed in bringing about a definite settlement our pleading with the two communities softened their hearts and prepared them for a final settlement.

You know my desire to have larger opportunities of serving the country and my people in the new field of political and social life which is opening out before our eyes to-day. In standing for the Madras Legislative Assembly as a Scheduled Classes candidate, I have followed the advice you gave me, and by the Grace of God and with your blessing I have succeeded. I leave the future in the same safe hands. I need not say how much I shall value any advice and support you give me in my present situation.

With best regards,

Yours sincerely,
M.C. Rajah.

25 AUGUST 1938

My Dear Mahatmaji,

I regret to have to bring to your notice the state of affairs in this Presidency as regards the Depressed Classes.

You remember how when most of my people were in favour of Separate Electorates so that they may express themselves faithfully and effectively in the Legislature, you staked your life on bringing them into the Hindu fold not only politically but socially and religiously. And I was in no small measure responsible for my people going in for a Joint Electorate with Caste Hindus on the express understanding that there was to be no interference with our choosing men who would faithfully represent our grievances and wishes. It was with this object that the Panel Election was instituted. All this you know as well as I do. But my object in recalling the fact is to show that while on our part we faithfully adhered to the Poona Pact, giving up agitating for a Separate Electorate, the Congress party men in Madras representing the Caste Hindus deviated from the Pact, so much so that our community in the Legislative Assembly have to follow the Caste Hindus blindly in every measure the Ministry may bring and to vote with them even in matters which deeply affect the interests of the community.

You perhaps remember that at the beginning of the elections I protested against the Congress Committee setting up candidates for the Panel Election among the Depressed Classes. You were good enough to say that I might allow my community joining the Congress on certain conditions placed before us by Mr. Satyamurthi. One of these conditions was that in matters affecting their community the Depressed Class members of the Congress Party need not vote with the Congress members but vote according to their judgment.

The recent debate on the Temple Entry Bill in the Madras Legislative Assembly has exposed the ugly fact that the whole Depressed Class members driven by the discipline of the Congress Party in the Assembly voted solidly against my motion for referring the Bill to a Select Committee. Could anything be more unnatural and more humiliating, proving as it did the subjugation of my community by the Caste Hindus represented by Mr. Rajagopalachari.

You know the provisions of the Bill. It was only a piece of permissive legislation making it possible for a majority of worshippers of a temple to allow Harijans to worship in the Temples. There was no element of compulsion or coercion in it. This Bill had your blessing. It was drafted by Mr. Rajagopalachari himself and approved by you.

At a previous session of the Assembly I introduced the Bill with the consent of Mr. Rajagopalachari who promised his full support to the measure. When I suggested that the Bill might be introduced by him as a Government measure he wanted me to introduce it. When I met him last, on the 12th July 1938, and informed him that I was giving notice of a motion for referring the Bill to a Select Committee he did not object.

I do not know what happened in the meantime, but two days before my motion for referring the Bill to the Select Committee came up before the House, Mr. Rajagopalachari sent for me and quietly asked me to withdraw the Bill, which I refused to do. When in due course I moved for the consideration of the Bill Mr. Rajagopalachari stood up and opposed the Bill and requested me to withdraw it, saying that he would introduce a Temple Entry Bill on the same lines only for Malabar and not for other Districts.

The effect of Mr. Rajagopalachari's speech was to defeat my motion with my own community men registering their votes against the measure introduced to secure their social and religious elevation. One effect of Rajagopalachari's opposition will be to strengthen the opposition in the country to Temple Entry as a whole.

All this makes me uneasy about the wisdom of our having been parties to the Poona Pact in the full belief that the Congress would really help us in our attempt to secure social and religious freedom. I am forced to think that our entering the Joint Electorate with the Caste Hindus under the leadership of the Congress, far from helping us, has enabled the Congress, led by Caste Hindus leaders, to destroy our independence and to use us to cut our own throats.

In the course of the debate I asked Mr. Rajagopalachari whether he had obtained your approval of the attitude which he so suddenly and unexpectedly assumed, and the speaker said that Mr. Rajagopalachari will be given an opportunity to answer the question after I had done. Though he was given the privilege of speaking after me he avoided the question and did not answer it at all.

I trust that you will give your most serious consideration to this question of the attitude of the Congress Ministry in Madras towards Harijan uplift, especially with regard to Temple Entry, and let me have your view before I answer my community men who are very much exercised over this question and are contemplating a repudiation of the Poona Pact and an agitation for a Separate Electorate accompanied by Direct Action of some kind.

With best regards,

Yours sincerely,
M.C.Rajah.

21 SETPEMBER 1938

My Dear Mahatmaji,

I thank you for your reply to my letter. I am sorry that you do not give your view of the action of the Congress Ministry and the Congress Party in Madras in rejecting the Madras Temple Entry Bill. Your silence leads me to think that you are not pleased with their action though you do not think it wise to say so. But you advise me to trust C.R. It is easy for you with your personal attachment to Rajaji to trust him irrespective of what he does and how he does it.

I confess I trusted him too to the last moment, but after the sudden blow given by him to the cause of the social and religious upliftment of my community, loyalty to my community prevents me from accepting your advice. I should request you on the other hand to give more serious consideration to the pledges given to my community during the Yerravada fast and to the way in which they are carried out by your plenipotentiary in Madras. That fast was undertaken by you in order to change the Communal Award providing Separate Electorates for my people and to bring them into Joint Electorates with Caste Hindus by promising to spare no efforts to remove Untouchability. And you have more than once said that Temple Entry is of the very essence of the removal of Untouchability.

So the question of our being in a Joint Electorate with Caste Hindus and the attitude of the Congress Ministry towards the raising of the social and religious status of the community are mutually and vitally connected.

If we are not free to enter into Hindu Temples we are no Hindus, and if we are not Hindus, why should we be in a Joint Electorate with them? Is it for swelling their numbers as against Muslims and other communities?

If you look at the situation in Madras from this point of view, you will realize that the rejection of the Temple Entry Bill is a gross betrayal of the Depressed Classes by the Congress Government in Madras.

Any amount of money spent out of public funds or even from private resources for the amelioration of the economic condition of my community will be no substitute for the removal of Untouchability, through Temple Entry. As you yourself once said, Temple Entry is the acid test of the sincerety of Caste Hindus in espousing the cause of the Depressed Classes.

Mr. Rajagopalachari's Malabar Temple Entry Bill, besides involving the tactical choice of a difficult district makes our community subservient to the will of the Caste Hindus, a policy which is given further effect to in the appointment of Advisory Boards to assist the Labour Commissioner in which Caste Hindus of the Harijan Sevak Sanghs of this Province are given Government facilities for guiding the destinies of my people. I do not expect you to agree with my views on the measures recently introduced by Mr. Rajagopalachari after rejecting the Madras Temple Entry Bill; but I expect you to give more serious consideration to the situation in Madras as regards the Depressed Classes in the light of the pledges given to the Depressed Classes during your memorable fast.

You are morally bound to make this a matter of conscience and not merely one of political strategy. I am sure that if you should seek "inner light" on this subject of Untouchability and Temple Entry you will speak out more plainly and make the necessary sacrifice to educate your followers.

I propose to send this correspondence to the Press, but I shall wait for any further word from you till the end of this month.

With best regards,

Yours sincerely,
M.C. Rajah.

17 OCTOBER 1938

My Dear Mahatmaji,

I thank you for your kind letter of the 5th instant written in the train on your way to Peshawar, under conditions of health none too good. It shows how deeply and intimately you feel for my community and for the removal of Untouchability. I wish your followers in general and your chief representative in this Presidency in particular felt one half of your concern in the matter. May I remind you that it is the fate of a religious leader like you who wish to direct political activities in the country to be surrounded by men who seem all right in your presence and perhaps are for the moment what they seem to be, but once away from you and left to themselves, follow their own natural promptings and forget their undertakings to you and their obligations to others. I am sorry to say it, but I have to say it, since I have to think of the interests of my community, that C.R. as he is revealing himself to us in course of his actions is different from what you believe him to be out of your affection for him. His innate prejudices assert themselves day by day, and so he finds it difficult to overcome what you call Sanatanist opposition.

You have attempted to convert the Sanatanists' heart, and you know you have not succeeded; and when you have failed, do you expect C.R. to succeed in spite of all his attempts to be reasonable in their eyes? If we of the Depressed Classes have to wait till C.R. effects the "conversion of the Sanatanist heart" we should wait till Doomsday. Knowing this, what he is doing is to yield to Sanatanist influence and to sacrifice our freedom and self respect in order to maintain his present position, even as Britain and France have sacrificed Czechoslovakia on the altar of so called Peace. He knows that public opinion is sufficiently strong to allow the passing of a minimum permissive legislation which would help reformists to overcome Sanatanist opposition himself, he has only to enable reformists to do it within their sphere of influence. If he had only allowed Congress members to vote according to their individual conviction instead of ordering them under Congress discipline to vote against it, all the preparatory work done by you and by others in favour of Temple Entry since your memorable fast would not have gone in vain. It would have borne fruit in the passing of the Madras Temple Entry Bill. But to the surprise of his own followers he declared himself on a sudden opposed to it, all because the small community to which he belongs – much smaller than ours – is Sanatanist to the core and that community does not want it. He is more sensitive to their opinion than to enlightened nationalistic opinion both inside and outside the Congress. Nor does he care for the feelings of my long oppressed people.

C.R. is tinkering with this problem of Temple Entry by putting it off and relegating it to a corner of the country where Sanatanist opposition is strong but will not tell upon his nerves. He is dodging the problem instead of facing it and going at it straightforwardly.

It is your duty now to sound a note of warning to a disciple who is going astray and to bring him back to the path of repentance and of justice to a community who have placed their trust in you and so far followed your lead in identifying themselves with the Caste Hindus. We do not wish to remain betrayed any longer.

It is no pleasure for me to differ from you, but when I see the cause which is so dear to you and me betrayed in action by one in whom you have implicit faith and whom you have helped to place in a position of power which may be used for good or for evil, for large ends or narrow purposes, I have no alternative but to say that your faith in which you wish me to share is misplaced.

With best regards,

Yours sincerely,
M.C. Rajah.

Speech on Labour by M.C. Rajah, MLA*

I deem it a great honour to be invited to participate in this function and let me at the outset say how very pleased I was to have received Mr. Nuttal's kind invitation to preside over this function. As one who belongs to the Depressed Classes my sympathies are naturally with the labourers, no matter whether they labour in the fields or in factories. I sometimes think the word labour is too narrowly used when it is applied to those whose labour is in mills and factories, forgetting that the bulk of the labourers are in the fields. Man's essential wants are food and clothing. If the agricultural labourer helps to grow paddy and gives us food to eat, labourers like you spin and weave cloth which is equally necessary.

As Mr. Anthoni has remarked I am not a stranger to these mills, my interest in your Buckingham and Carnatic Mills is not a recent thing. It dates back from the days when my public life began. I espoused the cause of the depressed and labouring classes amongst you so long ago as 1920 and did so with no little sacrifice and risk. But that is now ancient history. All the differences which existed then have disappeared, and I am glad to see unity and harmony prevailing not only between employers and employees but also between labourers of different castes and communities. Unity does not mean merely unity against others, but unity amongst ourselves. Unity within will lead not only to unity in external relations but to strength all round.

This unity has been brought about by the cooperation of all concerned.

I would also like to take this opportunity to pay my tribute of praise to the employers of the Buckingham and Carnatic Mills for the valuable contribution they have made towards ameliorating the condition of the working classes in this area during the past few decades.

*M.C. Rajah Papers, Nehru Memorial Museum & Library, New Delhi.

We talk of industrial development of the country. For industries on a large scale we require both labour and capital. One without the other will not carry us far. What can mere labour do? What can mere capital do? One is powerless without the other.

I remember the time when this welfare movement was started. When there was a tendency on the part of labour to overcome capital and when capital did not understand the wants and wishes of labourers – this movement was started for creating harmony and mutual understanding between these two factors of industrial development. This movement was however an explicit organization of endeavours which had been quietly and unostentatiously carried on in these Mills. I remember that Dr. T.M. Nair who was largely responsible for the appointment of the Factory Commission of 1912 putting it on record in the Factory Commission Report that of all the mills in India, the Buckingham and Carnatic Mills bestowed the greatest consideration and attention on the condition of mill workers.

I therefore appreciate the good work that is being done through this Welfare Association, and I thank you for inviting me to witness this demonstration of goodwill and good understanding existing in these Mills between capital and labour, capital studying and promoting the welfare and happiness of labourers, labourers endeavouring to make capital most fruitful in advancing the industrial development of the country.

I have referred previously to agricultural labourers. Though their condition is hard – in many ways you are happier than they – it shoud be remembered that their masters, the Mirasdars took personal interest in their welfare, by giving them cottages to live in, and a share of the produce besides paying their wages, by giving them presents on festivals like Pongal and Deepavali and helping them in their marriages, etc., and the farm labourers on their part worked with real zeal. It is the same kind of mutual interest that this Welfare Association seeks to promote between you and your employers.

The Report which the Secretary of the Welfare Association has read is a record of service of which any Association may be proud. The good work of which it is a record would not have been possible without the cooperation of the authorities on one hand and of workers of all grades on the other. This cooperation is based on sympathy and good will on both sides; the willingness to understand the other man's point of view and assist him in his difficulties. That the labourers have difficulties to overcome at home and abroad is known to and admitted by all. And every effort should be made to help them to surmount those difficulties, social, moral and economic, and the Report shows that every effort is being made in this direction. It is not however recognized that the employers too have difficulties and that it is the duty of the workmen and their leaders to view questions from the standpoint of the employers as well. Too narrow a view of the labourers' position without a comprehensive view of the whole economic situation in the country is not likely to improve matters either for the labourer or for his employer. We must cultivate the habit of what Lord Morley once described as getting into other's skins, or what we speak of as getting into their shoes, before coming to a decision on matters which involve other people's interests as well as our own. We must be just in all our actions. Do unto others as we wish that others should do unto us, is a golden rule – a safe guide in life.

I am firmly of the opinion that joint consultation between the workers and management is extremely desireable for the settlement of the diverse questions that arise in the relations between the management and the workers. And I fully believe that such co-operation and consultation will be necessary, whatever be the changes the organization of industry may undergo. Here I should like to state that the committee is not rival to the Trade Union.

Some of you are members of the Trade Unions. While you fully realize the advantages of your belonging to the Welfare Association, you will find it difficult to reconcile your gratitude to the Welfare association for every practical benefits you derive therefrom, advantages which extend over the whole field of life – over your home life, your use of leisure, and give opportunities of self-improvement for yourself and education of your children etc. – you are not able to reconcile your gratitude to this Association with the claims of Trade Unions. A little calm thinking will however help you to see that there is nothing inconsistent between the aims of two institutions. If I were you, I would throw myself heart and soul in the constructive and educative and ameliorative work of this Association because it addresses itself to the day-to-day transactions of your life, helping to build up into self-respecting individuals and advancing your economic and social interests as they arise in the course of every day life of workmen of these Mills. You have first of all to make sure of your ground here as protectors of your families and your children and as healthy and useful citizens. This you are enabled to do with the cooperation of the mill authorities. I would let nothing interfere with your internal relations as members of the Welfare Association. Trade Unions are of paramount importance to the workers and but for them the progress the workers have achieved throughout the world would not have been possible. I have been myself connected with different Trade Unions at different times. But I do not see any reason why a Trade Union and a Welfare Committee should not co-exist. Trade Unions address themselves to economic and social questions common to all Mills and Factories, such as require for their solution, politico-economic investigations and legislative enactments. I would not allow my relations or people at home to interfere with or to be dictated to by the outsiders. Nor would I allow my public life to be determined by my wife and children. The spheres of the home and of public duties are distinct. My happiness at home makes me an efficient public worker. So I would say to you enjoy full happiness in these Mills through your Welfare Association. Then and thus your participation in Labour Unions will do you good. Your experience in these Mills, which are praised all over the country as models so far as relations between labour and capital are concerned, will serve you to direct your Labour Unions wisely. The Labour Unions which deal with large questions relating to the whole industrial life of the country demand men who have graduated in such Welfare Associations, graduates mind, and not undergraduates or failed matriculates.

I am glad to hear that besides Welfare Committees, you have departmental Committees which deal with specific problems of different sections of the mills. All this shows that your interests are studied in detail and intensively, and specific remedies are sought and applied. You can have no grievance which will not be heeded and remedied as far as circumstances permit.

Seek first the kingdom of god and all other things will be added unto you. So said a great prophet. If you seek the welfare of the whole institution – your particular welfare will be secured.

Speaking about my community I have no hesitation in saying that but for the excellent educational facilities provided by the Mills and the social welfare activities carried on by the Welfare Committee, they would not have raised themselves to their present position culturally, economically and socially. I am extremely glad to understand that the opportunities for education and for social progress which are provided by the Management are being utilized by my community in an abundant measure. I have no doubt that the Management of these Mills have rendered an invaluable service to the cause of my community by preparing them to take their due place in the New India that is emerging into existence.

My last words to you this evening – will be an appeal to your patriotism, to your love of your country and your people, and to your love of freedom and peace. You know we are all in the throes of a mighty struggle and I am glad my friend Mr. Anthoni has referred to the War. Never before in the world's history has wickedness or evil organized itself so terribly against all that makes life worth living, against civilization and progress. What we are witnessing to-day is a gigantic struggle between Good and Evil. In it your interests and the interests of labour are deeply involved. That is why Labour Unions and Labour Conferences all over the world have proclaimed their condemnation of Hitlerism. The war is at the gates of India. India is becoming the Arsenal of the East. Our workmen are distinguishing themselves for their output of arms and ammunitions for defeating Germany and Japan. Our workmen are having a unique opportunity for showing their skill and strength. India is advancing industrially by leaps and bounds. I know you are making a mighty contribution in ways you know not of or dreamt of in the past. I have heard from the highest authorities who are directing war efforts that the Buckingham and Carnatic mills are foremost in producing textile supplies for the War. I would say to you, go forward, don't allow false philosophy or false patriotism to lull you to sleep or slacken your efforts. The War is India's as well as England's. It is world war. We cannot let slip this opportunity to sit on the Round Table Conference of Victory, for establishing the world on a footing of permanent peace which will bring happiness to rich and poor, to educated and ignorant. In short there will no longer be very rich people nor very poor people, no high caste or low caste. No rulers nor ruled. Democracy means that all will have a share in the power and responsibility of Government. In this noble work of implementing the highest ideals of mankind let us go forward without looking to the right or to the left, straight to Victory.

PART III

SPEECHES IN MADRAS LEGISLATIVE COUNCIL, CENTRAL LEGISLATIVE ASSEMBLY AND MADRAS LEGISLATIVE ASSEMBLY, 1921-1939

Discussion on the Budget, 9 March 1921*

Mr. M.C. Rajah: "Mr. President, Sir, I have a few suggestions to make. I find that a sum of twelve lakhs is set apart for advances to agriculturists. I suppose this will benefit those who have lands to cultivate but have no means to put in enough capital upon the land. May I now press the claims of the members of the Depressed Classes to whom *darkhast* lands have been given by the benign Government and who too do not possess the means for cultivating those lands. I suggest that a sum of about two lakhs be earmarked in that direction. What happens is that when my people get these lands assigned to them they are not able to make the necessary investment for the cultivation and improvement of the land and they are driven to the necessity of mortgaging, if not altogether parting with, the lands given by the sympathetic Government. It is to prevent this, Sir, that I make this request. Then I observe that there is a provision of five lakhs for the city and suburban improvements trusts. I would urge that a portion of this amount be expanded on acquiring lands for settling the Depressed Classes in healthy surroundings. We all know that in Madras there is a regular movement on the part of the landlords belonging to the higher castes to evict the poor tenants in the different cheris of Madras. Relief is badly needed for the Depressed Classes by way of being provided with lands acquired by Government on their behalf. This, Sir, I think will go a long way to improve the city and suburbs and should be regarded as an essential part of the scheme of the city improvement trust.

Coming now to education, the sympathy of the Madras Government towards my community is exhibited in the budget by a provision of one lakh for opening schools for the Depressed Classes. Sir, whereas I see—Honourable Members of this Council will not misunderstand me if I say that—the establishment charges for the year including salaries, allowances, contingencies, etc., for the Queen Mary's College, Madras is about Rs. 66,400. And there are only about 132 women

*Speech in Madras Legislative Council.

studying in the Queen Mary's College. Whereas the population of the Depressed Classes amounts to nearly eight millions. Last year the Government of Madras set apart two lakhs under this head for opening elementary schools for Depressed Classes. I do not know how much out of the two lakhs was spent actually for opening schools. This year the sympathy of the Government seems to have gone down a bit and now they have only set apart one lakh.

Mr. M.C. Rajah (continuing): "Even last year the sum of two lakhs was allotted for the additional schools to be opened. Now, this provision of one lakh is most inadequate. It ought to be increased. The allotment of six lakhs for the expansion of education and for improving the cause of district educational councils is I think unnecessary. Out of this, three lakhs should be set apart for opening schools for the Depressed Classes under the Madras Elementary Education Act. Again, Sir, I would press the Government to institute more scholarships for pupils of the Depressed Classes.

"Sir, in the report on Public Instruction in the Madras Presidency for the year 1919-20, under Education of Mohammedans (p. 11), I find the number of public institution chiefly intended for Mohammedans rose from 1,815 to 1,983 and under Education of Panchamas I find the number of public institutions rose from 5,958 to 6,438. Sir, now we all know that there is a special Inspecting Agency to look after the Mohammedan schools and I say it is very necessary. Seeing that the number of schools for the Panchamasis 6,438, I also wish that a special Inspecting Agency be established to look after this enormous number of schools. Sir, we are going to open a number of schools this year also. I say that under Special Education is included the Reformatory School at Chingleput. This institution earned a well-deserved reputation for fulfilling its function admirably when it was in charge of Mr. J.W. Coombes who was an educational officer. He was like an elder brother to the boys committed to his care and he brought them up on the latest principles of therapeutic psychology. Now that he is retired, an Assistant Surgeon is put in charge and the result is that the spirit of the jail predominated over that of the school and the home. Government should see to it that school is placed as speedily as possible under the management of an educational officer who knows how to use moral rather than physical force to wean boys from evil ways and evil habits. The budget provides a lakh of rupees for opening 12 new training schools. This is as it should be, for we cannot have in the present state of expansion in education too many trained teachers. But then those teachers should be of the right sort. It will not do to pick up boys and girls who have just come out of the primary stage and train them as teachers for primary schools. Seeing that the educational career of a boy or girl depends very largely upon the training given to him or her in the earliest years of his or her school course, it is essential that the teachers should be of very much higher standard than the pupils whom they teach. So I would suggest that the lower elementary training should be abolished, and that we should hereafter give up the training of what are called lower elementary trained teachers and insist upon every teacher being at least higher elementary trained. In this connexion I would request Government not to open lower elementary department in the 12 new schools they propose to start. I may perhaps be allowed at this point to draw attention to a petition submitted to the Director of Public Instruction by the teachers undergoing training in the Government Higher Elementary Teachers' Training Schools at Calicut in which they complain that they are put to very considerable inconvenience in the matter of finding suitable boarding and lodging since they belong to the untouchable community. Besides the disadvantage of untouchability, the stipend they get is too low to get even third-rate rooms for them. The Government maintain a hostel in connexion with this school in a palatial extensive building but the petitioners are denied admission there to owing to their caste which is subversive of the Government order recently issued to local bodies that public buildings on no account be opened to the exclusive use of certain community alone but thrown open to all sects and castes. If the so-called high-caste pupils cannot accommodate themselves in the same building with the Thiyya students, it is their duty to look out elsewhere. It is no business of Government to keep out any people on account of the so-called untouchability.

Under Widows Scholarship there is a provision for Rs. 14,580. Unless the Brahman Widows' Home is thrown open also for the non-Brahman girls or unless a similar building is put up side by side with the Kernan's Castle for accommodating non-Brahman girls, I will strongly object to this amount. Unless the Minister in charge gives me an assurance that equal facilities in the shape of boarding and lodging will be provided to non-Brahman girls as is the case with the Brahman widows, I will strongly vote for the deletion of this amount.

As regards the controlling staff, I find the Government is contemplating the appointment of one Inspector for each district and one Sub-Assistant Inspector for each taluk. It is no doubt necessary to have one Sub-Assistant Inspector for each taluk, but I do not think it necessary to have one Inspector for each district. It will be quite enough to have one Inspector to examine schools in more than one district.

Again, Sir, as the Honourable Member Mr. Macphail has rightly pointed out, the grants given to aided education are not sufficient. The grants to non-Government Arts Colleges are Rs. 2,81,000, and there are 33 Colleges with 6,183 students. The grants to Government Arts Colleges are Rs. 7,46,000, and there are only ten institutions with 1,981 scholars. I do not see any reason why we should not encourage these non-Government Arts Colleges. Once when I brought a resolution here, I was told that it was a thing for private enterprise and that it was the policy of Government that private enterprise should be encouraged. When private enterprise could do the work of the Government, it is our duty to help it. While the Government are spending for 33 non-Government Arts Colleges with 6,180 students a sum of only Rs. 2 lakhs, why should not the benign Government see its way to help private enterprise liberally and push it up?

Again, Sir, as regards grants to non-Government secondary schools, I see there is to be no increase in the special teaching grants for secondary schools. I wish the Government will also consider this and increase the provision for special teaching grant.

Under Medical, there is a proposal to concentrate all X-ray installation in this city in one place and a provision of Rs. 30,000 is made for it in the budget and this institute is to be located next to the proposed tuberculosis institute at Temple Gardens, Royapetta. At present there are X-ray installations at Royapetta, Maternity and General Hospitals and arrangements have already been made to have one in the Rayapuram Hospital. It is only right and proper that each hospital should have in it one X-ray installation and thus be completely equipped in itself, for the X-rays are an auxiliary to the surgical cases and their help is sometimes emergently and urgently required in the operation cases. That in these circumstances the patient should be conveyed to a central X-ray institute in close juxtaposition to the Tuberculosis Hospital is a most inconvenient and unnatural arrangement. I hope this idea of X-rays, like that of locating the Tuberculosis Institute in Temple Gardens, ought to be given up. I observe that a sum of Rs. 50,000 has been allocated for taking over the Victoria Caste and Gosha Hospital. I do not object to such a sum being spent over medical help for Indian women, but I do not understand why admission to this hospital should be confined to caste and gosha women only. Unless the Minister in charge assures me that in this hospital women are admitted irrespective of caste and creed, I will have to vote against this allocation. Under Medical Schools there is a provision of Rs. 90,000 for stipends and books of civil pupils and Rs. 4,648 for stipends, etc., of Madras-Burma pupils and Rs. 42,500 for instruments and chemicals. I consider these amounts to be necessary. I do not see any reason why stipends, books and instruments and free instruction should be given to pupils in medical schools. These items should be deleted and a certain amount of scholarships to deserving pupils belonging to Depressed Classes should be instituted.

Under Industries, I have just one suggestion to offer and that is that attempts should be made to teach cottage industries of various kinds to Indian women, so that they may ply the various little trades in their own homes. I do not see why something should not be done by way of training Indian women to earn a decent living for themselves by the use of their hands.

Under Labour the Government complain that a struggle has to be maintained to find time to carry on the work for the amelioration of the Depressed Classes in the face of the insistent demand for the settling of labour disputes etc. It should be remembered that the department was originally created for the protection of the Depressed Classes, but gradually the protector was burdened with various kinds of work. My community protested even at the very beginning against the diversion of this department's attention to other work then for which it was called into being, and I am not surprised that the protector of the Depressed Classes has been swallowed up by the Labour Commissioner. Government have either to abolish labour or to find a separate officer for labour. I may assure this Council that we the Depressed Classes have enough needs to find work not for one but for more than one officer, only he should be of a sympathetic nature ready to take infinite pains on our behalf for solving our many problems. I am glad that provision is made for three assistants. I would here strike a note of warning against appointing officers, Brahman or non-Brahman, whose ideas of personal greatness of official dignity and caste superiority make it impossible for them to enter into the skins of the Adi-Dravidas and feel with them, like them and for them. In conclusion, I would only urge the great necessity in view of high prices and the loud cries of subordinate officers for bread, more bread and bread in time that we should practise retrenchment, at least with a view to help those whose needs are most urgent. Whenever a claim is made on behalf of the poor, the oppressed and the hard-worked, the answer given is where are we to find funds, but when a proposal is made for incurring expenditure on behalf of high-paid officials, we accept the proposal quietly and silently in the name of efficiency. For instance there is a provision of nearly 4¾ lakhs for improving and extending Queen Mary's College. I am not opposed to the higher education for women, but why should such a large sum be robbed away in one year? Could not the expenditure be distributed over three or four years? A college like the Presidency College took nearly half a century, and why should the women's counterpart of the Presidency College be reached through at such short space? I find also an allotment of Rs. 32,000 for the improvement to the Madras University Student' Club. Those who are acquainted with this institution know the class and number of students who avail themselves of this institution. I am convinced that I cannot agree that such a large sum as Rs. 32,000 should be spent by those who are trustees of the people's money on an object which seems to be rather doubtful in its utility to the people of the whole Presidency. My plea, Sir, is for economy, a fair distribution of expenditure with greater sympathy for those who are suffering.

Madras Disturbances, 12 October 1921*

Mr. M.C. Rajah: Sir, as one who has suffered considerably during this recent trouble, I think I have a right to give my opinion on this subject. I welcome this opportunity of having the matter discussed in this Council. My community has no newspaper at their disposal, no means of expressing their grievances, and the few leaders of the community capable of speaking on their behalf are intimidated, calumniated and subjected to oppression and coercion, I myself having been driven away from my house in Royapetta. I suppose all the honourable members in this Council know this, and also that that was the reason why I was not able to come out of my house to attend the Council meeting last month.

It is not necessary for me here to recapitulate the events of the past. It will be sufficient if I say that there are over two thousand Adi-Dravida families in Madras, and the suggestion was recently made that these families should be packed like rats and put in trucks and deported out of Madras. Countless assaults, innumerable attacks have taken place, and every member of my community in the vicinity of Madras has spent many sleepless nights during the last four months. I have no desire here to palliate any act of my people going beyond the right of defence; there have been indeed very few such instances. It is due to the constant endeavours of the leaders of the community – as I said, even if they were not allowed to go to that area and they had to shut themselves up within their houses for fear of being assaulted – who induced the Adi-Dravidas to look to the law for protection. As regards the Labour department, I wish to say here that it has done the minimum that any civilized Government in this world can do to these poor homeless Adi-Dravidas. They did nothing more than that. As regards work in the mills I would like to say a few words. The Adi-Dravida workers in the mill did not join the strike at all. I want that to be impressed on the minds of honourable members here. It was, I think, on the 19th of June this year, it was

*Speech in Madras Legislative Council.

a Sunday, that a meeting of the Adi-Dravida labourers was held in Pulianthope, and I was present there. In my presence the Adi-Dravida labourers unanimously decided that they could not join the strikers at that time. There was no strike then; the workers were only contemplating a strike at that time. The reason for their decision was this: the Adi-Dravida labourers there told me expressly that during the previous strike, the one towards the end of last year, it was a strike continuing for about three or four months, during that strike the men of my community suffered considerably, and they had to part with the little jewels they had and even with their clothes. Mr. Natesan knows it, and Sir P. Thyagaraya Chettiyar knows it. And so, they said that after the three or four months strike – that was Mr. Wadia's strike – (laughter) what happened was that these labourers surrendered actually to the Mill authorities and my men on the 19th of June expressed that they could not submit themselves to any more strike like that. And they in a body wrote a letter to the President of the Labour Union stating that they were extremely poor, that they had no means of livelihood except working in the mills, and that they could not afford to join the strike since they had suffered considerably during the last strike when even the little property they had, had to be placed in the hands of the Marwaris. I state this plainly so that honourable members may understand the situation clearly. That letter was sent to the President of the Labour Union on the 19th June and no reply was received thereto. That was flouted, I suppose, and then the other members of the Union went on strike. But my men continued to go to work. They did not stop at all and for that they are suffering like this. My people only exercised their rights to give or withhold their labour as they thought best in their own interests. That right my community has maintained against the non-cooperators whose object, both manifest and avowed, is, as is well known to all here, simply to render Government impossible. That right my community intends to assert and to maintain in the future. My friend Mr. Tanikachala Chettiyar has said that not one Adi-Dravida was shot. For my part I am extremely sorry for the caste Hindus who have been killed. From the fact that no Adi-Dravidas have been shot, it is clear that these Adi-Dravidas were not in the disturbed areas; they were not the rioters and therefore they escaped shots. That is quite clear. If they had been with the rioters in their rioting, they would have certainly lost their lives. The very fact that no one Adi-Dravida was shot clearly indicates that the Adi-Dravida was not creating the mischief. He was aloof on the one side. But my friend Mr. Tanikachala Chettiyar has said nothing about the throwing of bombs, which has become the fashion of the rioters. How many lives have been lost by the throwing of bombs, who threw them, and who manufactured them, these are questions which my honourable friend ought to have put before the Council. I am sorry he has forgotten this aspect of the case. And then my friend Mr. Natesa Mudaliyar has said that certain representations by the champion of the Adi-Dravidas were made to His Excellency the Governor regarding the disturbances. I want to know what the representation is. I suppose he refers to the famous memorial, that partisan memorial, Sir, I say here, signed by Sir P. Thyagaraya Chettiyar and others. Sir, I should like to point out that it was said in that memorial that on a certain morning I was present at the Vyasarpadi camp with my friend Mr. Sundaracharlu. I say here that I was not there at all at the time. I think that morning, I was talking with a friend of the Hon'ble Mr. Venkata Reddi Nayudu, one Mr. Gnanaprakasa Rao. This person came with an introductory note from the Hon'ble Mr. Venkata Reddi Nayudu and asked me for a recommendation to Mr. Schmidt (laughter). And that day, Sir, as I was a little indisposed I did not leave my house at all. But I used to go to Vyasarpadi camp to advise my men to be careful and to restrain themselves. Unfortunately or fortunately I do not know, I was not there that day at all. I did not leave my house that whole Sunday. From this, Sir, you will understand what sort of a memorial that famous memorial is. And then my friend Dr. U. Rama Rao has said that the Adi-Dravida leaders advised their men to go to work. I suppose there is no harm in that. The leader of any community has got a right to advise his people to the best of his judgment; and if Mr. Rama Rao, as the leader of this community, is afraid to tell his constituents what his views are on any particular and pressing question, I do not know what to say about his right to be their leader. I am astonished, Sir, at a section of the party which claims to stand for the depressed and the oppressed classes countenancing the persecution and the reign of terror to which my community is at present subjected. I do not believe that this section voices the real opinion or attitude of the Council nor of the non-Brahman party throughout the Presidency. The position of my community is simply this. We believe at present the view of Mr. Tanikachala Chettiyar that the Government are siding the Adi-Dravidas is not shared by the members of the wide non-Brahman party in this country. If however they are, we have no option but to cut ourselves aloof from that party; and in doing so, I appeal with all the force at my command to all the moderate members of this House, to the non-Brahmans, the Brahmans and the Europeans alike in this Council to say that this campaign to excite public feeling against my community, to deprive them of their legitimate rights and to reduce them once more to the political, social and economic bondage of ages, shall cease.

Motion on Insertion of a Conscience Clause in the Grant-in-Aid Code, 16 November 1921*

Mr. M.C. Rajah: I stand to oppose this resolution. It will hit Christian Mission schools. Next to the Government, they are the greatest educational agency.

We of the Depressed Classes owe what education we possess to Christian missionaries. The four Hindu members that represent the Depressed Classes in this very Council were educated in Christian missionary schools. I spent my younger days in Wesley College and then came up for my high school and college courses to the Christian College. The missionaries will have no object in maintaining schools when they are not free to impart religious instruction to their pupils. They do not come here merely to teach History and Geography or Algebra and Geometry or Sanskrit to Indian boys and girls. The money which they spend has been given to them by people at home in order that they may have the opportunity of imparting Christian truth to non-Christians. Non-Christians are not compelled to send their students to their schools – they may send them to non-Christian schools if they please. If you say that you cannot help sending them to these high schools when and where there is one school and that the mission school, my answer is that in many cases even when there is a choice between the Christian school and the non-Christian school, parents prefer the Christian school. I was in Voorhees College, Vellore, in-charge of the lower school. Vellore, you all know, is an orthodox centre. Voorhees College and Mahant's high school were on the same road, opposite to each other. In Mahant's high school, Sanatana Dharma was taught and in spite of all that Hindu parents preferred Voorhees College and we used to have the full strength and some classes had to be divided into sections A, B, C and D, each section having the full strength of 40.

A knowledge of Christianity does not drive children into the Christian church, though it might make them Christians in the larger

*Speech in Madras Legislative Council.

sense of being lovers of all men, rich and poor, educated and ignorant, elevated and depressed, lovers of all that is good, pure and noble in life. In this sense are we not all Christians – though most of us are outside the Christian Churches?

I told you that I was educated all through in Christian schools and for the last 13 years I have been in mission service. What has happened to me? Have I become a Christian? Has my conscience been outraged? It is really a slur upon those educated in Christian missions to say that they become hypocrites by attending Scripture classes. On the other hand, they learn tolerance and that independence which comes not from slavish following of ancestral faiths but from a deliberate conviction arrived at by comparing what is taught in schools and colleges with what is taught at home and practiced elsewhere. 'Prove all things, hold fast that which is good,' that is the thing, Sir, that is taught in Christian schools.

'They are slaves who dare not be
In the Right with two or three.'

This is the motto of the Madras Christian College. Does this spell slave mentality? Does it sound like the outraging of one's conscience? Is this a lesson in hypocrisy? No, true independence comes from a widening of one's outlook on the world, with its many religious customs and civilizations. It is this loyalty to one's true self that comes from a knowledge of religions other than that in which the priests of one's ancestral religion would like its followers to confine their attention and their affection. I can assure my old Professor Rev. Meston that our conscience has not been outraged or tainted; but on the other hand, it has become pure and real by the influence of Christian missionaries.

The honourable member Mr. Govindaraghava Ayyar in his speech yesterday stated that it was not right that the general taxpayers' money should go to support those sectarian institutions. I believe Mr. Govindaraghava Ayyar is a member of the Pachaiyappa's College Trust Board and also a member of the Hindu High School Committee and the P.S. High School Committee.

Mr. M.C. Rajah (continuing): I know that Mr. Govindaraghava Ayyar was once a member of the Pachaiyappa's College Trust Board. And I believe, Sir, that in the Hindu High School, P.S. High School, Theological High School and Pachaiyappa's College pupils belonging to certain sections are not admitted. Yet these schools get aid from the general taxpayers' money. Is it right that the general taxpayers' money should go to support these sectarian institutions which deny admission to the sons of the soil in a far truer sense than Mr. Govindaraghava Ayyar and his friends can claim to be?

Mr. M.C. Rajah (continuing): Then again what about the Sanskrit schools which teach Vedas and exclude the non-Brahmans? Is it right for these schools to get Government aid? Sir, if we make attendance at Scripture classes optional, what will happen is this: Not that the parents will exercise their option freely and unhampered by extraneous considerations, but they will be subject to all sorts of more or less tyrannical influences brought to bear upon them by agitators who care very little for the good of the boys or their parents. In this land where fear of ex-communication and disapproval of neighbours operate powerfully in social and political matters as we see every day, it will be very difficult for a parent who thinks that attendance at religious classes does good to his boys to exercise his judgment independently. A national agitator has only to go about with a declaration form and get signatures of parents in opposition to missionary schools teaching Christian religion.

I therefore object to the resolution being passed.

Deletion of Terms "Panchama" and "Paraya" from Government Records, 20 January 1922*

Mr. M.C. Rajah then moved:
225. *That this Council recommends to the Government that the terms "Panchama" or "Paraya" used to designate the ancient Dravidian community in Southern India should be deleted from Government records, etc., and the term "Adi-Dravida" in the Tamil and "Adi-Andhra" in the Telugu districts be substituted instead.*

In doing so he said: Sir. We were for a long time called "Parayas". Whatever the derivation of this name may be, the word conveys everything that is mean and despicable. It means the opposite of all that is holy, and respectable. That is why a "Paraya" is regarded as unfit to be even touched with the hand and the so-called high caste man goes and bathes for what he regards as the sin of touching the Paraya.

As our sense of self-respect was awakened we protested against the old opprobrious name and wanted to give ourselves a better name. Some of the Hindus sympathizing with us suggested the name "Panchama". In our eagerness to get rid of the opprobrious epithet "Paraya" we allowed ourselves for some time to be called "Panchamas". But as our sense of self-respect increased we came to realize the sinister implications of the name "Panchama".

When there are only four castes, if you call a man "a man of the fifth class" it is really to call him an outcaste. So we wanted a name which would have nothing to do with that most inhuman of human institutions, namely caste, and would indicate the fact that we were the first inhabitants of Southern India. We wanted a name devoid of caste suggestions which would point to our race, origin and geographical position.

We are the original inhabitants of this land and we never submitted to the yoke of caste. We are the true descendants of the original inhabitants and the preservers of the original Adi-Dravidian civilization.

*Speech in Madras Legislative Council.

When this question of a name for my community which would convey no caste stigma was considered some thirty years ago; we decided that we should call ourselves Adi-Dravidas and we embodied our decision in the name of our Association. When some wanted to call our Association the "Paraya Mahajana Sabha", we decided to call our Association the "Adi-Dravida Jana Sabha". The Sabha was established in 1892 and incorporated under Act XXI of 1860.

There are some who say "What is there in a name? You are what you are. A bad name will not make you bad, nor a good name good". Such persons take good care to see that they are called by names which imply superiority and command respect. You know what a trade mark is how it is taken as a guarantee of the stuff that is sold. Similarly in this land of caste distinctions our name has a great deal to do with our position in the country and the esteem with which we are held. Among the various ways in which we have been kept down in the country is the name or appellation which has been given to us and which we in our poverty and ignorance accepted. We are a depressed community, and we are in need of greater facilities for improving our social status. So it is very necessary that we should remain a separate entity to get the required privileges from the Government to achieve our object. Mass meetings have been held in the various parts of the Presidency asking the benign Government to change the name "Paraya" or "Panchama" into Adi-Dravida.

We have just now circulated a pamphlet to the honourable members of the Council, and there it will be seen the names of the representatives of the community in this Council and elsewhere in the various district boards, taluk boards, municipal and educational councils in the Presidency, also honorary magistrates and other leading members of the community too numerous to mention here, requesting this Council to pass this resolution. We are all eager, Sir, to be called by this name. I hope the Council will pass the resolution unanimously.

Mr. M.C. Rajah moved:

227. *That this Council recommends to the Government that a committee consisting of educational officers, managers of schools and members of the teaching profession, be appointed to consider the ways in which the Grant-in-Aid Code may be liberalized.*

In doing so, he said: I do not propose to say much by way of commending this resolution to the acceptance of this House. For more than ten years past the cry has been, and it is as true to-day as it was ten years ago, that the Madras Grant-in-Aid Code is in most respects very stringent, more stringent than that obtaining in any other province of India and needs considerable liberalizing. Managers of mission institutions and mangers of indigenous schools have alike been complaining, and complaining justly, that amount of the aid they receive is totally inadequate to their needs. Writing in 1911, Dr. Miller pointed out that "financial aid to private effort has been more and more restricted in recent years", and this statement applies with truth to conditions obtaining to-day also. What is noteworthy is that the more important of the provisions of the Code, such as those relating to teaching grants for secondary schools, for example, are so vague that even some inspectors of schools, I am told, are not able to say how much a particular school might expect to get as teaching grant. What is the official or departmental meaning of the expression "contribution from private sources"? I am credibly informed that at one time within recent years this meant, besides what was paid by the managers from their private sources, any sums which were collected in the shape of fees over and above the standard rates. It appears that is not the interpretation now put on that term. What is the result? Some schools which as a result of the more liberal interpretation drew some decent sums as grants have been refused them now.

As the result of a number of questions raised and resolutions pressed in the local Legislative Council, the Madras Government appointed in 1916 a representative committee to consider the provision of the Grant-in-Aid Code and kindred matters. The report submitted by this committee was before the Government for nearly three years and at last, early in 1991, a Government order was issued. The most important point to note in it is that practically every recommendation made by that committee in respect of aid to secondary schools was disapproved. Some were totally rejected and others remitted to the Director of Public Instruction for further consideration and report. Thus in respect of Government aid to secondary schools we are now no better than we were a dozen years ago. If anything, we are worse off in certain respects. At the same time it is being freely asserted and acknowledged that secondary education is the backbone of our system of education. I strongly urge therefore that the question of the grant-in-aid should immediately be taken up for consideration and that a strong and representative committee should be appointed for the purpose.

One word more. I am afraid it is the fashion with the Government to discard the teaching profession altogether while choosing the personnel of committees of the kind that I suggest. I do hope that this time no such mistake will happen, and that a fair proportion of teachers will, in addition to managers and departmental officials, be nominated to the committee.

EXEMPTION FROM EXAMINATION FEE IN THE CASE OF DEPRESSED CLASSES

242. *That this Council recommends to the Government that candidates for the Secondary School Leaving Certificate Examination belonging to the Adi-Dravida and other depressed classes be exempted from the payment of the examination fees.*

Mr. M.C. Rajah, in moving the above resolution, said: Mr. President, I am sure that there will be no opposition to this request which I make on behalf of my community. Your sympathy with my people in their depressed condition, and with their attempts to raise themselves will, I have no doubt, prompt you to give the little relief which I ask for. You know perhaps in a general way, but you have probably not realized through experience what a sad plight my people are in – sunk in poverty and with none of the hopes and comforts which make life worth living. It is rarely that our people think of educating their sons, and if a few of them send their children to school, they withdraw them by the time they reach the first form. And you know the reason why they are withdrawn from school at such an elementary stage. They are not able to pay the school fees, even the half-fee which a benign Government and a sympathetic Council have out of the abundance to their goodness sanctions. How could they? Take the case of a domestic servant earning Rs. 17 a month with which he has to keep alive himself, his wife and two children, or a coolie earning 10 annas a day for 26 days a month. He has to pay a rent of Rs. 3 a month and to feed a wife and three children. Even suppose the women earn 4 annas a day. What does it all come to? About Rs. 22 a month. How can he manage to educate a son? You may ask : "Are there not men earning such low pay among the lower middle classes who manage to send their sons to school?" It should be remembered that they have in more cases than one some ancestral property to fall back on, some well-to-do relatives to help them on, etc. Our people live a hand-to-mouth existence. If the man or the woman falls sick, the relief they get is from the sowcar, with whom they mortgage their cooking vessels or their clothes and to whom they pay usurious interest.

I say all this just to give you an idea of the struggle against poverty our people have to maintain. The poor boy who amidst such poverty is sent to school is stopped from school by the time he reaches the first form. Why, because his earnings are required for the family.

It is a regular up-hill work the boy and the family have got to do, to continue his education till the sixth form, and where has the family got a lump sum of Rs. 12 to pay for the School Final Examination? Surely the Government can afford to excuse this fee in the case of our boys. It is not much they will lose, because it is not many boys that will need such help.

Referring to the report on public instruction published by the Government for the year 1917-18, we see on p. 30, vol. I, that the numbers of pupils belonging to the Depressed Classes reading in high schools appear as 77. Referring again to the reports published by Government for year 1918-19 on p. 32, vol. I, we find the number as 56 and referring to the same report the year 1919-20, the number of boys reading in the high schools, belonging to the Depressed Classes, appears as 70. These figures give us an idea of the number of boys, belonging to the community, reading in the high school stage. From this it is obvious that only a very few, say, about dozen, appear for the Secondary School-Leaving Certificate examination every year. On an average this will cost for the Government only a very small sum. It will be a great help, much appreciated in the darkness and poverty of our houses and will point the way of hope and encouragement to some few boys who may make up their minds to climb the ladder of education till they attain the degrees of the University.

If you wish well to my community, you will, I am confident, pass this resolution as gracefully as we shall view your acceptance of it gratefully.

Mr. M.C. Rajah (interrupting): Neither Mr. Madurai Pillai's son nor my son will ask for such a concession. My children are all reading in schools and they are paying full fees.

Mr. M.C. Rajah: I cannot exactly understand the Hon'ble the Minister for Education.

Mr. M.C. Rajah: Certainly, Sir, I will be the last person to ask the Government to help the boys, belonging to my community, who are able to pay their school fees. Although concessions in school fees have been granted for poor boys, it is only on the production of a certificate of poverty. As my friend, Mr. Rama Rao, said yesterday, there is a lot of trouble in securing one such poverty certificate. The Hon'ble the Minister for Education need not fear that rich boys will apply for this concession, and the Government will not grant this concession unless the boys produced the required certificate of poverty. I plead here on behalf of the poverty-stricken people and not for others, and since the Hon'ble the Minister for Education has given me the assurance that he is going to consider the matter I withdraw the resolution.

The motion was by leave withdrawn.

Discussion on the Budget, 8 March 1922*

Mr. M.C. Rajah: I cannot help thinking that the budget for the coming year presented to this Council is far from satisfactory – I am tempted to say, is disappointing. The defects in the budget of last year were apologized for by the Ministers saying that they were new to the Government and that they had to accept and pass on with their sanction figures prepared for them by the then purely bureaucratic Government. But I am afraid this year the same plea is not available to them. The popular party has been in power for over one year, and their Ministers and their friends in Council and in committees innumerable have had opportunities of acquainting themselves with the details of administration, and it is to me a sad spectacle to see that far from initiating any progressive measures, the Government is crying halt to several beneficent activities, and instead of marching forward, the popular Government is moving backward along with path of reactionary prejudice, social and political. I know it will be said in reply, "What can the Government do when there is no money in the exchequer, when there is a deficit already and a deficit to provide for?" "But whose fault," I ask, "is it that there is a deficit?" "It is the fault of the non-cooperators," is the reply of the Government. But the Government is a popular Government – there is a party in power, in virtue of a large majority in the Council, a party which claims to represent 97 per cent of the population. That non-co-operation should have spread among the people to such an extent as to cut down the revenue to the extent of 81½ lakhs and necessitated additional expenditure of 18½ lakhs, making a total loss of one crore, is no compliment to the party in power.

If the leaders of this party had only carried on effective educational work and vigorous propaganda in the country and disillusionized the people as to the fallacies of the propaganda carried on by the non-cooperators, do you think, Sir, that we would be confronted with this deficit which I cannot help regarding as the triumph of the non-cooperators and the defeat of the party in power. This party has a

*Speech in Madras Legislative Council.

majority in this Council at present; but unless they use this majority with regard for real justice, and not merely from an intoxicated sense of power which they wish to retain as long as possible, and unless they feel that it is their duty to enlighten and educate and elevate the masses, including the Depressed Classes, that majority will become a thing of the past. In this connection, I would remind the caste Hindus that we, the Adi-Dravidas, were the first to denounce non-cooperation in this Presidency. If the example set by us was followed by the non-Brahman party in general, the non-Brahman Hindus would have had timely warning. But what is the use of going to correct wrong notions when the poison has once been injected into the popular mind?

Besides, I remember how, soon after Mr. Wadia left Madras, I asked Sir P. Thyagaraya Chettiyar and other non-Brahman leaders to take the leadership of the Labour Union and prevent them from falling into the hands of the non-cooperators. What did the party in power do then? Was it not because they allowed the non-co-operators to capture labour in Madras that we the Adi-Dravidas felt it a duty we owed not only to ourselves, but to the Government and the public at large, that we should refuse to join the non-cooperation strikers? And instead of thanking us for refusing to join the trap set by the non-cooperation leaders who, instead of distinguishing between non-cooperation strikers and loyal non-strikers, divided the labourers into caste-Hindu strikers and Adi-Dravida blacklegs and asked the caste-Hindu non-cooperation strikers to go to the caste-Hindu leaders of the non-Brahman party and worry them to take their side against the loyal non-strikers. And these leaders, partly out of fright and partly out of flattered vanity, and partly in the hope of capturing labour, which had already been captured by the non-cooperators – they might as well capture a peacock by putting butter on its head – played into the hands of non-cooperators by attacking our community and extenuating non-cooperation strikers' acts of incendiarism, etc., against us. If only I had not at that time kept my people from joining the non-cooperation strikers, I leave you, Sir, to imagine what would have been the state of Madras with the non-cooperation Labour Union men in their full strength, when, for instance, the Prince of Wales came to Madras. Even as it was, how did the non-cooperators behave on that day? It was a fine compliment that they paid to Sir P. Thyagaraya Chettiyar when they paid a State visit to his house on the 13th January last and made it necessary for the valiant knight to take shelter in a house in Kappal Polu Chetti Street so that he could not attend this Council during the Prince's memorable visit to it, and prevented that stalwart Captain of the Volunteer Corps, I mean Mr. Tanikachala Chettiyar, from attending the reception at the Government House that night.

I need hardly say that if there are any departments of Government whose activities the non-cooperators dislike, they are the Publicity Bureau and the Labour Commissioners' office. They find the Publicity Officers a thorn on their side – coming out as he does with most commendable promptitude with corrections which put an end to the swift-footed lies of thc non-cooperators both in the press and in the bazaar; and the Labour Commissioner is an eyesore to them because he protects and elevates the loyal Depressed Classes and prevent labourers from growing wild and getting out of control by watching their every movement and obtaining for them all reasonable privileges.

I started with the saying that the budget is a disappointing budget. It is so, particularly from the standpoint of the Depressed Classes. When the non-Brahman party came into power, we, the Adi-Dravidas, expected a great deal from them. We thought that even without our asking and out of the abundance of their overflowing sympathy they will do a lot for us on their own initiative. But what is our surprise when we find they have not only not started any new lines of action, but they have knocked down the expansion of the work of the Depressed Classes already being done. The first and the foremost charge on the exchequer of all civilized Governments is the amelioration of the condition of what are called the Depressed Classes, who are the real producers of wealth. The mirasidars' pride is based upon the sweat of the labourers in the fields; the merchant fattens upon the profits earned for him by the despised coolie.

What the capitalist is to the factory labourer in the city, that is the mirasdar to the field labourer in the country. We find now that the so-called foreign bureaucracy was more benignant in its intentions towards our people than the new Government brought into existence under the Reform scheme. Our only hope lies in the British Government and in our helping to maintain the British character of the Government; besides our organizing ourselves as an independent people. This was the twofold message delivered to us by the late Dr. T.M. Nayar whose memory we always hold dear.

Under Public Health, there is a provision of Rs. 29,460 for the

Town Planning Trust. I would here give a warning to the Government that no proposal to oust or evict my people from their present localities should be countenanced. I know that on the Town Planning Trust Board there are no representatives of my community and there are capitalists and house-owners in plenty on that Board, and some of them being wealthy caste-Hindus do not like my people to live in their present localities. This Council knows that a body of caste-Hindus solemnly proposed to the Government that some of my community people should be removed from Madras and brought back by special trains. If such men should sit in the Town Planning Trust Board I shall not be surprised at their suggesting under the plea of relieving congestion that my people should be located outside Madras. Such proposals would be on a par with what Indians are protesting against in South and East Africa, at present in Kenya, the whites want to live in healthy places and relegate the Indians to low marshy places. Let us beware of reproducing Kenya conditions in Madras.

The Hon'ble Finance Member in his introductory summary of the budget mentions the expansion of the Labour department and the extension of the Publicity Bureau as things which he has closed down. These two departments seem to me as dykes to keep the inundations of the non-cooperation flood, and in refraining from strengthening them, the Government would only strengthen the hands of the non-cooperators and provide for larger deficit next year. Owing to the abolition in the current year of the office of the Deputy Commissioner of Labour, the staff of the Labour Commissioner has been considerably reduced and in order to get more work done by the department for my people two things are necessary; (1) more money should be given for work among my people and (2) the Protector of the Depressed Classes should not have other work dumped upon him. He should be a senior officer who could command the sincere cooperation of the district officers. My people are the real wealth-producers of the country, the real sons of the soil. I should welcome the separation of the office of the Protector of Depressed Classes from that of the Commissioner of Labour. The combination in one person of these two offices has led to a great deal of misunderstanding and when there is any strike going on the ameliorative work of my people is suspended for the moment and we have to wait till the strike is settled. If only our friends the non-cooperators wish it, they would keep the Labour Commissioner so constantly employed with strikes as to leave him little or no time to attend to our work. I would therefore urge that more amount should be set apart for the work of the Protector of the Depressed Classes.

In this connection, I would call the attention of this Council to the way in which my people's applications for the assignment of darkhast lands are at present disposed of. One objection against the grant of such lands is that they are required for grazing purposes. I do not see what obligation rests on the Government for providing the mirasidars and other landowners with grazing purposes. I do not see what obligation rests on the Government for providing the mirasidars and other landowners with grazing ground for their cattle. Why should they not set apart a portion of their own lands for their cattle to graze upon? Is it because the Government think that my people are lower in the scale of creation than the mirasdars' cattle, their applications for lands are being treated in this summary and contemptuous fashion. I find also that when assignments of land are made to my people they are asked to pay for the trees growing on it. When a poor farmer of my community starts life practically, it is rather hard to expect him to pay for these trees. I would request the Government to make an exemption of this payment in the case of the Depressed Classes.

At present a great deal of waste land is reserved as forest lands. These lands should be disafforested and given to members of the Depressed Classes either for cultivation or for house-sites as the case may be.

Another feature of the assignments made to my people is the introduction of caste distinctions even in classifying poramboke lands. In this caste ridden country, even lands are divided into high caste lands and low caste lands, the high caste lands being the better lands reserved for the so-called high caste and the low caste lands being inferior lands to be given away to the so-called low caste people. For instance, when my people apply for house-sites on an elevated place, they are offered sites on low marshy ground.

The Council will have noticed in the reply given last Saturday to my question as to the extent of lands given to my people in the Chingleput district during the year, when Mr. Vernon was the Collector that out of 18,000 acres of lands set apart for the Depressed Classes in that district, not one cent of land was granted in spite of thousands of applications sent to him by my people. This needs no comment. Mr. Vernon seems to have very curious notions of the priority of claims of caste-Hindus over the Depressed Classes. It is rumoured that when my people living in a certain village in Chingleput district applied for a burial-ground, he said that the caste-Hindus should be first provided with a better burning ground than that they had at present before the Adi-Dravidas should be granted a burial-ground. This gentleman seems to hold the view that no lands should be given to the Depressed Classes or other benefits bestowed upon them without equal benefit being conferred upon caste-Hindus. It seems Mr. Vernon thinks that if lands are granted to the Depressed Classes or other privileges bestowed upon them the caste-Hindus will all turn out non-cooperators. The caste-Hindus of Chingleput who are represented in this Council by my friends Mr. C. Arunachala Mudaliyar and our Council Secretary Mr. A. Ramaswami Mudaliyar, must be a wonderfully constituted people and their loyalty to Government must indeed be built upon over fragile foundations indeed that acts of social justice on the part of Government to people who have been kept down for years by landlord tyranny and caste arrogance should drive them into the arms of the non-cooperators. Either Mr. Vernon is mistaken or the caste-Hindus of Chingleput are wonderful specimens of humanity or inhumanity. If the protection of the Depressed Classes is left in the hands of a district officer of the type of Mr. Vernon (I rejoice to think that he is a freak of nature rather than a typical member of the noble band of civilians in this country), the future conditions of the Depressed Classes will surely be worse than their former conditions.

Mr. A. Ramaswami Mudaliyar (interrupting): May I point out to the honourable member Mr. Rajah that Mr. Vernon is a British Officer?

Mr. M.C. Rajah (continuing): That is known to all the world, Sir.

The caste Hindus cannot have a more powerful attorney to advocate their case. Even Mr. Tanikachala Chettiyar will have to play a second fiddle to him.

Coming to Education, Sir, I regret to notice that the allotment made for aided institutions is meagre. The reduction in grant for aided colleges is Rs. 1.24 lakhs less than the current year. In this connection, I see that grants to the extent of Rs. 1.1 lakhs have been cut out from under building, furniture, apparatus, appliances, hostels, etc. How can education be efficient or be conducted on healthy lines if these provisions are withdrawn? There is a provision of Rs. 20,000 for medical inspection. But what is the use of medical inspection if the pupils are not provided with benches and tables constructed on hygienic principles? For I see even under grants for non-Government secondary school, furniture, etc. grants have been reduced to the extent of Rs. 1.70 lakhs. I would request that a lump sum of Rs. 2,000 at least be set apart for helping students of my community to pay university examination fee. There is a provision in the budget of Rs. 20,000 for agriculture middle schools. While I welcome this, I confess to a misgiving at seeing the word 'middle'. For this suggests that this is intended for the special benefit of non-Brahman caste boys in the same way as primary education is meant to be shared largely by my community, and higher education suggests the largest beneficiaries of it being Brahmans. I hope that for the benefit of my community, who are the real agricultural people of this Presidency, agricultural schools will be started as well. For young men of my community, I request a separate lump provision should be made for enabling them to go to Europe and America for their general and technical education. A great deal is being done for instance in the United States for the educational progress of the Depressed Classes in the Booker Washington Institute at Kentucky. I am sure that if a few young men of my community are trained in that institution they will be able to point the way of progress in my community.

A great deal can be done to make the lives of Indian women of the middle and richer classes more useful and active. It will be a good thing if an educated Indian lady is sent abroad to study and report on the various ways in which the ladies make themselves useful to the country.

Under European education, I would urge that the same standard of fees should be charged for Indian boys and girls as the European children. The present distinction in the fees charged is invidious and ought to be stopped. I must, before passing over this subject, congratulate the Hon'ble Minister for Education upon making a beginning in the matter of vocational education. This has been a long felt desideratum, a beginning has, I am glad to say, been made in this direction under the regime of my friend the Hon'ble Mr. Patro. He had effected retrenchment in his department. Under Public Works he has cut down Rs. 6½ lakhs. I see he is also getting up a scheme for a provident fund for teachers. He is trying his level best to help elementary education and I am glad to note that he has also raised the scale of teaching grants for elementary schools. He is also trying his very best to Indianize the service.

Coming to the Police, Sir, It is very necessary to strengthen the police. I find a sum of Rs. 1.16 lakhs has been allotted for additional police for the city of Madras. In recruiting these men I would urge the claims of my community. I need not say how well they are physically and morally qualified for rendering faithful service, as has been established beyond doubt in the army. In conclusion considerable sum is collected every year by fines levied by honorary Presidency Magistrates in the city of Madras. Many of these cases fall under the committing of nuisance. It is only reasonable that a good portion of the fines collected should be spent in providing sanitary facilities for people who are otherwise driven to the necessity of committing nuisance.

Demand XXIV – Labour and Allied Departments, 25 March 1922*

Mr. M.C. Rajah: Sir, the motion on the agenda is to omit the allotment of Rs. 4,240 for Personal Assistant to the Commissioner of Labour. Sir, being myself a member of the Depressed Classes, I have closely come in contact with the work of the Personal Assistant to the Commissioner of Labour referred to in this motion, and I know somewhat the work which is carrying on in the office. I do not think any other Hon. Member in this Council except my Hon. Friend Mr. Guruswami knows the volume of work that is done by the personal assistant here in Madras. The personal assistant in Madras is not a personal assistant such as you see in other offices. Here personal assistant is also doing some executive work. The protector of the Depressed Classes being a touring officer throughout the whole Presidency, he is absent sometimes nearly for the whole month, and therefore during his absence it is essential that there should be a responsible officer in the office to carry on the work, of course, on the lines laid down by the Labour Commissioner. If you do away with this personal assistant, it would be simply to cripple the work of the Labour Commissioner, and we would consider that as aiming at the interest of our community. My Hon. Friend Mr. Ramalinga Chettiyar when he opened the debate said that he was not for stopping or arresting the progress of the work that was being done. But I ask, if you do not have efficient men, how can you carry on the work? Some of the hon. members tell me: "We are giving you, 10 and 15 lakh of rupees; why do you want officers." I answer them "You are giving us money to construct houses and at the same time, you are asking us not to employ efficient men to do the work; you would not allow us to employ good maistris or good engineers and you also ask us not to use good bricklayers." It is something like that when you do not want this personal assistant and yet you say "We are not against the progress of the Depressed Classes." My Hon. Friend

*Speech in Madras Legislative Council.

Mr. Ramalinga Chettiyar also said that the great non-Brahman Hindu community did not pay sufficient attention to these classes. That is the very fact, Sir, why you should pay particular attention now to these classes; that is the very reason why you should employ efficient men, and that is the very reason why you should spend more money on this special kind of work which requires a great deal of energy and enthusiasm. If you are not going to employ efficient men to do this work, you may as well abolish the Labour Department and leave things as they are. We consider this motion as an attempt to do away with the useful work done for the Depressed Classes. I am not speaking on my own behalf, the individual "Raja". I am ventilating here what my community has said in a conference last week. I am not going to swallow the pills that you are giving me, however sugar-coated they may be. I am responsible to my community, and I am simply voicing in this Council the instructions they gave me.

My Hon. Friend Mr. Tanikachala Chettiyar, the loud mouthed champion of the non-Brahmans, comes out and says that a *thousand* rupees was given to the Adi-Dravida Students' Hostel. I wish to know what his intention is. He says at one time: "Do not spend money over officers who protect the Depressed Classes"; at another time he says "I do not give money for starting a students' hostel". Is this the sympathy that he evinces towards the Depressed Classes?

Mr. M.C. Rajah: I will ask my Hon. Friend whether he is holding any brief for any section of the Depressed Classes and whether he had applied for any help on behalf of a section of my men to the protector of the Depressed Classes, and whether he was refused help by him. I am constrained to say, Sir, that I thought I was living in the year 1922: but now I see I am made to live in 1822. I am sorry I have to speak like this. I do not mean anything personally to my Hon. Friend Mr. Tanikachala Chettiyar. I am only giving out the feelings of my community.

Mr. M.C. Rajah: I do not say that I do not want a man from my own community to be appointed as personal assistant.

Then, you want cheap machinery to conduct the work of my people, and you want a very efficient and highly paid machinery for conducting the work of your own people. You do not go in for people with minimum qualification to attend to your work. You want efficient men, men with great intellect for your work. For Panchama work, you say: "there is no necessity for a deputy collector, an ordinary man will do". You know as a matter of fact, there are certain deputy collectors who are called "Panchama deputy collectors" because they do work for the Depressed Classes.

I know my Hon. Friend from Trichinopoly. He is a great friend of the Depressed Classes and he has been taken a good deal of interest on their behalf. I do not know these things personally; but that is what I hear from my community in Trichinopoly. I think my Hon. Friend wants that honorary men should be appointed to look after the interests of the Depressed Classes just as there are honorary co-operative assistant registrars. I wish to tell him that this work is none which requires constant attention of the worker from hour to hour and day to day. He will have to devote his whole time to look after the interests of the Depressed Classes. Spasmodic work and work done in spare hours as is done by the honorary assistant registrars will not do. I am myself an honorary registrar and I can devote only a few hours to that work.

Mr. M.C. Rajah: This is a special kind of work which requires the constant attention of good men, men specially endowed with ability as you see in public services. Unless you have able men, it is not possible to do this work satisfactorily. Therefore, I think a personal assistant to the Commissioner of Labour is quite essential.

Mr. M.C. Rajah: I think the members of the Finance Committee represent us and also represent the view of the Finance Committee. What I was given to understand was that the Labour Department sent in proposals for extension of the work. The Hon. Finance Member also has said in the memorandum which he read the other day that he cried halt to a certain extension of work in regard to the Depressed Classes. So I say, Sir, that the Council did not vote for more money to carry on work in other districts.

Mr. M.C. Rajah: I was not holding any conference with the Labour Commissioner to know all those details. What I know, I say. I know he has sent up proposals for additional districts and the money was not granted.

Sir, some of the Hon. Members were of opinion that this work could be left to the revenue officers in the districts. I should like to read from that Government Order published by the Board of Revenue some years back. This experiment was tried for over three or four decades and was found to be unsuccessful. My community has been agitating for a special agency. As my Hon. Friend Mr. Vandanam has said, by means of resolution passed at various conferences the Telugu districts have asked for a special agency. And in one of the conferences, in that held at Amalapuram, one of my Hon. Friends Diwan Bahadur R. Venkataratnam Nayudu has presided and, I believe, a Minister was also present. All that I would like to say, Sir, is that this work is of a special kind and requires a special training. Moreover, Sir, one reason why Mr. Arulanandam got a bad name in Tanjore was, if I understand it correctly, that he was trying to pull down the slavery of my community. Slavery is existing, Sir.

Mr. M.C. Rajah: All that I want to drive at is that a man of sufficiently high status is required to do this work. You know, Sir, in the mufassal parts the influence of the local magnates overrides the influence of the petty officials and therefore if the officials appointed to do this work there are of sufficiently high standing, say of the grade of a deputy collector, of a gazetted officer, such people alone can acquire land according to the Land Acquisition Act, and I think, Sir, the work will be carried on successfully. On the other hand, if the work is to be left in the hands of the deputy tahsildar or the revenue inspector who is only a reporting officer, he will have no power at all for acquiring sites. All that he will do is he will go to the spot and write a report and sent it to the office. The deputy tahsildar cannot send a communication direct to the Collector. He must send it to the office. The sarishtadar is in the office and he puts a note and sends it to the Collector. He may say the deputy tahsildar reports so and so. We cannot accept this. The paper should be sent to the revenue district officers for further investigation. You know, Sir, what that means. In this connection I should like to point out certain incidents that took place in the South Arcot district during the time of Mr. Guppy. I have got the proceedings here, Sir, Swami Sahajananda applied for the acquisition of some lands in South Arcot. Of course, the Revenue Department put in a number of obstacles in the way of acquisition. But the Swami persisted in it and the sympathetic Collector went and inspected the spot, and here is his statement. He says: "I therefore resolved to inspect the land and did so. All reports in the file are misleading. More correct reports are found in another file not shown to me before inspection. The northern portion is the highest and is no use for storing water. The middle portion is low and is required for draining off surplus water of Kunnamangalam tank. South of this is the bund on which there is an Ayyanar temple. South of the bund is a swamp along the western margin of which runs an irrigation channel to take Kunnamangalam tank to wet fields." The notes later on read, "The Mirasdar, Mr. V. Velayudam Pillai is the chief opponent of the alienation. Knowing that I inspected the land, he gave up the contention that the northern portion is required for water spread and says that it is required for village site. The contentions, of persons who offer contradictory arguments of this kind are not worth anything." So, Sir, you will find what sort of support the report of the deputy tahsildar is likely to give to my people and what support they are likely to get from the revenue department. And further, Sir, as regards the Chingleput district, you remember that in the budget speech, I spoke something about Mr. Vernon. At a conference in Chingleput district my people have passed a resolution in which they say:

That this Conference resolves that in the interests of the community it is desirable and necessary that Mr. A. Doraiswami Mudaliyar, Deputy Collector and Personal Assistant to the Collector of Chingleput, should be immediately transferred from the district, since there is reason to fear that he exerts his influence against the progress and prosperity of the Depressed Classes in that district.

My people in that district come and say that because there is Mr. Doraiswami Mudaliyar as personal assistant they are not able to get anything from the Collector. I am placing all these facts to show how people throw obstacles in the way of the progress of my community. Unless we have a special agency set apart there is no salvation for us; and to relegate us to the tender mercies of the revenue inspectors or the deputy tahsildars is the same as bringing on our destruction. Mr. Tanikachala Chettiyar said something about Mangadu. I should like to ask my Hon. Friend who said that these people went there and put up huts in one night, whether he has seen my people also there and asked them what the matter was. If he had seen Adi-Dravidas and the mirasidars on opposite sides, then I would agree to whatever he says.

Mr. M.C. Rajah: I therefore say, Sir, that the Hon. Member is saying all these things under instructions given to him by one side and that he has not seen these things. I have come here to represent a big community and if we want to do efficient work in this Council, it is our duty that we should consider the interests of all the parties concerned and come to a conclusion instead of taking sides with one or the other.

Mr. M.C. Rajah: It is not the mere assurance that we want but actual work to be done.

A Bill to Provide for the Reorganisation of the Madras University, 15 November 1922*

Rao Bahadur M.C. Rajah: Mr. President, Sir, I am sure the Council will not be surprised if I view this question from the standpoint of elementary education which is my special field of work and of the Depressed Classes whose interests it is my birthright to defend. Others may view it as it affects the independence of colleges in Madras or the importance of those in the mufassal. Some may consider the question whether the Bill is revolutionary in character or evolutionary. Some may question the possibility of the Bill achieving its professed aims. All view it however from the standpoint of finance and ask whether it is not a costly experiment, whether the game is worth the candle, and above all whether there is enough candle to keep the game going. I am sorry my revered professor the Rev. Meston, who so vehemently supported the Bill yesterday, did not consider the financial aspect of the question. It is the duty of each and every member of this Council to see if there is sufficient money to push through the scheme successfully. Where is all the money to come from for the hostels and the laboratories and the professors' quarters, the university professorships and the technological institutes which are necessary for converting the existing examining university with its affiliated colleges partly residential into a purely residential and purely teaching university which will absorb and swallow the existing colleges in Madras to constitute itself at their expense into a teaching and residential university? In this connection one doubt rises in my mind which I hope the Hon. Minister in-charge would kindly try to solve. The Government colleges impart no religious education but they are allowed to dip their hands freely into the public purse. But others get a large portion of their support from religious bodies in England, Scotland and America, not to speak of those which derive income from endowments made by religiously minded individuals in

*Speech in Madras Legislative Council.

India. Does the Hon. Minister cherish the hope that such bodies and such individuals would continue to feed any of these colleges when they have become constituent's parts of his new-fashioned university? What provision does he make for allowing such colleges to make their peculiar contribution to the moral and spiritual culture of India? Does the Hon. Minister who has conceived and brought forth this Bill imagine that without any such appeal the constituent colleges or the university will be able to draw money from people's pockets? I can understand the offering of memberships and of life-memberships will become sufficiently seductive when the university has succeeded in establishing itself in the veneration of the people or in capturing their imagination or in appearing to their highest instincts. What glamour will this university have to attract the vanity of persons whose sole qualification to be members or life-members will be, that they have money to part with for this more or less legitimate purpose? I am afraid that the Minister's hope that he will be able to attract benefactions is not one justified by past experience. The money will have to come from the Government or to put it the other way the Government will have to bear the burden of having to feed this white elephant of higher education, namely, the re-organised University of Madras City with provincial affiliated colleges. And this at a time when there is no immediate prospect of an overflowing exchequer. And even if at any time there should be money enough to spare in the Government purse for education, what branch of education has the largest and most immediate claim upon the Government? Is it higher education, or secondary education with vocational training, or elementary education? What is the order of political and democratic importance in which these branches of education should be fed out of the public purse? Is it not elementary education, compulsory and universal, first and foremost, and then secondary education next only in importance to primary education, and last the least in its claims on the public purse is university education, the expenses of which all wise and just statesmen have felt should be met out of public benefaction? Is it easy to say that the claims of higher education should not be brought into rivalry with those of elementary and secondary education. But we live in a world of limited means in which arithmetic plays the tyrant with our desires and ambitions. If we spend large sums upon higher education, every little item of which is costly (with the sum spent upon erecting a laboratory one might erect and manage a hundred primary schools for the benefit of the poor and the ignorant), very little will be left for elementary and secondary education. This goes without saying. In this connection there are so many things requiring to be done for improving and expanding elementary education. The status and pay of elementary schoolmasters require to be improved. My Hon. Friend Mr. Patro said that the salaries of elementary teachers have been raised. May I ask him, if he is aware of the fact that this daffadar gets better salary than an elementary school teacher? It is not financial reasons only that I plead for elementary education. For university education to produce its best results on the people it should be the main object of consideration in all legislative measures that there should be a foundation of universal elementary education. It will not do for a few municipalities here and there to have resolved to introduce compulsory primary education; nor will it do for the Educational Minister of to-day to profess equal, if not more, zeal for primary education than for university education. The Hon. Mr. Patro may not be the Education Minister always nor will he be the same Education Minister as he is today. What is wanted is that for at least a whole generation or a quarter of century compulsory education should have diffused its blessings of universal intelligence throughout the various communities of South India before large expenditure out of public funds on the university education could be justified or become popularly fruitful.

When retrenchment in the salaries of schoolmasters and inspecting agency and the curtailing of grants to schools and colleges is the order of the day, to think of incurring new expenditure on a large scale on university re-organization seems to me to argue misplaced zeal. If only the Education Minister would show half the zeal to incur financial responsibility on behalf of elementary and secondary education as he does on behalf of university education he will earn the undying gratitude of countless generation of the common people including the Depressed Classes whose interests are most intimately connected with the introduction and the sustained and zealous maintenance of compulsory elementary education. I do not forget that the Hon. Minister for Education has been very solicitous of the welfare of my community – more solicitous than his colleagues in the Ministry. The Hon. Mr. Venkatareddi Nayudu's sympathy with my community is like a light hidden under a bushel. As for the Hon.

the Raja of Pangal, I need not sing his praises in this respect, since they have recently been sung loudly from house-tops and hill tops, in the *rajagoshtam* of a ministerial tour from Malabar to Vellore.

If my vote depended merely on personal considerations of gratitude and appreciation, I should certainly vote for Mr. Patro's Bill. But I owe a duty to my people and when I find that their immediate and distant progress is bound up with elementary education, how can I support a Bill whose effect, sure and certain, will be to divert funds which ought to be spent on education suitable to their needs and which will thus lead to the neglect of my peoples' educational interests?

I cannot help looking upon the introduction of this Bill as a reversal of the original policy and as a departure from original principles of the party now in power.

One of the first things which Dr. Nayar did in elucidating the special policy of the non-Brahman party was to write a series of articles in *Justice* entitled "The Social Iniquities of the Educational Policy",– in which he pointed out how overwhelmingly disproportionately large sums were spent upon the higher education of a comparatively small number, while the total sum spent upon secondary education was utterly inadequate to the needs of the country that which was spent upon elementary education was paltry and meagre, not to say niggardly and beggarly.

Then again when in the budget debate of 1921 the ministerial section of the House were challenged to say how their policy differed from that of the rest of the House, the Hon. Minister for Development stood up and valiantly pointed out that while opponents were most insistent upon the claims of university education, he and his followers laid greater emphasis upon elementary education which benefited the many as distant from the few. This was two years ago when the party had not forgotten its democratic principles. What has happened in the meantime, I do not know. What need is there for this reorganization of a university which has not been doing badly, I do not know either.

The only thing I know is that: that the party now in power having succeeded in placing the Depressed Classes under the trampling feet of the rich and the well-to-do by making their economic and their social progress depend upon the sweet will and tender mercy of local opinion brought to bear upon the District Collector – having once I say tasted the blood of the Depressed Classes – is hungering for more of their blood – this time by crippling their mental growth and educational progress through the strategic move of a measure intended to benefit the higher and the higher middle classes at the expense of the lower middle and the lower classes.

I cannot help looking upon this measure as one step forward towards a new oligarchic goal and one step further away from the realization of democracy in the Presidency. As it is, the Indianization of the services in the Presidency will mean more and more the filling of important posts with the friend and the followers of the caste-ridden leaders and the exclusion of the Depressed Classes from schools on the score of deference to so-called respectable public opinion. The process of developing the non-Brahman movement into an oligarchic and anti-democratic movement will be complete, when funds which might be spent on elementary education are spent on university reform.

In conclusion let me confess to you, however much I am grieved beyond measure for my people, that all this is the direct realization of the fears we entertained when the Reforms Scheme was first promulgated. Listen to the almost prophetic words used on this very subject of education. When the Adi-Dravida Jana Sabha of which Mr. P.V. Subrahmanya Pillai is the venerable president was asked to give its views on the Montagu-Chelmsford report, it said:

> We are averse in the present condition of public opinion and in the present stage of social and moral progress and with the ideas which now rule the social relations of communities to the establishment of a dual Government in this country. We are therefore opposed to any department of the administration being transferred to popular control. We would particularly protest against education being vested in Ministers. These Ministers would look after the interests of their particular community and either neglect us or train us in such a way that we may look upon them for ever as our masters!

General Discussion on the Budget for 1923-24, 3 March 1923*

Rao Bahadur M.C. Rajah: Mr. President, I am at a loss to know whether I should congratulate the Hon. Finance Member or condole with him in regard to this budget. I sympathize with him in his inability to make both ends meet and in his having had to bring in a deficit budget. I congratulate him however on the skill with which he has made the deficit appear so small.

While I do not agree with the cynical remark of the member of the Indian Legislative Assembly that the Madras Government should set their house in order before asking for a remission of their contribution, I cannot help thinking that the administration is top-heavy, and that, while an increase of salaries in the lower grades of service is regarded as a great burden, comparatively little attempt is made to do away with unnecessary high posts or to reduce the salaries they carry.

In this respect, I must express my unalloyed appreciation of the fact that the leader of this House – I mean the Hon. President – has given a real lead to the Government in the matter of retrenchment, by offering to forego one-third of his salary. It is an act of pure self-denial on his part; for, he has no electioneering prospects or want of prospects before him and cannot therefore be accused of making a virtue of necessity and appearing virtuous on the eve of a new election.

Nor should I fail to congratulate the Ministers on following his noble example by consenting to forego one-fifth of their salaries. I am glad that no considerations of the indispensableness of Rs. 5,333-5-4 for maintaining prestige, have stood in the way of their consenting to receive a lower salary. I am glad that they have come to realize, though late in the career, that it is a sin for elected representative of the people, belonging especially to a party with large democratic pretensions, to receive salaries much above Rs. 2,000, and that prestige

*Speech in Madras Legislative Council.

is not the result of being a burden on the taxpayer, but the natural reward of character and conduct.

Honour and shame from no salary rise:
Act well thy part, there all the honour lies.

It is by befriending the weak and the depressed that a Minister maintains his prestige and not by moving in motor cars or traveling with a group of more or less dependent followers in a Government saloon. I say this in the interests of a true democratic ideal and in the interests of the people at large, so as to apply to popular Ministers all over the country.

For we of the Depressed Classes are more interested than any other class in the Government being conducted in the true democratic spirit, and the progress of the country on true democratic lines is bound up with our interests; and the success or failure of a ministry is not to be gauged by measures like the Madras University Bill passed to benefit the well-to do classes, but by the number and sufficiency of scholarships enabling the Depressed Classes to come up to the level of oppressing classes, not in respect of ungrudging industry, but in respect of general enlightenment and economic well-being.

You should, therefore, excuse me, Mr. President, if I say that, considered from the standpoint of the Depressed Classes, this ministry, which seemed to have begun well under the impetus and direction given to it by the residuary influence of the late Dr. Nair, has been moving backward under the influence of leaders more responsive to vested interest, social pride and aristocratic affection than to principles of justice and democratic progress. We of the Depressed Classes can never forget nor forgive the set-back given to the caste Hindus in the expansion of their social sympathies, and to the Depressed Classes in securing social and economic justice in this country, by the party leaders and their obedient followers in this Council depriving the Protector of the Depressed Classes of the services of intelligent and independent gentlemen acting as his agents in different places.

I find there is a provision in the Budget for expanding the work of the Labour Commissioner in new districts like Trichinopoly, Krishna, Guntur, Cuddapah and South Kanara. I am glad that this is done, though this is only a tardy response to the demand we made in successive Adi-Dravida Conference that there should be a staff of workers under the Labour Commissioner working in every district; and it is to be hoped that in the next Budget the remaining districts will also be served in the way – with a special staff under more efficient superintendents. I must urge, however, that all this additional expenditure will not bear full fruit unless the operations are placed in the hands of officers of the grade of Deputy Collectors.

I am glad to see that a provision of Rs.10,000 is made for an Adi-Dravida Hostel in Madras. That such an institution is a long-felt want goes without saying. In this connection, I find that a letter over the titled signature of Rao Sahib M.C. Madurai Pillai has appeared in the newspapers asking me to give an account of the Adi-Dravida Hostel started with the help of the Labour Commissioner in 1921. If my learned colleague was really anxious to get the information, he knew where he could have obtained it, namely, from the Labour Commissioner who has got detailed accounts of all the facts and figures. This officer has also in his possession all the furniture bought not only with the Government grant but also with the donation from my friend, Mr. T.S. Ramaswami Ayyar, B.A., B.L. In the letter referred to, my learned colleague is represented as being ignorant even of the location of the hostel. May I refresh his memory by reminding him that he visited the hostel more than once? – Once with my Hon. Friend, Mr. R.T. Kesavulu; and again at the time when the Labour Commissioner, Mr. T.E. Moir, happened to call on me at the place. The fact that my Hon. Friend Mr. S. Somasundaram Pillai, could not tell my Hon. Friend, Mr. O. Tanikachala Chetti, where the hostel was situated, was *his* misfortune and not *my* fault.

It is a matter of satisfaction that Rs. 30,000 are provided as free grants for putting up 200 houses for labour at Puliantope.

It is to be hoped that the funds sanctioned for educational, commercial and industrial scholarships for the Depressed Classes will soon be made available.

In the matter of granting *darkhast* lands to my people, I am informed that objection is often raised on the ground that the applicant has plough and no oxen and that therefore the lands cannot be granted. This is surely putting the cart before the horse. When a man applies for land he wants it for ploughing, and to ask him whether he has the plough and the oxen at the time of application are to raise unnecessary difficulties in the way of the poor man.

I am sorry moreover that in some districts, presidents of local bodies have become more bold in ignoring the claims of the Depressed Classes for representation on their respective councils. When these grievances are brought to the notice of the Hon. Minister for Local Self-Government we are told that the nominations are in the hands of presidents, and sometimes that Government have no information, and that we had better appeal to the particular president; a case of appeal from Philip Sober to Philip Drunk, – drunk with a sense of chuckling triumph. Such is the plight to which we have been reduced; and for this, our eternal thanks and blessings are due to the Minister for Local Self-Government.

If my people have to appeal to the very perpetrators of wrong in such cases, what I venture to ask, is the Minister for Local Self-Government for? Has he not even the power of sanction and remonstrance, seeing that in many cases these presidents are his own nominees? Can he not even obtain information? Or is it a case of collusion? I am informed that in some instances that is the case. Mr. Galletti, the Collector of Chingleput, recently sent up two names of the Depressed Class men for nomination to the Saidapet Muncipal Council. The Minister, for reasons of his own, thought it fit to nominate only one. I am therefore compelled to think that the fact that more men of my community are not appointed to several local bodies and municipal councils is due to the reactionary prejudices of the Minister for Local Self-Government. I hope that he or his successor, whoever he be, will pursue a more liberal, a more progressive, a more enlightened and a more democratic policy in the future.

It is not that I do not want to give him credit where credit is due to him. I am glad, for instance, that in the Medical Department one lakh of rupees has been provided for a leper colony at Chingleput. In the pre-Reform Council I moved a resolution for the starting of such a colony and the present provision comes none too early. I am sorry however that no attempt is being made to remove the Tuberculosis Hospital from Royapetta.

Under education, I find there is an increase of 1,35,500 in the allotment for Government Arts colleges, whereas the increase in the case of non-Government Arts colleges is only Rs. 36,600. This seems inexplicable to me, especially now when all colleges are going to be more intimately associated with the University. How can non-Government colleges become residential and parts of a teaching university unless they are more liberally provided with funds? Then, again is it not the educational policy of the State to work through aided colleges rather than directly undertake educational work?

I am sorry to see that in spite of the assurance given to me last month by the Educational Minister that he would consider sympathetically the claims of non-gazetted subordinate Educational

Officers, no provision is made for a better scale of pay for them in the present Budget. The lot of teachers is very pitiable indeed.

I shall here quote what the Committee appointed to consider the applicability of the recommendations of the Calcutta University Commission to South India has said in its Report embodied in G.O. No. 239, dated 14th February 1923:

> It is accepted on all hands that the position and prospects of the members of the teaching profession are anything but satisfactory. Indeed, perhaps there is no profession where discontentment seems to be so rife.

The President of this Committee on page 25 of the above Government Order says this:

> I feel that only a halting word has been accorded by the Sub Committee to the position and prospects of teachers. It is a subject of the great moment; and I plead with this Committee to give to it the most earnest and sympathetic consideration and to enunciate a policy calculated to place the teaching profession on a sound financial basis.

I find, on the other hand, a provision of .07 lakh for increasing the pay of Assistant Professors of Law College though these gentlemen are allowed to practise their profession.

A lump sum of Rs. 1,15,000 is provided for vocational training. I hope the whole of this amount will be spent this year unlike last year when only Rs. 30,000 was spent, out of an allotment of Rs. 1½ lakhs.

Regarding scholarship for the Depressed Classes, I must take this opportunity of recording my emphatic protest against the speech of the Educational Minister the other day when I asked for an enhancement of their amount in view of the extreme poverty of the boys of my community. He told us then that poverty was not the monopoly of the Depressed Classes and that Brahman boys too were poor. I wonder when and where he discovered these facts, whether before or after he assumed office. If Brahman boys were poor, why did he not press their claims as a non-Brahman leader, and if the Depressed Classes were not the only classes suffering from the pangs of hunger, why did he and his party make a specialty of the advocacy of their claims? Does he see no difference between the poverty of the Depressed Classes and the poverty of other classes? Does he not know that the poverty of the Depressed Classes is due to age-long oppression by other classes? And is it not bare justice that we ask when we ask for special encouragement being given to them? If he has forgotten the first lessons of his political school, shall I read to him what the recent Report and G.O. No. 239, referred to above, say:

> The Committee considered the needs of special classes and communities and agreed, so far as the Depressed Classes are concerned, that adequate boarding and fee facilities should be granted to them. It was felt that the position at present occupied by the members of these classes was due in a large measure more to the peculiar customs and usages of the country than to any inherent defects of the classes themselves. Viewed from this point, the education of the Depressed Classes became a matter of national duty, and public funds should in justice be available to all reasonable extent in serving their interests.

Let me say in conclusion that his speech the other day was the most graceful speech I have ever heard from the lips of a responsible Minister in the House.

The Hon. Minister called my attention to the poverty of the so-called backward classes. I find that whenever I press the claims of the Depressed Classes, certain so-called backward classes are brought forward to minimize the claim of my community. I wonder who these backward classes are so distinct from Depressed or Untouchable Classes. I suppose they are all caste Hindus. Under these classes come communities to which belong at least two of the Ministers. I do not know whether the Hon. Mr. Patro is a Nayudu or an Oriya. At college we used to look upon him as a Brahman and that is why perhaps he brings forward their claims to thwart the claims of my community. Are these classes to be compared with the Depressed Classes in their poverty? Under backward classes in the Educational Rules are included classes which are educationally backward but economically flourishing. Does the Hon. Mr. Patro wish to compare these classes with mine? He also speaks of the labouring classes as distinct from Depressed Classes.

Does he realize that my community forms the main bulk of the labouring classes, especially of the agricultural labourers? I might have answered the Educational Minister then and there, but I wished to see how this House would treat his reply to my resolution without any severe remarks from me. I was surprised to find that only fifteen supported me. The rank and file of the caste Hindu members were neutral; but my Hon. Friend, Mr. O. Tanikachala Chetti, stood towering above them all and voted against my resolution. My learned colleague and helpmate in this Council, Rao Sahib M.C. Madurai Pillai, quietly went out of the Council as I was moving the resolution and as quietly came in soon after the poll was announced, thus furnishing an object lesson in serving one's own community.

Under Public Health, I observe an allotment of Rs. 12,77,800. This includes I believe town-planning and extension. I wish to say in this connection that there are persons who under the plea of town-planning and extension wish to vent their social prejudice against my people by proposing that they should be asked to quit their quarters and live outside municipal limits. Such proposals should not be listened to. The labouring classes should live near the industries in which they are employed. They should live within the reach of public institutions, schools, hospitals etc., so that they may share in the benefits of these institutions. Government hospitals are intended for the poor and not for the rich. In Government schools the standard rates of fees are enforced. It does not matter where the rich live. Distance is no matter to them. It is hard on the other hand for people getting low wages to have to walk long distances early in the day; for they cannot afford any other means of locomotion. (Here the gong was sounded as the Hon. Member had reached his time limit.)

If the Government is anxious to build quarters for their servants or police constables, they should acquire sites from those who live in spacious compounds. Let the habitation of the poor be by all means improved but their quarters should not be removed.

Demand XXV – Labour Including Factories, 21 March 1923*

Rao Bahadur M.C. Rajah: Sir, I wanted to bring to the notice of this House one particular point, and that is when the Department was started in 1919, it was intended for the sole purpose of protecting what are called the Depressed Classes, and consequently a number of functions were assigned to the Protector of Depressed Classes, so much so that this officer was swallowed up by the Commissioner of Labour, and now for the last three years we have been agitating for the bifurcation of this Department. There may be a separate Protector for the Depressed Classes and separate Commissioner of Labour to look after the labour affairs; but, Sir, for want of funds, the Council was not able to have this. As my revered friend, Diwan Bahadur Venkataratnam Nayudu, pointed out, we form one-sixth of the population of the presidency; we are more than 65 lakhs, and that is the reason why we require a separate officer with a separate department and a separate staff. Also, Sir, a Council like this should see that the first charge upon the Government is to improve the status of Depressed Classes. It is a national concern. Unless the Depressed Classes, or a large portion of them, are brought to the level of the progressive classes, I do not think we will be nearer what all people call Swaraj. Unless opportunities are given to us to come up to the level of the progressive classes, I am sure the country will not progress. When we have popular Ministers and popular Government and democratic councils, I do not think that there is any cause for despair. Therefore what I ask is that a considerable amount of money should be spent and a considerable amount of attention devoted to these matters. Moreover the Commissioner of Labour has got so many departments in his charge. He has to supervise labour, supervise the work connected with emigration, take steps for the amelioration of the Depressed Classes by helping them to form cooperative societies and purchase house-sites, by opening schools and making free grants and the

*Speech in Madras Legislative Council.

amelioration of condition of backward tribes like the Kallars. All these things will occupy a lot of his time, and the poor Labour Commissioner will have no time at all to look after the work of the amelioration of the Depressed Classes who form a population of 65 lakhs. Moreover, at present the work carried on is only in Madras, Tanjore, Godavari, Chingleput and South Arcot.

The motion was by leave withdrawn.

General Discussion on the Budget, 6 March 1925*

M.C. Rajah: Mr. President, Sir, I re-enter the Council with great pleasure, and I should like to record my overwhelming sense of gratitude to His Excellency the Governor who has been kind enough to nominate me in place of Mr. Paddison. Although I can not boast of the prestige and authority which is attached to Mr. Paddison, I feel I have one advantage which Mr. Paddison did not possess; I am myself a member of the community I represent, which community he sought to serve, and served with such real sympathy and winsome tact. If you find in me a little more fire than you were accustomed to in Mr. Paddison, I hope you will pardon me and put it down to my consciousness of the burning grievances under which my community labours. I hope, however, that if I get the sympathy and support of all sections of this Council including the Ministers I shall be able to do some real good to my community, which fact shall not be lost sight of by the electorate when the time comes for an appeal to be made to the electorate with a record of real work done.

The Hon. Finance member while introducing the Budget for 1925-26 said that there was no immediate prospect without the return of a part of our contribution to the Central Government of appreciable progress towards nation-building.

We are happy to hear, Sir, that the Central Government proposes to give us a remission of Rs.126 lakhs. So the work of nation-building should be pushed on vigorously. What is nation-building if it does not include the amelioration of the condition of the Depressed Classes who form more than a sixth of the population of the Presidency, who are denied even the rights enjoyed by the brute creation? Unless and till the work of ameliorating the condition of the Depressed Classes is taken up in right earnest and carried on in every nook and corner of this benighted Presidency no nation-building work worthy of the name can be done. We form more than one-sixth of the population

*Speech in Madras Legislative Council.

and at least one-sixth of the remission of Rs. 126 lakhs shall be earmarked for this most important part of nation-building work.

Sir, I now appeal to the good nature, to the benevolence, to the love of distinction in well-doing, if not to the patriotism, and the religious fervor of the caste Hindu Members of this House to make some slight reparation for the age-long wrongs done to my community by setting apart at least one-sixth of this amount to do work for the social emancipation, economic uplift and political liberty of my people in this Presidency. Then, and then alone the prosperity of our province will be assured.

I see that the land revenue comes to Rs. 750.67 lakhs and the excise revenue amounts to Rs. 499.23 lakhs. It is generally said that my people do not make any contribution to the State in the shape of taxes. But let me assure this House that it is my people and it is their hard-sweating work that enables the landed aristocracy to pay such large revenues to the State. And it is they that contribute the lion's share of excise revenue. Since we are responsible to a great extent for the revenues of the State, we require the greatest attention and the greatest care in the hands of Government. There was a time when it was said that once Indians get power into their hands all the wrongs would be righted. Now let me ask you, the Hon. Members of this House, are we any nearer to the time when we will think with shame of such things having once existed in this country? Is not the very fact of the existence of the Depressed Classes an unquestionable indication of the depth of barbarism to which the Indian has sunk, and the enormous resistance that any attempt at their amelioration meets with is a further sign of how utterly incompetent they are for even an approach to Self-Government. Let me not be misunderstood here. Do not for a moment think that I am against the reforms; but I maintain that no greater harm could be done to the country than by the introduction of these reforms, before the country is ripe to receive them. Therefore I earnestly appeal to the Hon. Members of this House to push forward schemes, I mean nation-building schemes, to make the country fit to receive further instalments of reforms. If you only earnestly, sincerely and whole-heartedly take up first and foremost the work of the amelioration of the condition of the Depressed Classes in this Presidency, and thus bring these submerged millions to the level of the oppressing classes, then, and then alone, your nation-building work will progress, and then, and then alone, the country would be fit for full responsible Government.

In this connection, I would call your attention to that most necessary and useful department of the Protector of the Depressed Classes which now goes by the name of the Labour Commissioner's department. I do not know if all of you are aware that this department was first started in 1919, solely for the amelioration of the conditions of the Depressed Classes in this Presidency.

M.C. Rajah: Yes, Sir. The Protector was saddled with other duties and he is now called the Labour Commissioner. From 1919 I have been appealing to the Members of this House that the Protector should not be saddled with other kinds of work and that he ought to be a whole-time officer and should only do the work of the amelioration of the condition of the Depressed Classes. All these years I have been told that it was not possible to give a separate officer owing to want of funds. You know very well that the work of the Labour Commissioner has now increased to a very extent, and we expect him to push on his activities in all the districts of this Presidency. If that is also the intention of this House, I ask you if it will be possible to do appreciable and useful work by an officer who is saddled with other multifarious duties? Since the provincial impost is substantially reduced by Rs.126 lakhs, I pray that you would give us a whole-time officer for this most important work, and also make further additional grants to enable him to carry on the work in all parts of this Presidency without any difficulty.

When Government could find men from among the community to fill places in Legislative Councils, Municipal Councils and local bodies, can they not find suitable men to be appointed as honorary district labour officers?

Glancing through the labour budget I consider the amount set apart for Depressed Class work very meagre, seeing that this amount is intended for seven millions of the population. I must say I am astonished to see under Depressed Classes the item "maintenance of sessional schools for backward classes" on page 337 of the Civil Budget Estimate. Surely backward classes do not come under Depressed Classes. They are all caste Hindus, and if I am not mistaken, the communities to which two of our Ministers belong come under these classes. Backward classes are those communities that are educationally backward but are high up in the social and economic scale, whereas the Depressed Classes are those communities who are educationally, economically and socially backward; and this is due to the systematic tyranny and social oppression of the so-called higher castes. And so that item must be removed from the Depressed Classes budget and if necessary be transferred to the education budget. Whenever I tried to press the claims of the Depressed Classes they always bring in as a counterweight the claims of the so-called backward classes, who are backward from sheer idleness, self-imposed ignorance, inactivity and slumber.

I now wish to make certain suggestions as regards the educational policy on which the present Ministry has been concentrating its attention and powers. The importance of elementary education is something that is nearly a commonplace acceptance of all modern statecraft. It is thc basis that stabilizes the towers and domes of higher studies. We all want the shaping and realizing of a sound system of elementary education. Has elementary education become more general and popular? Has its influence extended? Are more people restoring to it? Are more parents urged to send their boys to elementary schools? Are the elementary school teachers better off themselves and more sanguine of the future of education? These are the questions that will strike one interested in the youth of the country. The elementary school teacher is not a professor who goes to his duty at fixed hours and returns with the sense of pride of a fine lecture delivered. He has to be an educator of parents. He has to coax, persuade and convince them of the benefit and necessity of schooling. He has to go round and collect pupils but no school teacher will care to be an enthusiastic recruiting sergeant when the reward is not adequate. We all know that the elementary school teachers are half-starved and may I say half-naked also? What is the use of starting more and more schools and introducing the element of compulsion when there is a dearth of trained teachers? That a trained teacher is anywhere and any day better as a general rule than an untrained one is a statement that the Minister and everybody must only too well recognize. But under the present order where is the incentive for teachers to get themselves trained? The supply of trained teachers is not now more than before. The Minister should take steps to make more provision for training schools for the training of teachers.

Then again, grants given to aided schools are very, very meagre. We expected the district educational councils to be more liberal. We thought they would safeguard the aided private schools. But all in vain. Unless this question is taken up immediately, I am afraid all the aided schools will die. The Hon. Minister will, I hope, look into this vital question and set right matters. No doubt it is very gratifying to note that separate allotments for the Boy Scout movement, development of public libraries and medical inspection of schools have been provided for. But no provision is made for giving a mid-day meal to poor boys that attend elementary schools. Since we are expecting a remission from the Government of India I sincerely hope that my friend the Hon. Sir Patro will take up this scheme on hand and push it through successfully.

Coming to the department of Local Self-Government, I wish to say a word regarding the representation of Depressed Classes on local boards and municipal councils. It may be that the Hon. Raja of Panagal might have issued instructions to give representation to these classes on these bodies. But what we want is proper and fit and adequate representation. It is not enough that every Tom, Dick and Harry should find a place on these bodies for the simple reason that he belongs to this community. That is not what we want. It is said in *Mahabharata* that Dhritarashtra one day called Duryodhana and Dharmaraja and gave each some money and ordered them somehow to fill their houses as best they can. Duryodhana's house was crammed to bursting with straw; and the other with lights and celestial odour. The former is what is happening now here. We want the presidents of district boards and taluk boards to follow the footsteps of Dharmaraja in selecting proper self-respecting representatives from my community. I sincerely hope that the hon. the minister for Local Self-Government, in future at least, will scrutinize the names sent up for confirmation by the presidents of these boards.

The cry for Indianizing the services sounds very patriotic indeed. The agitation for wholesale Indianization of the services is made only by a handful of educated Indians and it is for the purpose of satisfying the ambitions of a few Indians at the top of the services. The process of Indianizing the services and of the elimination of the Britishers from Government should be proceeded with slowly and carefully with an eye to the progress of the Depressed Classes. As long as there is caste in this country, so long will there be the necessity for the British character of the administration through the agency of the British people.

Adequte representation should be given to these classes in the public services. In a country like this where caste has not relaxed its iron grip on the people and where social culture has been mistaken for and identified with religious tenets, the predominance of any particular class in the public services is a danger to the country. If men belonging to the Depressed Classes are appointed, the grievances of the community will be attended to more readily and people who wish to ride rough-shod over their rights will think twice before they make up their minds to do so. A strong Depressed Class element alone in the public services will raise this class in the estimation of others as being invested with all the privilege and authority of the governmental machine. As a matter of fact, considering the gross injustice that has been meted out to them, it would be bare justice to allow the public services to be entirely recruited from them for at least a quarter of a century to come, and then the bitterness that has been rankling in the minds of these men on account of oppression by the other castes, through ages, will be softened, and the time may come when the Depressed Classes will gladly march hand in hand with the other communities towards the goal of Self-Government. India will then become one happy family with joy radiating from every home, and England will then be only too glad to invest her with full responsible Self-Government.

A Bill to Amend the Madras City Tenants' Protection Act, 24 August 1925*

M.C. Rajah: Sir, I beg to second the motion. I need not in this connection refer to the grievances of the Depressed Classes generally or how they are proposed or supposed to be remedied either by the Labour Department or by the party in power. The amending Bill is simple in scope but wide in its usefulness. At the time the Madras City Tenants Protection Act was passed, the Government Member in charge made me clearly to understand that it was only a tentative measure and that amendments as a result of expansion were inevitable.

Now the amending Bill introduces amendments gained by experience on six points. Three of these are simply due to judicial pronouncements on the Act and two out of the three follow the decision of the Full Bench. These are (1) a definition of land which will include endowed lands; (2) indeed the rest, are absolutely non-controversial and have, as a matter of fact, been viewed in the very light in which they are presented in the amending Bill by the Full Bench of the High Court of Madras. There are several hundreds of houses built upon the so-called religious or charitably endowed lands and the hon. members will agree with me in holding that the varamdars and other lessees and sub-lessees of these endowed lands should not be allowed to play the Shylock or perhaps the Machiavelli with us poor tenants.

The third point (39A) arises out of the common-sense principle that where one party to a contract is given a privilege, the same or a similar privilege should be conferred on the other party. The landlord under the Act as it stands has the power to apply for eviction and sale of the land when the economic conditions are favourable to him. All that we ask is that a similar permission should be given to us to seek redress in a court of law when the same conditions are favourable to us.

*Speech in Madras Legislative Council.

I have now disposed of three of the six points raised. Of the remaining three, one is simply that the value of the land directly enhanced by the activities of the city fathers like my friend Dr. Natesa Mudaliyar should not be taken advantage of to enrich the owner of the land. Another is that while the landlord has the power under the law to have his rent increased, there is no provision under it by means of which the tenant can obtain redress by a reduction of rent where the price of land has fallen.

Hon. Members are no doubt aware that the price of land at present has fallen considerably and yet these poor tenants are continuing to pay the rent that was fixed when the market value of the land was high and land was difficult to obtain.

The last point I have to refer to is merely one to correct an inaccuracy in the definition of the word "improvement". "Improvement" at present includes only the superstructure and the trees. There is no earthly reason why a tenant who plants trees in his backyard and gets their value while vacating the site should be deprived of a similar benefit if he converts a swamp into a habitable place or cuts shrubs and prickly-pear and makes a place habitable or puts up a fence round his borrowed site or digs a well for the benefit of the permanent owner of the site.

Hon. Members will thus see that the amendments proposed are largely unambitious and such as will command universal acceptance.

I am aware however, Sir, that a petition signed by Mr. Narayanappa Nayudu and some others has been in circulation for some time and several of the Hindu Members of this Council are aware of it. I need hardly traverse the allegations contained in it as most of them are just as valid objections to the existing Act itself. There is one point there however to which I must refer and that is the objection of the signatories to the proposed amendment of not mulcting the tenant with the value of the improvements effected by the City Corporation.

I have but to mention this objection for Hon. Members to see the untenable nature of the objection. Take the case, Sir, for instance of Swami Naickencheri where my people incessantly through the Labour Department and otherwise have obtained for their cheri corporation lights and metalling of the roads. If as a result of these civic activities, which mark you, Sir, characterize the tenant in occupation and not the absentee landlord, the value of the lands in the cheri goes up, why should the very promoters of civic amenities be punished by being asked to pay for the extra value? The signatories quote a proverb in their petition. I am tempted to quote another. Such a way of paralyzing tenants who are active and ensure proper attention at the hands of the Corporation is to kill the goose that lays the golden eggs.

General Discussion on the Budget for 1926-27, 6 March 1926*

M.C. Rajah: Mr. President, Sir, the first and foremost charge on the exchequer of all civilized governments is the amelioration of the condition of what are called the Depressed Classes. They are the real producers of wealth in this country. It is they that enable the landed aristocracy to pay heavy taxes to the State. The Mirasidars' pride is based upon the sweat of the labourers on the field and the merchant fattens upon the profits earned by the despised coolie. Are not these Depressed Classes responsible for the land revenue of 746 lakhs and Excise revenue of 485 lakhs? On the whole it is they that enable Government to realize a revenue of 1,231 lakhs out of a total revenue of 1,634 lakhs. Under these circumstances, is it not just and proper that a considerable amount of the revenue should be earmarked for my people and spent in relieving their distress and in giving their children better education with an agricultural bias and in improving their status and their present deplorable condition for which they are not responsible? If this is done, my people will be in a better condition to produce more wealth in the country and thus enable Government to realize more revenue in the shape of land revenue, as agriculture is the mainstay of the country, and as my people are employed in the productive industries of the land. Nation-building should be directed towards the amelioration of the condition of one-sixth of the population that have been kept down by the caste-proud Hindus for ages. Nation-building will all be tall talk if the activities are not directed towards the uplift of these wailing millions who are the real sons of the soil. After all, was it not the bureaucratic Government that created the department of the Commissioner of Labour, called at the initial stage as the department of the protector of the Depressed Classes? It has been in existence for the past eight years. If you take stock of what the department has achieved for all these years you will find it is very little. If at this rate the department is going to function its

*Speech in Madras Legislative Council.

work, and it is a very difficult work indeed, it will take ages for the department to reach all parts of the Presidency. Now, I wish to draw attention to the slowness and slackness which prevails in the Labour department with regard to the work of amelioration among the Depressed Classes. It is not perhaps fair to blame the officials in the labour office; but the system under which they have to work, a system for which the party in power was then responsible, is so devised that efficient work cannot be carried on under it. The work that is now done by the department is so half-hearted, subject to uncertainties and whimsicalities of so many persons and parties and communities that it stands in ominous contrast to the straightforward ethical directness of the activities of the department under the old bureaucratic Government. The Labour Commissioner assisted as he then was by the deputy collectors, men of influence, initiative and command, was an embodiment of the conscience of the State with regard to the wrongs under which the Depressed Classes suffered from time immemorial. The first concerted action of the British Government for the uplift of the Depressed Classes, the fruit of nearly a quarter of a century of discussion, was rendered ineffective by that vote of this Council in 1922. I refer to the abolition of the posts of assistant Labour Commissioners. During the past four years the department had a chequered career and deputy tahsildars acting under the orders of District Collectors have been appointed for introducing and carrying out ameliorative measures. It is a notorious fact that these men do not command one-tenth of the respect and influence the deputy collectors acting as agents of the Labour Commissioner did. The abolition of the posts of the Assistant Labour Commissioners was a death-blow to the department. These assistant Labour Commissioners were able to see things for themselves without being carried away by the glamour of interested persons. These were men who were able to bring into play the courage and independence moderated by the tact and patience so essential for carrying on the beneficient work entrusted to them. To deprive the Labour Commissioner of the services of such men is to paralyse his work. Unless and until such men are appointed to do this real nation-building work, the department, as it is now manned by deputy tahsildars and tahsildars, will not be able to carry on the original good intentions for which this special department was created. We are thankful to His Excellency Lord Goschen for the interest and sympathy which His Excellency all along evinced in the welfare and progress of my community. His Excellency knows better than many Indian politicians that India's progress and attainment of Swaraj depend upon my people being uplifted. Hence his patriotic sympathy towards us. I know how grateful my people are to His Excellency for his direct influence in averting the eviction of the Adi-Dravida tenants from Mackay's Gardens in Madras. This is but one example of His Excellency's statesmanlike kindness towards us. It is a melancholy fact that in the distribution of the remitted provincial contributions no allotment has been made for the Labour department and yet if there is one department of Government which may be said to be a nation-building department it is the department which is to look after the Depressed Classes. The fact of the matter is that the Depressed Classes are not regarded as children of the soil, as sons of India, but as aliens within the house who ought to be kept down so that they may not raise their heads. When such is the attitude of the powerful classes in this country what moral right have they to protest against the treatment accorded to the Indians in South Africa? If we were really in earnest about qualifying the country for Swaraj by raising the Depressed Classes, we would have a Labour Member in the Cabinet whose sole and exclusive attention will be confined to the labouring classes. There are a thousand things to be done for them, educationally, economically and so on.

Education is the most crying need of the Depressed Classes more even than of the other classes. There are a number of scattered schools conducted by the Labour department but they have no separate inspecting agency to maintain a high standard of efficiency. I do not want them to be handed over to the Education department, but I propose that a special inspecting agency should be created under the control of the Labour Commissioner for supervising schools for Depressed Classes.

The other day the Education Minister when confronted with the amount of drunkenness among the poor and labouring classes said that education was the best cure for drink. But if there is any sincerity in that plea, I should like to see more schools and much better schools for the sole benefit of these classes than are to be found to-day. The allotment set apart for the amelioration of the Depressed Classes is not at all encouraging, seeing the great bulk of the people, their deplorable condition and the immense work that lies before us. The work of the amelioration of the condition of the Depressed Classes is now being carried on in the districts of Tanjore, Godavari,

Chingleput, South Arcot, Krishna, Guntur, Bellary, Trichinopoly and South Kanara. It will be interesting to know how far and in how many taluks in each of the above districts the operations have been really carried on. Here also it is not fair for me to belittle the work of the district labour officers, for, as I said just now, they are either tahsildars or deputy tahsildars with a very limited establishment under them. I hope at least from this year the hon. Members of this Council, I mean the Members who have been ceaselessly fighting for provincial autonomy and for Swaraj, will not starve out this nation-building department and in the distribution of grants will give the first and foremost consideration to this department.

Looking through the Education Budget, I am glad to note that the Minister for Education has extended his hand towards non-Government institutions that require substantial aid from Government. Were not these missionaries the pioneers in the field of education in this country? Is it not to them that we owe a debt of gratitude? Education ought to be the first demand on the State purse, and I am glad my Hon. Friend, Sir Patro, has taken a lion's share this year and wisdom demands that the State should aid, and aid liberally, these private agencies which have generously and from pure public spirit stepped in to aid the Government in doing work which they ought to do themselves, and which if they try to do they will have to spend four times of what they now give to private agencies. It is a mistake to call private managed schools aided schools, as if they receive aid or alms from Government. They are not *aided* schools but *aiding* schools, for they really aid the Government. Although I see some improvement in the figures in the Budget, yet they are not adequate. I am glad to see an increase in the scholarships. May I request the Hon. Minister for Education to issue special directions to the officers concerned to consider the claims of Depressed Classes while awarding scholarships. Nothing gives me greater pleasure than to see a provision of Rs. 1,000 for the boy-scouts' association and a provision of Rs. 3,000 for the girl-guide associations. One special feature for which I wish to congratulate the Hon. Minister for Education is the provision he has made in this Budget for a special offer for Mappilla education. This is a step in the right direction. I have asked many a time in this Council for the creation of a special inspecting agency for Depressed Class education. Our claims for this are much greater than those of the Mohammedans and Mappillas. Our population is 7 millions and that of the Mohammedans is nearly

3 millions. There are 3,250 institutions for Mohammedans with 172,362 pupils. And there are 987 schools for Mappillas with 6,992 pupils. Where as there are 9,609 schools for Depressed Classes with 265,206 pupils. These figures clearly point out the necessity for a special inspecting agency for looking after the education of the Depressed Classes.

I find that though an order was passed in 1919 that no school maintained solely from public funds should be allowed to refuse admission to pupils of the Depressed Classes, yet in 1925 a Government Order issued by the Education Ministry says that in the districts of Krishna, Chingleput, South Arcot, Ramnad and Salem there are local board schools located in places inaccessible to the Depressed Classes. I would suggest that, in the case of such schools, subsidies by Government should be withdrawn. This would automatically compel local bodies to conform to the orders of Government in the matter of admitting Depressed Classes pupils.

The Government Order from which I have just now quoted says that the solution of all problems of elementary education can be solved only by introducing the element of compulsion. I may say that whether compulsory education is necessary for other classes or not, it is absolutely necessary for the Depressed Classes. If it is said that Depressed Classes parents are more anxious to send their children to wage-earning occupations than to schools, that only shows that their economic condition prevents them from availing themselves to the full of the educational facilities provided by Government. The remedy is that the economic burden on the parents should be lightened by a small subsidy being paid to the poor parents who send their children to school. If this is too large a proposition for some of the Hon. Members with their traditional and hereditary apathy towards my people, I would suggest as a minimum relief to parents that a meal be provided at midday to pupils who attend schools. This will act as an attractive incentive to pupils and parents alike.

Another department of Education which requires more effort on the part of the Government is girl's education. There are not sufficient secondary schools and efficient ones for the large number who pass through the elementary course. It may be urged that it is difficult to find suitable women teachers for the purpose. In this connexion it is important that the widows home started with the idea of educating a class of women who would otherwise remain a burden and an eyesore in the Hindu society, so that in course of time – not within a few years but in the course of two or three decades – a large group of women teachers might spring up amongst them, should be maintained in full strength. There was a time when the institution was subjected to a great deal of criticism on account of its sectional bias; but now its constituency has been widened and widows from all classes are receiving education in it. I trust that ample funds will be found for extending the usefulness of this most benevolent institution. When talking of widows, one's thoughts naturally turn to orphans. For what does the Bible say: "Pure religion and undefiled before God and man is this: to visit the fatherless and widows in their affliction, and to keep oneself unspotted from the world." I understand that in the matter of giving support to orphanages, Government makes a distinction between orphan destitutes and non-orphan destitutes. I wish to point out that a child may have parents living and yet be an orphan, that is to say that the parents may be so feeble and disabled that their children are as bad as orphans. I understand that such children are treated and rightly treated as orphans in European orphanages. I submit that the same comprehensive policy of orphans may be followed with regard to Indian orphanages.

I hope I may draw attention in this Council to another class of unfortunate humanity who require the help of the Government. I refer to the deaf, the dumb and the blind for whose benefit a few institutions have been started in this Presidency. It is a pity that Government have not thought it fit to start such institutions themselves. The best thing that they could do is to help those who are doing this work. All these institutions are maintained and managed by private agencies. The Government may discharge its duty in this respect by giving liberal aid to them. I am glad to mention that the Canoness' Mission of St. Augustine have started a school for the blind, the deaf and the dumb under the able management of Rev. Mother M. Arsen in Mackay's Gardens where my people live in considerable numbers.

In conclusion, I would invite the attention of this Council to the working of rule 92 of the Madras Educational Rules which professes to help pupils of backward and Depressed Classes by insisting that they should be charged half-fees where the parents are so poor that this concession is necessary to enable them to continue their education. The Government undertake when this concession is made by aided schools to make good the other half of the fee. But the aid is calculated at standard rates of fees which are lower than the rates charged by aided schools in the interests of efficiency. Thus the school which gives this concession suffers a loss in the case of each boy of the amount of difference between the standard rate and the actual school rate. The temptation in such cases is to refuse admission to pupils of Depressed Classes, and I am afraid it is coming to that, since their admission is a source of loss to the management. As things stand at present, the only schools where Depressed Classes are freely admitted are the mission schools, and by the working of this rule 92 they are penalized by the department for helping the Depressed Classes. This is as it should not be and the sooner the Government undertakes to make good the loss sustained by the schools for doing a work which the Government are morally bound to do themselves the better will it be for the country as a whole.

Demand on Education, 23 March 1926*

M.C. Rajah: I want to be very brief in my remarks. I am glad to learn from the Hon. Minister for Education that Government are very anxious to do all that they can for helping the Depressed Classes. In the Government Order issued in 1925 by the Education Ministry, I see it is stated that it is difficult for the Depressed Classes parents to send their children to school, for they are poor and they are anxious to send their children for wage-earning occupations. That is not my view, but that is the view taken by the Government. This the Government themselves clearly indicate in their order. If that is the case, how can you expect the pupils of the Depressed Classes to pay half fees according to your rule? That is the very point which the hon. Mover of this motion wanted to impress on this hon. House. (Hear, hear.) The point is this: the Depressed Classes are clubbed along with other backward communities under rule 92. As I have very often said, the Depressed Classes are economically poor and the backward classes are well-to-do classes and the Government cannot place the Depressed Classes on the same level with the other flourishing and well-to-do classes of people. We have come here to respectfully urge before this House to consider the claims of the Depressed Classes who have been all along kept low and who have been all along kept economically in a backward condition so that the Government may render all possible assistance to those pupils who seek education. We would be thankful to the Hon. Minister for Education who has been characterized as a bold and mighty Minister and subsequently as a sympathetic Minister and who has been in office for the last five years – I hope he will be our future Minister also – if he will make a standing record of his Ministry by giving as much concession as possible which we well deserve. It is all very well for every one of you to say "that we are all very anxious to elevate the Depressed Classes". It is all very well for you to say "that we sympathize with your aspirations". Sir, I would only request you to

*Speech in Madras Legislative Council.

translate your sympathy into action by immediately changing this rule 92 by granting full fee concession to the pupils of the Depressed Classes. Certainly, Sir, I am not objecting to the system of asking for poverty certificates. I am not going to take advantage of the grant of the concession in the case of my children although I am not rich. Other members of the community who are able to pay will surely pay the fees, even the full fees. I am not saying that every boy and girl belonging to the Depressed Classes will take advantage of this hospitality of the Government and avail themselves of the full concession. As regards the girls, however, the hon. Minister himself knows that it is very difficult to get these girls educated and if at a time like this you are going to impose fees also on them, it will be very difficult for them to go to school. Once more, on behalf of the Depressed Classes, I appeal to my old Friend, Sir Patro, who is now a valiant knight, to amend the rule and do this humanitarian piece of work for the benefit of the Depressed Classes, so that the members of the Depressed Classes might get full concession in the schools.

General Discussion on the Budget,* Legislative Assembly, 4 March 1927

M.C. Rajah: I am extremely thankful to you for giving me this opportunity to lay the grievances of my community before this august Assembly. But before doing so I would offer my thanks, sincere and heartfelt, to His Excellency Lord Goschen and to His Excellency the Viceroy for kindly sending a member of the class that has long been raising its voice and always failed to secure a hearing into this august Assembly. I take it as an honour done to the community – not merely an honour but a manifestation of a desire on the part of the Government to give recognition to that portion of the population of India which is considerable not merely in numbers but as forming the backbone of the whole country which is nothing if not agricultural; a recognition which it has never received at the hands of its own countrymen, whose long and gruesome tale of untold wrongs I will not regale you with relating at present, for they are patent to the world. The very word has passed into a byword of scorn into all the European languages. Therefore I say I feel doubly and trebly thankful to the Governments of India and Madras for sending me into this Assembly.

M.C. Rajah: It is too terrible to contemplate the condition of the Depressed Classes or the laws the Indians established, whereby one section of the country was kept in perpetual bondage to serve the interests, to minister to the pleasures and vices of the rest of them. In every country in the world a certain portion of the people through their own fault or through social arrangements naturally and automatically sink to the bottom, but here in India laws were passed so as eternally to keep down some millions of their countrymen – they form 60 millions now – never to give them, their children, or children's children down to the uttermost generation an opportunity to rise. They were put out of the pale of humanity; they were to be treated worse than animals, they were to be starved; they were not

*Speech in the Central Legislative Assembly.

to be allowed to breathe pure air; they were not to be allowed to drink pure water. They were not to live with the rest of them, but were segregated and housed like pigs. They were not to go or walk on the same roads, nor worship in the same temples, nor read in the same schools, nor live in the same cities, nor eat the same food. This, Sir, is the tyranny to which they were subjected for ages and would have continued for ever, but Providence, which though slow, is sure to hear at last, heard the desolate cries of despair of the hopeless millions that rent the air and sent the Britisher to India.

M.C. Rajah: We have been subjected to the most cruel wrongs, wrongs from which, thanks to an ever merciful providence, it is Britain's mission in India to rescue us. With the advent of the British our emancipation commenced. He too has been tardy, very tardy indeed, in moving his little finger to right this wrong, but I say I am deeply grateful to him. After all, is it not to the foreigner that we owe what little of education, material prosperity and personal liberty we possess to-day and not to our selfish countrymen, the caste-proud Hindu calling himself our kith and kin, exploiting our labour for the fulfillment of his selfish ambition and giving us only a pittance. My friends are transported with rage at the treatment accorded to their countrymen in South Africa. Is it because we are nearer at home that the eye is blinded and cannot see, or is it a wanton attempt to distract attention from irregularities at home that they are trying to fix the attention of men abroad? It sounds odd, very odd indeed, in the mouths of these people to speak against injustice in South Africa when they have brutalized and are keeping still in a state of bondage a vast section of their countrymen. Sir, they all cried for Indian Ministers. Let our representation of the atrocities that they were committing disturb one night's sleep for them? No, Sir, I wish they had never got this power. Well, Sir, as a matter of fact what has this Legislative Assembly done all these years to alleviate the sufferings of these voiceless millions? What have the provincial Councils done for them? There was a time when it was said that once the people of India get power into their hands they would help forward the oppressed classes in India. Are we any nearer to the time when the caste Hindu will think with shame of such atrocities having once existed in this country? I have often heard within the four walls of this House an accusation leveled against the Britisher by the Opposition Benches that the British Government has crushed the freedom of Indians and has deprived them of the rights of citizenship.

But freedom of person is totally denied to the oppressed classes by the caste Hindus, for their law allows it and the court supports it. Can India get Self-Government before our social wrongs have been set right? Social equality, social liberty and social fraternity should be enforced among the people who clamour for political equality, political liberty and political fraternity. Labour in India can be broadly classified under two heads, agricultural and industrial. The public agitate and the Government legislates for the latter, because that is largely a foreign concern, whereas the former, who form the greater portion of the labouring population of India, do not receive the attention of anybody. Why? In that the politicians take no interest, and the Government do not interest themselves in that either for there is no politician to engineer an agricultural movement. If indeed there was one, he would be caught by the neck and ducked in the nearest pond by the first landholder he met with.

M.C. Rajah: I am just asking the Government to legislate on that. He will go away with the lesson never to renew his efforts again to improve the lot of the agricultural labourer. Now, Sir, it is here where we want the help of Government and of my friend the Honourable Mr. Joshi. The landlords are the most powerful body in the country. The agricultural labourer forms the bulk of the labouring population in India; these are half famished and partially clad men, being given wages that could hardly keep body and soul together. Upon their industry the idle landlord fattens and thrives. The Indian politician will never come between them and the owners of lands, for, as I have said before, he will raise a hornets' nest about his ears if he attempts it. Hence the necessity, the absolute necessity, for the Government to legislate and thereby permanently improve the miserable lot of the agricultural labourers. When that is done, Sir, emigration will cease and the thorny questions, like the South African question, which has given so much trouble to South Africa and India and England would never arise. Here, Sir, I wish to offer a word of explanation for my adverse vote when the House considered the question of the appointment of a committee for investigating the causes of the Bengal Nagpur Railway strike. Such a committee I know would do positive harm to the labourer, embitter their relations with the employer. Why? Because the evidence of the really aggrieved labourer would not be forthcoming. It is the man set up and tutored by the executive who would come forward as a spokesman and repeat like a parrot what he was taught to say.

Now, Sir, all over the country the cry has been raised that the services ought to be Indianized. Now, what can this Indianization mean? It would mean a few more highly-paid jobs for the caste Hindus and the mass of the people will be left untouched; and the presence of these Hindus in those top places will be a hindrance to the advance of the masses, for the Indians have been blinded by the age-long caste prejudices; and even if a few had the extraordinary courage they would be hooted down by their own countrymen and thus incapacitated from doing any good whatever to the country, whereas the Englishman, who has none of these disadvantages, sees clearly and seeks the shortest road to remedy these. The first and foremost charge on the exchequer of any civilized Government is the promotion of human happiness and of the widening of the opportunities for a good life for many crores of the people of the country. Is it not proper, Sir, that out of the surplus amount a considerable amount of the revenue should be set apart and earmarked for my people and spent in relieving their deplorable condition for which they are not responsible? The Government of India should take up this question immediately. Nation-building should be directed towards the amelioration of the condition of the one-sixth of the population of the country that have been kept down for ages. Nation-building will all be tall talk if the activities are not directed towards the uplift of these waiting millions, the real sons of the soil. The first concerted action of the Madras Government for the uplift of the Depressed Classes was the creation of the office of the Protector of the Depressed Classes. This was due to the Government of India. In their letter to the Government of Madras published in their Resolution No. 1835 (Board of Revenue), dated 13th September 1916, the Government of Madras created a separate Department called the Department of the Protector of the Depressed Classes under a special officer with a separate staff. This officer was gradually saddled with other work and was ultimately transferred into a Labour Commissioner with multifarious duties, one of which is to look after the Depressed Classes. Sir, this is not as it should be. This Assembly should set apart a certain sum, progressively increasing, for the improvement and advancement of the one-sixth of the population who have been wantonly held back. The office of the Protector of the Depressed Classes should be created in every province and the condition of these millions should be remedied. Next, Sir, provision should be made in the Budget for giving scholarships to promising young men belonging to my community to enable them to go to England or Japan or America for higher studies. We all know the usefulness of that great institution at Tuskegee. I mean that famous institution founded by that noble son of American, Washington. If only we send them abroad for training will they not on their return be able to point the way to progress and usefulness for the Depressed Classes? Sir, it is a national loss to keep the Depressed Classes in the condition in which they are to-day. If you give them your hand of fellowship, they will be a national asset to you tomorrow.

The Statutory Commission, 16 February 1928*

M.C. Rajah: Sir, I stand up to oppose the Resolution of Lala Lajpat Rai and to support the amendment of Sir Zulfiqar Ali Khan. Sir, it is a painful task for me to have to oppose the Resolution of Lala Lajpat Rai, because I know that Lala Lajpat Rai has been doing some work on behalf of the Depressed Classes. Sir, Lala Lajpat Rai told us that the Government had created the Depressed Classes in 1917. I agree with him, for till 1917 the case of the Depressed Classes was not brought before the Government, because the so-called high caste Hindus remained as a screen between us and the rulers of this land. Sir, he asked us what have the Government done for these Depressed Classes. What have they done as regards their education and schools? Sir, let me answer these questions first. No doubt Government could have done more for us if the higher classes had not positively stood in the way of our advancement. (An Honourable Member: "How do you know?") I will prove that, Sir. That is exactly what I wanted. In the year 1915 in the old Imperial Legislative Council the Honourable Mr. Dadabhoy, a Parsee gentleman, brought in a Resolution for the amelioration of the Depressed Classes. Sir, when the debate went on, one of the trusted leaders of the Indians, I mean, no less than the Honourable Pandit Madan Mohan Malaviya, taunted him by saying:

> So far as the elevation or depression of that status rests upon social or socio-religious causes, the Government would rightly abstain from making any attempt in that direction.

Sir, when the trusted representative of the Indians, in the absence of a representative of my community in the Legislative Assembly, comes forward and threatens and tells Government to abstain from making any attempt in that direction, what can you expect Government to do? Then, Sir, poor Mr. Dadabhoy in reply said:

*Speech in the Central Legislative Assembly.

Sir, I find myself in a very peculiar and unfortunate position. There are two parties in this Council, and they are both on their defensive on this occasion. My justification for bringing in the Resolution, if any justification was needed, is to be found in the unenthusiastic and half-hearted support which I have received from my Resolution. If I could possibly have avoided it, I would have very cheerfully and very willingly done so. This is the sixth year of the life of this Reformed Council, as Honourable Members are aware, and the second term is now approaching expiration. During the major portion of that time – the five years that I have been in this Council – I anticipated that the champions of public liberty, public spirit and public enterprise and culture, men like my friends the honourable Mr. Surendra Nath Banerjee or the honourable Pandit Madan Mohan Malaviya – would take the trouble of moving a resolution to this effect. I waited all this time to see if one of these enthusiastic members would bring in a resolution for the amelioration of the Depressed Classes; but when I found that none of them had taken up the matter – though at times this matter is discussed even in the Congress pandal in a certain manner; when I found that it was not taken up in this Council – I thought it my duty to do so.

And, therefore, Sir, it is not right for us to blame the Government for not doing much for us. Sir, we had no voice in the Legislatures of this land prior to 1919. We were shut out from this Legislature as untouchables, and who were our spokesmen in those bodies prior to 1920? Sir, our case was not brought before these Councils and the caste Hindus stood as a screen between us and the rulers. My present position in this House is due to the Britishers and the presence of the representatives of my community in the Provincial Councils is also due to the Britishers. In the Madras Legislative Council a prominent member of the Congress party, who was the Chairman of the Reception Committee of the Madras Congress, moved an amending Bill to the Madras Local Boards Act in which he had brought in an amendment for doing away with nomination, the only door through which the members of the Depressed Classes and minority communities could get in. From this, Sir, you can gauge the depth of the heart of the Congress men; they do not want us to be there.

You are afraid of us because we will expose you. If the Congress men represent the real India, they would have by this time put in for election some of the members of the Depressed Classes. Have they? Even to-day, Sir, the Honourable Mr. Jayakar had tabled a motion for the amelioration of the Depressed Classes and if the Congress party had their sympathies with us they would not have asked him not to move his Resolution. This was an opportunity for you to have shown your practical sympathy and if you had allowed Mr. Jayakar to move his Resolution you would have got our votes at your command and with the support of us all you could have passed the Resolution.

Sir, as it is, I also find that there is an amendment tabled which asks for a Round Table Conference of seven elected Members of the Central Legislature. I wish to draw the pointed attention of the House to the word "elected". The nominated non-official Members, of course, deserve nothing more than mere ignoring. That shows, Sir, what this country can expect at the hands of these self-appointed plenipotentiaries of India who are anxious to meet the plenipotentiaries of Great Britain. That, Sir, is only a straw, but it is a straw that indicates the way the wind blows. Sir, we welcome this Commission. We feel that there is a possibility of its proving a blessing to us. We feel that a mixed Commission would have been suicidal from our point of view. Yet let me make my position perfectly clear. I yield to none in my patriotism and love for the country. In fact, representing 60 millions of the Depressed Classes. . . . (A Member of the Congress party: "Do you?") Yes, I do. Who else? I say that our love and patriotism has been translated into a thousand acts of sacrifice on behalf of the country. Is there any one in this Assembly who seriously doubts the fact that we form the backbone of the country? Is there any one who can canvass the position that our community is a really wealth producing community in this country? Is there any one, I ask, who can deny the fact that we have given our share – nay, more than our share – in the Great War recently fought? And yet what is our position to day? My friends, the politicians, ask us to boycott the Commission. May I ask them on what grounds their demand is based? What is the insult that has been offered to us by Simon Commission more than that which every day we are suffering at the hands of our so-called high caste brethren? The Simon Commission has come to this country to judge the real position here and to see how far Self-Government can be advanced without causing any trouble to the least advanced communities and how far the educated classes of the so-called higher castes are in a position to safeguard the interests and advance the progress of the Depressed Classes? Sir, I can very well understand the position of the high caste Hindus and their anxiety not to cooperate with the Commission. It is but natural. They are in the position of accused persons. It is their conduct that will come up for inquiry. It is their misrule of centuries and social oppression that will be the subject of investigation and the members of my community will be in the position of complainants and prosecutors. We have full faith in the Simon Commission. We shall tell them that it is the latest fashion of high caste men to speak of the removal of untouchability but that not one 'jot' and title of practical work has so far been done. We shall tell them that their Congress are immersed in political questions and in the solving of the Hindu-Moslem tension, but beyond passing pious resolutions about removing untouchability, nothing is proposed to be done by the most advanced of political parties. You talk of a Round Table Conference and you talk of removing communal differences. Whoever in this country – the Congress men, Liberals or Moderates – has so far thought of a Round Table Conference between high caste men and the Depressed Classes? Whoever has so far proposed the formation of a pact between the Hindus and the so-called Depressed Classes? You will not face realities. You know full well that the Depressed Classes cannot accept the humiliating position they are in and yet you expect them to join you in boycotting the Simon Commission. Our views have been well known to you, you say, and that with an air of superior wisdom and smug self-satisfaction.

M.C. Rajah: Sir, we form one-fifth of the humanity in this country. We may be treated as slaves, but we are bound to be counted upon and we shall say to the country and to the world that the race is not always to the swift nor the fight always to the most vociferous. We shall go before the Simon Commission to place our case frankly and tell them that, unless social equality is assured, political freedom and even the suffrage will be a mere mirage unless the present hopeless position of affairs is improved and that there is no possibility through the cooperation of the high caste men to work together.

M.C. Rajah on the Statutory Commission, 18 February 1928*

Thank you very much, Sir.

On Thursday my Honourable Friend, Mr. A. Rangaswamy Iyengar, interrupted me by asking why we should not come in by the door of election, of which he ought to know perfectly well there is as much chance as the river Jamuna flowing into the river Cauvery. Might I ask him, Sir, and his Leader, Sreeman Srinivasa Iyengar, why the Congress party in Madras did not put up a member of the Depressed Classes either for the Assembly or for the Provincial Council?

M.C. Rajah: Why should we ask them? You pose yourselves as the leaders of the people.

M.C. Rajah: That clearly shows that in the Congress camp there cannot be found even a single member of the Depressed Classes. (An Honourable Member: "that is quite wrong".)

M.C. Rajah: No. That is quite right.

M.C. Rajah: That might be, but not the Depressed Classes. Have they ever ventured to put up a candidate from the Depressed Classes for the municipal elections of which not less than ten take place every year in Madras? Sir, it is a blessing in disguise that there is no mixed Commission, for we are now enabled to know the mind of Great Britain towards India undeflected by any mixture of Indian element on it. There can be only two possible schemes. One on the basis of a Commission collecting evidence to study relevant records by associating with itself, by close conference, the Committee of the Legislature. That is the scheme that has now been adopted in the constitution and procedure of the present Commission. The other scheme is a round table conference. The honest issue before us is, whether a scheme that provides for an inquiry as well as a conference is not far better than a mere round table conference of half a dozen representatives of Great Britain and half a dozen representatives of this House without any inquiry which is indispensable. A handful of

*Speech in the Central Legislative Assembly.

politicians may give and take across a round table, may redistribute provincial boundaries and proclaim that they have come to an agreement. But is there the ghost of a chance of the people concerned, agreeing to these arrangements, forgetting realities in a moment of absentminded political idealism? India wants, so far as I could see, the continuance of British rule for a long, long time to come. (An Honourable Member: "No.") Excepting a microscopic fractional fraction of the country, India thinks that its future lies in working out its salvation by a wider and better directed diffusion of the benefits of British rule under British responsibility, so that India may become eventually one people politically. If a round table conference is to be held, it ought to be not with these elected members. (An Honourable Member: "With nominated Members.") – Wait, I will tell you – but with those who are of the people, live amongst the people, toil from day dawn to nightfall, not known to the leaders and not knowing the leaders also. Let the round table conference without a round table take place in innumerable hamlets and villages, under banyan trees of ancient lineage and immemorial standing, on the tank bunds, in harvested fields. And let the plenipotentiaries learn from the lips of the masses what they would want first and foremost and under what terms they will agree to the transfer of responsibility and power from the British into Indian hands. Sir, it is our feeling for the country and our legitimate desire to have some place under the sun that makes us adopt this attitude. Rather than criticizing us, if you are only honourable and search your hearts, you will find room for criticizing your own conduct and deploring your sentiments and that complaisance which leads you to such boycott resolution.

Sir, I feel that we have a case to present before the Simon Commission. Shall we be denied an opportunity to present our case? Shall we gain by taking up the attitude which has been suggested by some of the politicians? The problem of the Depressed Classes to the Simon Commission will not be in vain. If they could tackle that one single problem, I am certain that all the sacrifice that Sir John Simon and Lord Birkenhead have made would not have been in vain. So we the members of the Depressed Classes will do our duty by ourselves and our country by appearing before the Commission, which is no respecter of persons, which welcomes to its bosom, the Pharasee and the sinner, it will judge the motives of all, and before whose eyes I am certain that the conduct of myself and of my community will stand.

Proceedings of the Round Table Conference in London, 7 March 1931*

M.C. Rajah: Sir, it is a matter of profound satisfaction to me and the members of my community – the Depressed Classes – whom I have the honour to represent in this House, that the Indian delegates to the Round Table Conference have laid the general ground plan for the future constitutional reforms. Talking on a momentous occasion like this, let me tell this House that the Depressed Classes are in no way behind any other section of this country's inhabitants in their desire for political advance. Rather they appreciate freedom more than anybody else, just as the caged bird longs for freedom all the more keenly because it has known the limitations of a cage or restrictions on its liberty. I may go further and say that we are more anxious for the freedom of this country than others, because we are the original inhabitants of this land, and the country's interests and ours are closely associated.

I can assure this House that we are happy that we are on the road to responsible Self-Government, a government of the people, for the people and by the people. The outcome of that government, we believe, will be the largest amount of good to the largest number of people. Since we the Depressed Classes form a large section of the population, we expect the largest amount of good to our people. It is with this expectation that the reformed constitution will bring in new hopes and increased happiness and liberty to the 45 millions of the Depressed Classes in this country, a vast mass of humanity, that we welcome the change. But we certainly do not favour that kind of political concessions which if given will only benefit the intelligentsia and will not enable the Depressed Classes to participate in them with equal benefit with the upper ten of the community.

Sir, all of us are eager to raise a magnificent constitutional edifice, as my Honourable Friend Diwan Bahadur Rangachariar has said, "A new house", in our beloved country. In my vision of the building of

*Speech in the Central Legislative Assembly.

such a constitution I had occasion to view the plan, and to survey the materials out of which this grand edifice has to be built, for it has to be admitted that no solid and harmonious structure can be put up without a preconceived plan, and that no amount of political phrases or catch-words, however ethereal they may be, can conjure up a concrete and stable machinery of government. During my survey of the plan and materials, it has struck me that a splendid mansion of constitutional government can be raised in our country upon four corner stones, namely, the caste – Hindus, the Muslims, the Depressed Classes and the other Minorities. But unless each of these communities is sound and strong, how can they support a lasting superstructure? Sir, I am qualified to speak at least of one of these, namely, the Depressed Classes. Can you say with truth that an important section of your country the Depressed Classes, who form more than one-sixth of its population, are given the privileges which are enjoyed by the rest of their countrymen? Nay, are they not denied even the most elementary rights of mankind and condemned eternally to live in squalid surroundings, the hotbeds of dirt and disease?

Now I say to you who are really interested in the country and in the welfare of the nation that you should prepare yourselves for responsible Self-Government, and more especially for social solidarity through the breaking down of the caste system as it obtains at present in our country, and this can be brought about by a moral revolution, the sacrifice of selfishness; and the sooner this ban of untouchability is removed, the nearer will you be to the goal of complete Dominion Government for India. Unless you do this, India cannot be free, no matter how much Self-Government she obtains now. And in the words of Mahatma Gandhi, "You will gain Swaraj only to lose it the next month". Sir, patriotism is good and noble, but I ask what is patriotism without love for your neighbours?

In January 1921, ten years ago, the Indian National Congress passed a resolution for the removal of untouchability. Commenting on this Mahatma Gandhi wrote in *Young India* that the removal of this blot on Hinduism was necessary for the attainment of Swaraj, and that "it was a reform not to follow Swaraj, but to precede it". Just a year ago, in March, 1930, Mahatma Gandhi is reported to have said:

> We want to rule the untouchables, and on the other hand the Government want to rule us. Both are thus equal. If this goes on we do not deserve

Swaraj. I am really pained to see this. If you do not allow the untouchables to mix with you, then rest assured Swaraj will go far away from you.

The late Lala Lajpat Rai and Dr. Moonje both have affirmed that Swaraj and untouchability are incapable of reconciliation. What did the late lamented friend of the Depressed Classes, Lala Lajpat Rai, say? He said: "I believe that India will not be fit for Swaraj unless this blot on the fair name of Hinduism has been completely washed away."

And I am sure the House would also like to know the opinion of Dr. Sir Tej Bahadur Sapru, the leader of the moderates, who played a most important part in the Round Table Conference. He remarked thus:

> I do say what is my most sincere conviction, that unless you are able to solve your own social problems about the Depressed Classes and the untouchables, I do not see any real prospect for real genuine constitutional advance and any constitution that you may get will certainly not arouse any interest in me, because I do feel, however good, however perfect, howsoever ideal your constitution may be, unless you have got the support of the minorities and unless you command the confidence of those whom in your vanity you may describe as Depressed Classes, your constitution will not be worth a day's purchase.

And my friend Dr. Moonje was right in saying that if there was a real desire for Swaraj, the removal of untouchability was not a big Himalayan task, for it is not a Herculean task to root out this oppressive system, and especially its most cruel feature, namely, untouchability. Where there is a will there is a way. If the British enjoy a form of government which allows the maximum amount of liberty and fair play to individuals, it is because through every century of their history, and especially during the last, they have set themselves to remove the oppressive features in their social structure, whether they affected capital or labour, children, women or the poor.

If Japan again has made the most remarkable progress, it is because the privileged classes, the Samurai, had voluntarily given up privileges which wrought injustice on others, with the single-minded aim of benefiting the country as a whole.

Even when the English nation as a whole was unripe for reforms, or violently opposed to it, a Shaftsbury was able to get laws abrogated which worked oppressively on women and children. A John Howard succeeded in affecting improvements in prison life and a Wilberforce spent his lifetime in winning freedom for slaves even in the teeth of opposition from powerful quarters.

If only the smallest percentage of the efforts expended all over the country for the recent salt-making campaign and the methods of defying the Government were directed towards excising this canker of untouchability, which veritably eats our social and political system, untouchability would soon be a thing of the past.

Sir, from what I gather from the study of the history of our country, India has not suffered so much from the want of knowledge of the ideals of government as from the evil of disunion among its people. This evil genius has been at work in destroying the glorious destiny of our dear land. It was not the want of physical power to resist the invader that was the cause of the defeat of our people. It was disunion pure and simple and it has continued down to this day, and it will continue in the same groove till doomsday unless we cry, halt, and turn over a new leaf in our history – but not a new leaf in a paper constitution, which after all might be termed "a scrap of paper", but a new leaf in our moral effort. India can be the India of our dreams, "if it chooses", not in paper, but in its conscience.

Sir, the British have given a definite assurance to fulfil their promises, pledges and obligations. It remains for the Indians now to fulfil their promises, pledges and obligations to the Depressed Classes. Sir, we are glad safeguards have been promised to us. I fully hope and trust that they will be properly incorporated in the constitution. We no doubt want adult franchise, and what is more important, representation through Separate Electorates, and that on a population basis.

Sir, the caste Hindus ask us: "Why do you want safeguards? Why do you want Separate Electorates?" Might I ask them, Sir, in reply, what would they want, if like us they were held in subjection by long standing custom by the domineering classes against their will? What would they want if they were exploited? If they were intellectually starved? If they were denied the benefits of schools, roads, wells, temples? If we now ask for safeguards, it is not our fault. That fault is to be laid at their doors. Sir, for the successful working of responsible government, the contentment of all classes is very essential and it would be only wise to grant the community its desire. Why force an unwanted system upon us? It would be far better to foster the growth of confidence by removing all suspicions of majority manipulations, by granting to us Separate Electorates. The moment our confidence in their sense of equity, justice and fair play grows to such an extent as would render Separate Electorates unnecessary, rest assured, we will not hesitate to join them in joint electorates. At present as the community is so weakly represented in the electorates and so little versed in the craft of the politician, it should be given the protection and the sense of security afforded by the Separate Electorates. Sir, we are a separate community, though we are labeled as Hindus. We are not allowed to take part in Hindu ceremonies; we are not allowed into a Hindu temple to worship a Hindu god; we are not allowed to read the Vedas, the Hindu scriptures, and it is also said that we have no place in the Hindu heaven. In consideration of our separate interests, our numerical strength, our political importance and our undoubted disabilities, we press our undoubted right as a distinct community to elective representation on the Legislatures, by means of Separate Electorates.

In this connection I may point out to this House that the Depressed Classes did not boycott the Simon Commission. Depressed Classes Associations throughout India appeared before the Indian Statutory Commission and placed before them their considered opinion. In para 79 of the *Indian Statutory Commission's Report*, vol. II, it is said:

"Most of the Depressed Classes Associations which appeared before us favoured Separate Electorates with seats allocated on the basis of population, though one or two still wished to retain nominations."

It will interest the House that the two delegates nominated by the Government to represent the Depressed Classes at the Round Table Conference held in London are not from those associations that favoured Separate Electorates, though the Government of India also in paragraph 35 of their Despatch on proposals for Constitutional Reforms had pointed out that, "Recent meetings of Depressed Classes Associations have re-affirmed their belief in Separate Electorates".

Sir, we want also an adequate share of Governmental responsibilities, particularly a fair share of public services, both civil and military. All that we want is our manhood, our rights.

Sir, on an occasion like this, I will not be true to myself if I do not publicly acknowledge that it is the presence of Englishmen in India that has brought to us a sense of our rights as men. They have been our friends, and we are thankful to them for this. Now that political power is passing from the British into the hands of those who have oppressed us and have been oppressing us in the past, we feel that our position in the future would become intolerable and that under Swaraj or responsible Self-Government, they would look after the interests of their particular communities and would either neglect us or train us in such a way as to look upon them for ever as our masters. This is why, Sir, we urge for safeguards.

The moment they infuse confidence in us, the moment they bring in a real living feeling of common brotherhood based on equality, the moment they destroy, root and branch, the oppressive and inhuman caste system, the moment we see that real change in them, the change of heart, I assure you, Sir, we will say, "no more of these safeguards". We want them only as a temporary measure until real democracy is established, till conditions improve and a real national outlook is developed. I do not put Separate Electorate as an end in itself, but only as a means to an end, the object being effective representation in the Councils for the Depressed Classes. But we do not believe in social unification by means of formulas, speeches, resolutions and conferences.

Now that we are going to get responsible Self Government, I wish to sound a note of warning to the majority communities in this land. When you get power into your hands, see that you do not misuse it, I am afraid a day may come sooner or later – or it may not come at all as it all depends upon how you conduct the affairs of the State with reference to the Depressed Classes. I say a day may come when the Depressed Classes will agitate for their legitimate rights and privileges, and if you then resist or repress their legitimate demands, they will then start non-cooperation and civil disobedience movements against your Government. See that you then view their demands and aspirations as you wish the present British Government to view your present civil disobedience movement. After having obtained power into your hands, see that you do not use it as a giant. Do not bring in section 144 against our leaders, and do not promulgate ordinances to send our men to jail.

In conclusion I hope that the Depressed Classes will secure their voice and representation in all future negotiations and collaborations with Government and that their point of view will always be considered.

Representatives of the Depressed Classes, Round Table Conference, 5 September 1932*

M.C. Rajah: Sir, I am extremely thankful to my Honourable Friend Sir Cowasji Jehangir for giving the House certain information as to what the representatives of the Depressed Classes demanded in the first Round Table Conference. He said that my friend Dr. Ambedkar demanded only Joint Electorates at the first Round Table Conference.

M.C. Rajah: Yes, with reservation of seats and that certain force of circumstances made him demand Separate Electorates at the second Round Table Conference. I do not know what those circumstances were.

M.C. Rajah: Whatever they may be, Mr. President, let me to-day voice the sentiments of all sections of the Depressed Classes in expressing our deep disappointment and dissatisfaction at the British Cabinet's solution of the communal problem in India. I say the sentiments of all sections, because unfortunately before the so-called Communal Award was given, there were two voices heard on behalf of the Depressed Classes. One was in favour of Separate Electorates and the other was for Joint Electorates with reservation of seats. Thanks to the decision of the Cabinet, the two sections are now united in expressing disapprobation of the proposed arrangement. Both of them had proceeded on the assumption that their interests would be adequately protected by their getting representation at least in proportion to their numbers, if not in greater proportion considering their social status. Taking this for granted, they concentrated their attention on the question of Separate or Joint Electorates. The communalists, especially, at the Round Table Conference, were able to persuade the two delegates of the Depressed Classes in the Conference to join them and prepared a pact, called the "Minorities Pact" to which they were able to secure the signature and support of the Depressed Classes delegate. It looked at that time that the union

*Speech in the Central Legislative Assembly.

with the other minorities would greatly strengthen the Depressed Classes. But when the allocation of seats to the several communities proposed in the pact was studied closely, it was found that in most provinces the Depressed Classes were getting less than they should get on the population basis, whereas the other minorities like the Muslims and the Europeans made themselves sure of getting as much and even more. This gave room for serious thought among the Depressed Classes and other leaders outside the Conference. They began to suspect and the suspicion soon came to be a conviction that they were being let down by the Depressed Classes delegates at the Conference and their interests unwisely sacrificed. For, how could the other minorities get what they wanted, some of them out of proportion to their numerical strength, except by cutting down the representation of the poorest of the poor minorities, since there was a limit to the paring down of the representation of majority communities. This is what often happens when the weak make common cause with the strong against those whom they consider to be stronger than them all. It is the old story of the fox asking the goat to get down the well and after getting on the back of the goat and getting out of the well, leaving the foolish goat in the lurch. If you think the parable is not just to the other members of the pact, let these communities, the Muslims and the Europeans, come forward now to denounce the Communal Award for the injustice done to the Depressed Classes and agree to forego some of the seats assigned to them in order to secure adequate representation to the Depressed Classes. I hope they will do this. They are in honour bound to do so, and a representation proceeding from them on behalf of the Depressed Classes will go a long way to get the Award changed so far as the Depressed Classes are concerned. A pact means that all the parties to it bind themselves to sink or swim together and not leave one behind while themselves rushing ahead. Mr. President, this disparity in the representation proposed in the Round Table Conference minority pact opened the eyes of my community to the futility of Separate Electorates and made them consider whether they would not do better to throw in their lot with the majority community in Joint Electorates only making sure that sufficient representation was secured to them through reservations to give them an effective voice in the Councils of the land. It was felt that being an integral part of a general electorate with safeguards in the shape of the reservation of at least a proportionate number of seats was better than being a separate community with a separate electorate with less number of seats. It was at this time, Mr. President, that the Prime Minister on the 1st December 1931, declared in England that whatever else of the present constitution making was to materialize or not, autonomy in the provinces was as good as a settled fact. This meant that the protecting arm of the bureaucracy was to be withdrawn and that the Depressed Classes should stand on their own legs and make themselves felt in the body politic by influencing and being influenced by the other communities constituting the majority. For this purpose they should be an organic part of the Joint Electorate with sufficient seats reserved for them. They should get the candidates of their communities approved and supported by other communities and the other communities should get their candidates approved and supported by our community. This reciprocal arrangement we thought was more conducive not only to nationalism but also to the leveling of the various communities and the social, economic and intellectual uplift of our community. It is by engaging in a common task with others that we can break down prejudices however deeply rooted they may be and not remain untouchables in a Separate Electorate roll. As a minority community with a Separate Electorate our influence will be circumscribed, whereas, as a strong section of a general electorate our influence will be unlimited. Sir, we are glad that the British Government has realized this and put us in a Joint Electorate, but under what conditions? We could vote for members of other communities but other communities could not be compelled to vote for our candidates. This has been our grievance and the cabinet chooses to have this grievance unredressed and satisfies us with giving us a double vote – a complimentary vote and a vote which gives us a candidate from our community who is not likely to command the support of other communities in the Council. Sir, this Communal Award is going to make us politically amphibious, strong neither on land nor in water, numerically weak in a Separate Electorate and politically ineffective in a Joint Electorate. This Award satisfies neither the clamourers for Separate Electorates nor the advocates of Joint Electorates. It sets the seal upon the betrayal of the community by the members of the Round Table Conference minority pact. Sir, look at the number of seats given to the Depressed Classes of the Punjab. It is nil. In spite of the recommendations of the Indian Central Committee on which there were two distinguished sons of the Punjab, my Honourable Friend Sir Zulfiqar Ali Khan and Sardar Sivhdev

Singh Uberoi, in spite of the recommendation of the Simon Commission and in spite of the recommendations of the Lothian committee, His Majesty's Government thought it fit to ignore the Depressed Classes of the Punjab. No greater injustice could be done to the poor Depressed Classes of the Punjab than this. Sir, what we want therefore is primarily an increased representation, at least proportionate to our numbers in each province. About this the whole community is unanimous. For numbers count in councils as well as elsewhere. How does it profit our community if you shut them up in a Separate Electorate and cut down their numbers or if you allow them to vote in a Joint Electorate in which you do not guarantee the election of a sufficient number? Number, number, number is the essence of an election and number through a general national electorate will be more effective politically, socially and economically than through a purely communal electorate.

Motion for Adjournment, 13 September 1932*

M.C. Rajah: Sir, never in the annals of the history of India has the issue of the Depressed Classes assumed the importance it has to-day. For this, we of the Depressed Classes must for ever be grateful to Mahatma Gandhi. He has told the world in words which cannot be mistaken that our regeneration is the fundamental aim of his life. If world conscience cannot be roused even now to the realization of the position of the Depressed Classes, then we can only conclude that all instincts of humanity are dead in the world to-day.

Let me remind the House that ours is an All India problem and not confined to some provinces as it is in the case of Muslims and Sikhs. I have heard it repeated often that the Muslim claim and the Sikh claim to special consideration is because they are martial races. So have we been in the ancient history of India. If they claim that they have been rulers in this country, so have we been in ancient times. But, Sir, what we claim is that we have, in addition, been the most law-abiding and loyal citizens. Even when social laws degraded us to a position of untouchability, we never took the law into our hands and depended upon the moral conscience of our countrymen being roused to a realization of the grave injustice and inhumanity practiced against us.

The question before the House is the situation created by Mahatma Gandhi opposing the grant of communal electorates to the "Depressed" Classes. I am sure, there is no Member in this Honourable House who will not regret that circumstances should have forced such a great personality to take a vow to play on his life. But, Sir, the correspondence shows that Government had enough warning. If they did not attach full importance to our considered views expressed in our conferences and in the pact I had the honour to sign with the President of the Hindu Mahasabha, they should have taken at least the grave warning given by Mahatma Gandhi and desisted from the course of creating Separate Electorates for us.

*Speech in the Central Legislative Assembly.

Sir, the situation as it confronts us to-day is as follows. The British Government has given their communal decision. They declare that it shall hold the field for 20 years in respect of the Depressed Classes unless there is unanimous request made before the constitution is framed or ten years after the constitution has worked. I wonder what is meant by unanimous request. Has in the political history of India or any country such literal unanimity ever been attained on any issue? Are the British Government sure that the Britishers are unanimous in giving India a further measure of responsibility? Are even the National Government sure that the conservatives as a whole back their Indian policy? This condition of unanimity is thus a dodge to keep us perpetually divided. I claim that my community is already in favour of common electorates and I will prove my contention by a few quotations.

You all know that the British Government sent two delegates to represent the Depressed Classes at the Round Table Conference – Dr. Ambedkar and Rao Bahadur Srinivasan. Dr. Ambedkar presented the case of the Depressed Classes in Bombay before the Simon Commission and he presented the statement of his Sabha where he said:

> System of election – Free election in general constituencies is, in the opinion of the Sabha, out of the question so far as the Depressed Classes are concerned. On the other hand, the Sabha does not wish to ask for communal electorates. In its opinion it would be sufficient if the Depressed Classes are provided with reserved seats in the general constituencies.

This was what Dr. Ambedkar said before the Simon Commission.

Again, in his minute of dissent to the Report of the Bombay Provincial Simon Committee, he demanded Joint Electorates with reservation of seats.

As regards Rao Bahadur Srinivasan, when he appeared before the Simon Commission in Madras, to a question put by a member of the Commission whether he wanted Separate Electorates for the Depressed Classes, he said "Not at present" and his reasons were:

> Our people are not yet advanced to have Separate Electorates. Unless you give adult franchise the Depressed Classes should have no Separate Electorates.

This was in 1929. When he went to the first Round Table Conference, the Depressed Classes Federation of Madras, of which he is the President, passed a resolution supporting Joint Electorates and giving him that mandate for being placed before the Round Table Conference.

In this connection let me remind the House that even Dr. Ambedkar demanded Joint Electorate with reservation of seats at the first Round Table Conference.

When the Indian Central Committee's Report was published giving the Depressed Classes Joint Electorates, with reservation of seats, for all provinces except Madras, there was no hue and cry, and when the Simon Commission's report embodying Joint Electorates with reservation of seats was published, there was no protest raised against it. My friend, Dr. Ambedkar, while speaking on the recommendations of this Commission, welcomed this system as an advancement in the interests of the community and raised objections to the system of panels from which the Governor was to select candidates for the Depressed Classes. Indeed Dr. Ambedkar, speaking at the Kamptee conference, in 1930, declared:

> No share of political power can come to you so long as the British Government remains where it is. It is only in a Swaraj constitution that you stand any chance of getting the political power in your hands.

He said in the same speech:

> Swaraj is going to be a system of Government in which you, the Depressed Classes, stand the chance, other things being equal, of being amongst those who will be installed as political sovereigns of this country.

I do not know what brought about a revolution in the state of mind of Dr. Ambedkar and Mr. Srinivasan at the second Round Table Conference, when they sacrificed the system whereby they would have obtained the right to be political sovereigns and secured, instead of expression of minimum voice for a people who deserved the maximum electoral power, to direct the Government from within.

Now, Sir, it will be clear to the House that Joint Electorates were acceptable to my community from the time they understood that there was to be transfer of power to Indian hands. The position we took was that, under a scheme of government in which Indians will rule, our safety lay not in finding channels for voicing our opinions but in taking our due share in the governance of the country. Indeed this is my chief attack on the premier's letter to Mahatma Gandhi. He tells us that he has given the Separate Electorates for 20 years to enable us to get a minimum number of seats, so that we may place our views before the Government and the Legislature of the day. I contend that this privilege we have already enjoyed under the Montford reforms, which have enabled us to get representation in numerous local bodies and in the Legislatures, both Provincial and Central. We are sufficiently organized for that purpose, and do not need either special pleading and special succour in future. What we do need, as a real remedy for our uplift, is a definite power to elect our representatives from the general constituencies and hold them responsible to us for their actions. I do not know why the Prime Minister calls the scheme of Joint Electorates with reservation of seats as impracticable. It is already in force in local bodies in Madras and some other provinces and has worked very satisfactorily.

I contend, Sir, that the scheme enunciated in the communal decision involves our segregation and makes us politically untouchable. I am surprised at the argument of the Prime Minister that there is no segregation because we can vote for caste Hindus who will have to solicit our votes. But, Sir, how can we bring about common ideas of citizenship when the Depressed Class representatives are not to solicit votes of the higher castes. There is, Sir, another tragic side to the controversy. When we claim special protection from Government for some share in official services, such as is already given by the Government of India to other minorities and backward classes, we are told that we are classed as Hindus to have no special claims, and when we declare that in the matter of legislative representation we would like to join the general body of Hindus, we are told that we are a separate community.

Sir, the sufferings which my community has undergone at the hands of the caste Hindus have been acknowledged by the caste Hindus themselves and I am prepared to admit that there are a large number of reformers among them who are doing everything possible to improve our status and position. I am convinced that there is a change of heart and a change in the angle of vision of the caste Hindus. We, the Depressed Classes, feel ourselves as true Hindus as any caste Hindus can be, and we feel that the moral conscience of the Hindus has been roused to an extent that our salvation lies in bringing about a change from within the main body of Hindu society and not by segregating ourselves from them. The course adopted by Government would certainly arrest the progress of this most laudable movement and process.

I must say, Sir, that the Prime Minister's letter in its entire conception and expression has disappointed me most. He argues, for instance, that reservation of seats under Joint Electorates would not get a genuine representation for us. Does the Prime Minister know that the Simon Commission, consisting of seven chosen Britishers, held, after a most thorough investigation on the spot, that such a system would produce genuine representation for us? Even the fear expressed by the Prime Minister is resolved by Mahatma Gandhi who has said that he is ready to enroll every adult member of the Depressed Class as a voter and impose a stricter test on the caste Hindus. May I ask, why the Premier is not prepared to consider this solution?

Now let me summarise the position. The Premier's Award is Separate Electorates, solely to secure a minimum number of spokesmen for the Depressed Classes. Mahatma Gandhi's decision is for over representation of the Depressed Classes in Joint Electorates. My pact with Dr. Moonje of the Hindu Mahasabha gives my community reservation of seats on the population basis through Joint Electorates.

In conclusion, let me add that I have known and studied the question of the Depressed Classes in all its bearings all over India during the quarter of a century of my public life. I was privileged to review it fully during our tour with the Simon Commission. I would, therefore, ask the Government to take this assurance from me that our best interests require that we should not be dissected from the Hindu community, but that we should have our due representation in the legislatures on the basis of reservation. The crisis that faces us to-day is very grave. There hangs in the balance the future of millions of the down-trodden people of this country. Are Government going to take the responsibility for killing the one, and reducing the other to perpetual servitude? Let them make their choice well and wisely.

The Hindu Temple Entry Disabilities Removal Bill, 24 August 1933*

M.C. Rajah: Mr. President, the reason why I intervene in this debate is to clear certain misconceptions that are lurking in the minds of some of my friends in the House. Sir, I am extremely sorry that my revered leader, Raja Bahadur Krishnamachari, is not here today. The other day on the 24 March 1933, while opposing this Bill, he said that as far as human memory could go, these gentlemen (referring to Depressed Classes) never entered a temple and that their entry would desecrate the temples. Sir, I shall presently show to the House that the Raja Bahadur was not correct in this.

It is most unfortunate that there should be in this country a class of people who believe that the exclusion of certain classes from temple worship is based on the true interpretation of the precepts of Hinduism. Little do those belonging to this class, realize the injury they are inflicting upon the religious and political well being of the Hindus. It will be out of place to go into the very debatable question of how far the ancient and sacred books support the case for or against the untouchables. It will be more interesting to consider that such a sentiment is purely of a historical growth and was an evil growth of certain political conditions that existed in this country in the past. This inferiority was a political condition caused by the conquest of the country by the White Aryan races and it is no wonder that the White races effecting a slow domination over the coloured races developed a sentiment of superiority over the conquered, nothing inherent in the nature of the people to justify such a permanent assignment of a place of inferiority. It can be easily understood by those who have a knowledge of historical growth of institutions and customs. Sir Herbert Risley writing in the *Census of India* (1901) remarks:

"In Madras, the Mala, the Nair and the Pariah of whom the last retain the traditions of a time when they possessed an independent organization of their own had been delegated to a low place in the Hindu social system."

*Speech in the Central Legislative Assembly.

Sir, the Depressed Classes represent the earliest civilization of India. Long before the Aryans came to India, the Depressed Classes had their own political and social institutions:

"A time before this when the Aryans came to India" says F.A. Steel in *India Through Ages*, "they found a people in India civilized enough to have towns and disciplined troops; to have weapons and banners; women whose ornaments were of gold; poisoned arrows whose heads were of some metal that was probably iron."

These were the ancestors of the present Depressed Classes, a tawny race as compared with the white skinned Aryans. The Aryans called them: "the neglectors of sacrifices, who decorated with gold and jewels" and "dwellers in iron cities".

These are at the present day some relics of their ancient rights and privileges which show beyond doubt the former greatness of these people, which are still to be found in the village organizations. Their decision in disputes concerning ownership of land is considered as final. Mr. W.F. Sinclair calls the Mahar as the guardian of boundaries and of public peace and health.

In an inscription of the eleventh century A.D., we find recorded the decision of one Vesali Parian and his councillors to be a final one in a civil case concerning the ownership of a piece of land belonging to a temple. The special privileges the Depressed Classes enjoy even to this day point to their former greatness. At the annual festival of the tutelary Goddess of George Town in the premier city of Madras, the Thali or marriage badge is tied round the Goddess by a member of the Depressed Classes in the name of the entire community. A member of the Depressed Classes officiates as priest at the bull games at Dindigul; during the great Hindu annual festival at Conjeevaram, Srivilliputtur, Kumbakonam, Trivottyur and other places in the South, the members of the Depressed Classes are allowed to pull the ropes of the huge cars containing the idols. During the festival of Siva at Tiruvalore in the Tanjore District, the headman of the Depressed Classes is specially honoured by being placed on the temple elephant along with the God and made to carry the Chowry in his hand for fanning the idol. In the famous temple of Krishna in Melkote, in the Mysore State, members of the Depressed Classes are accorded special privileges.

Pandit Satyendra Nath Sen: Where do you get all these? Why special privileges?

M.C. Rajah: You are ignorant of facts and figures, and yet you call yourself a Pandit. Your ancestors were more sensible than you are and so they accorded special privileges. Melkote is the chief seat of the Sri Vaishnavite Brahmins and the place where Sri Ramanuj lived in the 12th century. They enjoy a similar privilege at Sriperambadur in Chingleput district. In the case of a number of temples, there is a periodical admission of the Depressed Classes even under the present practice. Yet Raja Bahadur Krishnamachariar says, as far as human memory could go, these gentlemen never entered a temple. The Valluvars, a section of the Depressed Classes, were priests to the Pallava kings, before the advent of the Brahmins and even for some time after. Sir Harold Stewart, in the Census Report of 1891 quotes an unpublished Vatteluttu of the 9th century which says that Sri Valluvar, the temple minister, will employ six men daily and do the temple service.

Dr. Gustav Oppert in his book, *The Original Inhabitants of Bharatvarsha or India*, says:

> Valli is a well known female name common among the Pariahs and Pallars. Subramanya, the South Indian representative of Kartikeya, the son of Siva, is credited with having chosen a South Indian girl called Valli as his wife. That Subramanya's wife, Valli, was a low caste South Indian woman. Parvati, the wife of Siva and daughter of the mountain Himalaya, is even worshipped as a Pariah woman in her disguise as Matangi.

Sir, there are many sacred places and many holy temples, in south India, but for inspiring the pure joy of religious ecstasy there is perhaps no place equal to Chidambaram where the Divine Essence of the Universe is represented as engaged in an eternal dance of delight. Here, Nanda, belonging to the Depressed Classes whose very existence is one long story of unremitting toil rewarded by poverty, social degradation and religious excommunication panted for a glimpse of that God whose heart is love and whose feet, ever active and ever moving and ever balanced in joy. Did not god release Nanda from bondage to a master who was both an orthodox Brahmin and a landlord? Did not Nanda aspire for a vision of God while he was still enclosed in flesh? The image of Nanda is found in all Saiva temples and is worshipped even to this day by the devotees. Among the 63 Nainars or Saivite Saints who are worshipped as Gods the well known Nanda and the holy Thiruvalluvar belong to the Depressed Classes. Did not god order the Brahmin priest to carry Tirupan Alwar, the untouchable Vaishnava saint, on his shoulder right into the temple? Do not the orthodox Brahmins accept that Tirupan Alwar has become one with God Sri Pangunatha at Srirangam in South India? Do not the Vaishnavite Brahmins chant the verses in the famous work of Tirupan Alwar *Amaran Adhiparan* in all Vaishnavite temples side by side with the Sanskrit hymns? Is not the image of the Tirupan Alwar now found in all the Vaishnavite temples in South India and universally worshipped? Among the twelve Alwars or Vaishnavite saints who are now being worshipped as Gods in Vaishnavite temples the famous Tirupan Alwar and Maraneri Nambi belong to the Depressed Classes. Ravi Das of Oudh, Choka Mela of Maharashtra and Hari Das of Bengal have all sprang up from the untouchable classes. So also Arundhati, the wife of Brahmarishi Vasisth, one of the Sapta Rishis, who was famous for her chastity.

An Honourable Member: Where do you get all these from?

M.C. Rajah: I am surprised that these people should call themselves orthodox Pandits and yet are quite ignorant of Hindu history and Hindu religion. These honourable gentlemen come here in the name of religion to defend Hindu religion and it is a shame that they are ignorant of these things. When Abhimanyu, son of Arjun, was hit by an arrow, what did Subhadra, his mother, do? She invoked the blessings of Arundhati and her son recovered. What does this show? This shows the high veneration with which she was held by women of all classes. Jambavan, who was called a bear in *Ramayana* by the Aryan poet in his conceit, belonged to the Depressed Classes. Jambavan was the custodian of all ancient learning and a mighty warrior. Yet, Sir, Raja Bahadur Krishnamachariar says that the entry of these gentlemen into the temples would desecrate these temples. Sir, these facts show that the so-called untouchables were intimately connected with the important Hindu temples in India and that these temples originally belonged to them. All the ancient Hindu temples in India belonged to the Depressed Classes and not to the Aryans. They were gradually taken over from the Depressed Classes. The following extract from O'Malley says:

> A curious example of the way in which Brahmans become associated with non-Brahmanical worship may be mentioned. In Bengal there is a Godling, called Dharmaraj, who is now worshipped in the shape of a stone and credited with powers of healing. His priests are commonly men of the scavenger castes, such as Hari and Dom. In one district some Brahmans suffering from diseases believed to be incurable turned in despair to Dharmaraj, vowed to make offerings if cured, and were miraculously cured. They had to redeem their vows but would not make their votive offerings through the established priest, who was an untouchable Hari. A way out of the impasse was found by installing a low Brahman who was ready to associate himself with the

Hari in order to make it a living. The two became partners, each having a clientele of his own, but the Brahman was predominant partner, for he forced the Hari to make his sacrifices of pigs and cocks in the jungle behind the building housing Dharmaraj. Finally the Hari family died out and the Brahman remained in sole possession.

Sir, this was how these temples which belonged to the Depressed Classes passed into the hands of these cunning Brahmans. Sir, in this connection I may also lay certain facts before you to show that God does not make any difference between untouchables and the high caste men. Have you heard of the "Midday Pariahs", a Brahmin sect of old cursed by God Shiva and made outcastes for 90 minutes every day? This curse continues to this day in Tiruwalur in Tanjore district from where my leader Raja Bahadur Krishnamachariar comes. Certain high caste priests in Tiruwalur once decided upon holding a *yagna* or great sacrifice and to request Ishwara or God to be present on the occasion and to receive the offerings in person. A deputation waited on the presiding deity. But the deity would not think of moving from his place, but wanted the offerings at the temple. Through the intervention of the Goddess word came to them that God Shiva would be present at the function, but that he would not be dictated to as to the mode of his dress. The priests agreed saying, "Oh yes, let him come as he pleases; what difference can it make to us?" The priests were dressed in immaculate dress. The sacrificial fire was glowing and the smell of butter hung heavily in the air. There were only a few seconds more for Shiva to arrive. But no signs of his coming. But just at twelve, the appointed hour, the priests saw an outcaste, carrying a carcass on his back and followed by four dogs with his wife in Pariah garb. To avoid their being getting polluted by this outcaste and his wife they took to their heels not caring what became of their *yagna*. But the deity, for it was He who had come with the Goddess in that dress with the four Vedas as the dogs, symbolically accepted the gifts, blessed the really pious and departed in haste. But He 'outcasted' the priests who had fled. Through the intervention of the Goddess, Shiva laid it down that they shall be untouchables only for half a *jama* (90 minutes) a day. All men are equal in the eyes of God. God is for the sinners and the oppressed and not for the orthodox who think they are righteous.

Sir, these clearly indicate that such a low state was never a natural state and those responsible for creating such a state could have easily sought and found an authority for such a state in the ancient and sacred books. The state of law was in so confused a condition, so capable of being lent for any interpretation, that it was no wonder that any number of texts could be found in the ancient books by those who were anxious to search for it to prove that the ancestors of these untouchables were real devils. Imagine in what state these authorities must have been in those dark ages when the white races flushed by the sense of conquest sought to create and render permanent its own superiority and the corresponding inferiority of the conquered races. How easy would have been the task and are we for ever to be in a state of religious serfdom because of these texts? Sir Thomas Strange, whose monumental contribution to the development of Hindu law is well recognized, writes thus:

> To those who have made the Hindu law a part of their study, it cannot appear strange that it is so unsettled and contradictory. Many of the opposing writers as in point of credit equal to each other, and regardless of consistency texts are adopted for each for the purpose of sustaining his own end. The obsolete is confounded with the acknowledged law. The context is often omitted and passages which ought to be relatively considered are quoted as if they are absolute and independent in themselves. We cannot therefore wonder that so little satisfaction is obtained from authority. Nor can we but lament that some effort has not long since been made to distinguish and separate those which are not rules of action.

These remarks of a great scholar in Hindu law correctly describe the state, and one wonders how any correction can be centred on a state of law in this condition. We believe that ignorance alone can justify blind a faith and the objection from the class that swears on the holy books may be set aside as unworthy of consideration.

The learned author of this Bill considers the impossibility of the disability being ever removed by any method beside legislation. The final pronouncement of the highest judiciary in the land in 35 Indian Appeals, 176 shattered the hopes of those who believed that by a series of judicial designs this much desired removal of disability could be effected. But the pronouncement of the Privy Council would be no surprise to those who knew the unwillingness of the British jurist to interfere with the personal usages and customs of the people of India. Though those now trained in a system of democratic jurisprudence realize all the inequity of certain rules of law they are unwilling to interfere. But whenever the legislature did intervene to correct such inequities they have been benevolent measures. In actual life we have experienced the benefits of legislation and we need have no apprehension for the future in putting this Bill on the Statute book. The sooner this disability is removed the better for our religion and the sooner these ancient barriers are broken, the ancient gulf is bridged, the earlier will be the unity of the race of Hindus realized.

Sir, there is no ingredient in the universe separate from Brahma, this to look upon the world of merits and demerits with an eye of absolute equality is the only means of liberation, that to view all things as Brahman is the only means of salvation. To the pure all things are pure. This is the basic principle of Hinduism. What did Sree Krishna say in the *Gita*?

> See me in every one. If you insult any one, you insult me in him. If you disdain any one, you disdain me in him. If you love me, love every one, for then alone do you really and fully love me.

Sir, the Bill confers on millions of untouchables certain benefits and removes from them the age-long stigma of inferiority, confers on the emancipated a sense of self-respect and is the greatest contribution towards the abolition of untouchability in this land.

With these words, I support the amendment of my friend, Mr. Sarma, that the Bill be circulated for eliciting opinion thereon by the end of June 1934.

The Untouchability Abolition Bill, 5 September 1933*

M.C. Rajah: Sir, I beg to move. . . .

Pandit S.N. Sen: Sir, I rise to a point of order.

M.C. Rajah: What is the point of order? I have not said anything yet.

S.N. Sen: I rise to a point of order, Sir.

Mr. President (The Honourable Sir Shanmukham Chetty): What is the point of order?

S.N. Sen: Sir, I beg to submit that this Bill for the abolition of untouchability among the Hindus is *ultra vires* of this Legislature. I take my stand on the notification of the Government of India under section. . . .

S.C. Mitra: Nothing has been moved so far. The point of order is premature.

M.A. Ali: Sir, how can the Honourable member raise a point of order at this stage? The Honourable the Mover has not said anything so far.

Mr. President (The Honourable Sir Shanmukham Chetty): The Chair understands that Pandit Satyendra Nath Sen wants to raise a point of order that the Bill is *ultra vires* of this Legislature; is that so?

S.N. Sen: Yes, Sir.

Mr. President (The Honourable Sir Shanmukham Chetty): Let the Honourable Member, Mr. M.C. Rajah, move his motion first.

M.C. Rajah: Sir, I beg to move:

That the Bill to provide for the abolition of untouchability among the Hindus, be referred to a Select Committee consisting of the Honourable the Law Member, the Honourable Sir Harry Haig, Diwan Bahadur Harbilas Sarda, Mr. C.S. Ranga Iyer, Mr. Gaya Prasad Singh, Mr. T.N. Ramakrishna Reddy, Mr. S.C. Mitra, Mr. B.V. Jadhav, Mr. B. Rajaram Pandian, Captain Rao Bahadur Chaudhri Lal Chand, Rai Bahadur Kunwar Raghubir Singh, Rao Bahadur S.R. Pandit, Mr. R.S. Sarma and the Mover, and that the number

*Speech in the Central Legislative Assembly.

of members whose presence shall be necessary to constitute a meeting of the Committee shall be five.

Sir, in so doing, I appeal to Honourable Members unanimously to cooperate in facilitating the progress of this belated effort to do justice to the Depressed Classes. If I enter into an analysis of the acts of omission and commission on the part of my fellow Hindus that have produced the degradation to which my community is condemned and brought about the shame and humiliation of Hinduism itself before the world, it will take hours. I do not want to embitter feelings by recapitulating the past when I see that a great and welcome change has come over the Hindu mind as a whole. This Bill is based upon the principle that the law of no civilized country can recognize or give its support and assistance to an anti-social usage opposed to humanity as well as national interests.

S.N. Sen: What is the procedure followed here, Sir?

Mr. President: Order, order. The Honourable Member can raise his point of order after the Honourable Mr. Rajah has finished. He will not lose his right.

M.C. Rajah: That an inequity is old is no reason for a day's further delay in redress, but for greater speed in penitence and restitution. Such a measure, we expected, would be taken up by Government with alacrity seeing how much popular support has been wholeheartedly given to it, and how earnestly popular organizations plead for its enactment. I am inclined to press for a Select Committee, if not enactment of the measure in this Session itself, it being a non-controversial and belated recognition of a well-known principle of Jurisprudence as well as the barest negative justice to the oppressed Community that I represent. But as some members desire circulation, I have no objection if the House desires to do so. I hope the Bill will in time receive support from all and set right an intolerable wrong in the administration of the laws of our country.

Sir, the cause of the Depressed Classes combines in it the best of religion, the best of humanity and the best of nationalism. It is a cause worthy of the best energies and the most strenuous efforts of a large number of Indians who believe "life is a mission and duty its highest law", and the best fulfilment of that duty lies in the service of uplifting of those whom human tyranny and prejudice have practically put out of the pale of humanity. No sin is greater than that of attempting to keep human beings in a state of perpetual bondage. It is infamous beyond measure and galling to the very soul of men, to deliberately and persistently keep a section of the people – God's own children – and removing them by brute force or by religious and social duplicity to the level of beasts.

The vision of the future from the heights of legislation discloses the Hindu Race so rich in culture and philosophy, united and inseparable for all time with no more dividing walls between the two great sections of caste and no-caste.

Untouchability Abolition Bill, 1 February 1934*

M.C. Rajah: Sir, I thought my task was easy as I was all along under the impression that I had to answer only two Honourable members of this House, but this morning up sprang the Honourable the Law Member who tried to throw certain bombs at my Bill. Sir, it is surprising to me that the bulk of the opposition comes from a province, Bengal, where they say there is no untouchability, but I shall first deal with my revered leader, Raja Bahadur Krishnamachariar. He seems to attribute the genesis of this Bill to Mahatma Gandhi. Let me straightaway tell this House that this is an incorrect statement. The Raja Bahadur is not aware of the real origin of this Bill and his statement merely misleads the Members of this House.

M.C. Rajah: In this connection I should deal with two aspects of the question, the genesis of this movement and the genesis of this Bill. The first attempt at the reclamation of the down-trodden classes was made by the European Christian Missionaries. The Christian Mission schools are democratic institutions, where the low and the meek, the depressed and the oppressed, the poor and the struggling are treated with equal attention with the high and the rich, the progressive and the flourishing, the socially high and the politically strong. The Christian Mission schools open their door wide to all, but especially to the outcaste and the down-trodden fulfilling Christ's sayings: "He that is least among you the same shall be great", and "Blessed are the meek for they shall inherit the kingdom of God". "At present" says Henry Whitehead, formerly Bishop of Madras, in his book *Indian Problems*: "83 per cent of the Indian Christians throughout India are illiterate and, at the same time, ignorant, illiterate outcastes are being swept into the Church at the rate of 2,000 a week."

The restoration of civic and political rights in a measure were vouchsafed to us by the British Government. The British administration has all along been struck with the peculiar disabilities of the

*Speech in the Central Legislative Assembly.

untouchables and had been doing their best to ameliorate their sufferings.

In His Excellency Lord Willingdon we have a true friend of the Depressed Classes. It will be interesting to mention that His Excellency was the first in India to appoint a member of the Depressed Classes to a Provincial Legislative Council and that was in 1919 during the pre-reform days. It was His Excellency that inaugurated the special department in the Presidency of Madras for the protection of the interests of the Depressed Classes when he was the Governor of that Province and appointed the late Sir George Paddison, the Protector of the Depressed Classes. Sir George Paddison, with his Personal Assistant, Diwan Bahadur S.K. Sunderacharlu, did a great deal of ameliorative work on behalf of the Depressed Classes in that province.

Coming now, to the non-official side, it was the late Dr. T.M. Nair that gave an impetus to the movement for the removal of untouchability and placed it in the forefront of his political programme, when he organized the non-Brahmin movement in the Madras Presidency in 1917. Individual social reformers like His Highness the Maharaja of Mysore, the Maharaja of Pithapuram, Sir Venkataratnam Naidu, of the South, His Highness the Gaekwar of Baroda, the late Justice Chandavarkar in Bombay, the late Lala Lajpat Rai in the Punjab and Swami Shradhanand of Delhi in the North took growing interest in the amelioration of the Depressed Classes of India.

Later, under the inspiration of Mahatma Gandhi, the Congress took up the question and passed a Resolution for the removal of untouchability at its Session in January 1921, and included the item of the removal of untouchability in the programme of the Congress. As a matter of fact, I have been accusing Mahatma Gandhi for not taking up the cause of the untouchables in right earnest, until so late as November 1931. For the information of the House, I should like to read a passage from my speech delivered at the 9th session of the All India Depressed Classes Conference held in the Punjab on the 31st October 1931. There I said:

> The Indian National Congress had been functioning for over 46 years. About ten years ago, they adopted a Resolution for removal of untouchability and a few years later, Gandhiji included the item of the removal of untouchability in the programme of the Congress along with prohibition and khaddar. I would like to ask Mahatma Gandhi if he and his followers have devoted one-hundredth as much attention to the removal of untouchability as to the

promotion of khaddar, though many of them know that khaddar is a poor economic proposition by the side of mill-made cloth. Khaddar is, no doubt, immediately useful for wresting power from the British people, whereas the removal of untouchability is not useful for such a purpose though it is even more useful and more permanently useful for establishing Self-Government in this country.

Then I asked:

Why does not Mahatma Gandhi direct his energies to removing the oppressive features in our social structure, and, in particular, to removing the canker of untouchability before he makes any further attempt for Swaraj, since he himself had wisely admitted on more than one occasion that this reform should precede Swaraj?

Therefore, Sir, you will understand that it was not Mahatma Gandhi that first took up the cause of the untouchables. Then, coming to the genesis of this Bill, let me remind this House that it is not a new Bill. A similar Bill, called the "Hindu Untouchable Castes Disabilities Removal Bill", and Lord Irwin, the then Viceroy and Governor General of India, without any difficulty whatsoever, accorded previous sanction to it on the 30th of December 1929, that is more than four years ago. Unfortunately, my friend, Mr. Jayakar, did not continue his Membership in the Assembly, and so was not able to pilot that Bill. Subsequently, you, Sir, sponsored it and His Excellency Lord Willingdon, the present viceroy, gave you the previous sanction, and that too without any difficulty, on the 6th of August 1931, that is, more than two years ago. It is significant that the orthodox section of the Hindus did not raise any hue and cry then against that Bill. But, Sir, I can understand the feelings of these orthodox friends. They always cry hoarse whenever any custom of theirs, however injurious to society and however useless it may be, is sought to be modified by an act of the Legislature. They respect these customs, whether good or bad, and they always feel it too much to part with any of them. Sir, in his speech, my revered Leader, Raja Bahadur Krishnamachariar, complained that I failed to mention the abolition of untouchability in my note attached to the report of the Indian Central Committee. This, too, I beg to add, is an incorrect statement.

M.C. Rajah: But I observe that, whenever the Raja Bahadur makes a statement, he does so "subject to correction". But, Sir, this is not the way a responsible Member of this House, rich in age and experience, speaking on important subjects, should mislead this

Honourable House by making inaccurate and misleading statements "subject to correction".

M.C. Rajah: For the benefit of this House, however, let me read what I have said on this particular matter in my note attached to the Report of the Indian Central Committee. Sir, this is what I said:

> The general remedy that suggests itself is the immediate and total withdrawal of legal and administrative recognition to the superstition of population. The laws, as they are administered today, uphold these superstitions and punish the untouchables who dare to disregard them.

And, then, Sir, I said on page 385:

> The peaceful progress of the untouchable classes is a *sine qua non* of the orderly development of Indian nationalism. Paradoxically as it may sound, the aim of the Depressed Classes and those working for their future should be their abolition. They are an excretion of the Hindu society and they must aim at becoming one with it. The ideal should be to become not merely an integral part of it, but to become an indistinguishable part.

This report was published in the year 1929 – long before Mahatma Gandhi thought of getting a Bill like this introduced in this House. Sir, I make bold to say that we are not piloting the Bill at the behest of Mahatma Gandhi; yet we cannot but be grateful to him for taking up this question at this time and thus rendering a great help to our cause.

Sir, my revered Leader, Raja Bahadur Krishnamachariar, says that I advanced certain fantastic arguments during his absence from the House in connection with the Temple Entry Bill. Sir, I made that speech six months ago and up till now I have not seen any adverse criticisms in any of the papers, even in the Sanatanist papers. Sir, I stand by every word I said in that connection and I can prove them by records. In this connection Raja Bahadur Krishnamachariar gave the House to understand that Saint Tirupanalvar's parentage is not exactly known. Sir, this is the usual characteristic way in which Brahmins, when they find a saint in a so-called lower community, say, "he does not belong to that community", or "he was born in it by a mistake". (Interruption by Raja Bahadur G. Krishnamachariar.) I am not giving way.

M.C. Rajah: But, at the same time, he accepts the theory that this saint from his boyhood was being brought up in an untouchable's house. Sir, the very fact that he was brought up by untouchables from his babyhood raises a strong presumption that Saint Tirupanalvar belonged to that community. Sir, in this connection, my revered leader, Raja Bahadur Krishnamachariar, said that when saint Tirupanalvar was singing the praises of the Lord until he was about thirty years of age, one day God gave orders to the temple priest to bring that devotee to the temple, and my revered leader, Raja Bahadur Krishnamachariar, avoided saying why on that particular day God ordered the temple priest to bring that devotee to the temple. Let me say why. Raja Bahadur Krishnamachariar, my revered leader, is a Vaishnava like myself and I challenge him to disprove my statements, I shall at once give way. One day, Loka Saranga Muni went to the river to fetch water for the morning *puja* of the God. On his way to the river, he saw Tirupanalvar sitting on the bank of the river chanting hymns in praise of Sree Ranganadha. He shouted to Tirupanalvar to move away. Tirupanalvar was absorbed in contemplation and heard him not. Seeing that Tirupanalvar did not move away, Loka Saranga got incensed and threw a stone at him.

M.C. Rajah: It hit Tirupanalvar on his forehead and he began to bleed profusely, and then he moved away. When the Muni went back to the temple, he saw Sree Ranganadha similarly bleeding on his forehead. He tried to stop it, but could not. He felt the God was angry over his behaviour to the Saint Tirupanalvar. He deeply reflected and the call distinctly came to him from God Sree Ranganadha not only to go and apologize to Tirupanalvar, but to carry him on his shoulders to His presence in the temple. He obeyed, went and fell at the feet of Tirupanalvar and carried him on his shoulders to the temple. I challenge my revered leader, Raja Bahadur Krishnamachariar, to contradict this.

M.C. Rajah: You did not say this. Again, Sir, my revered leader, Raja Bahadur Krishnamachariar, said that the temple priest took the devotee to the temple as far as he could be brought and God exhibited his presence. This is another perversion from truth. What was the order of God? The order of God was to bring him to the temple where God was actually bleeding in his forehead and the temple priest carried him to that very place, not as the Raja Bahadur says to the place up to which he could be brought.

With reference to Saint Nandanar, I am glad that my revered leader did not dispute his parentage and he admits that Saint Nandanar was admitted to the *sanctum sanctorum*, for the Raja Bahadur said that God said: "Light a fire in front of my *sanctum sanctorum*". And the Raja Bahadur, I am glad to say, had explained why Saint Nandanar was asked to walk on the fire, although I do not believe this part of the story which is a mere concoction by the clever Brahmins of those days. The Raja Bahadur also explained that he was asked to go through fire so that he could become one with God. Let me tell the Raja Bahadur that we are not for becoming one with God, but we are for having Deva Darshan. At the same time, let me also remind him that in the temples in the South no one – not even my revered leader, the Raja Bahadur – is allowed in the *sanctum sanctorum*. Again, with reference to Ramanujacharya and the Melcottah Temple to which I made reference in my speech, the Raja Bahadur, while accepting that the members of the Depressed Classes are allowed into the temple for three days in a year, asserts that a purification ceremony is performed immediately after the third day to bring Godhead again to its proper place. This is really wonderful and Sree Ramanujacharya was a great saint and, I am sure, he would never have placed God in that precarious condition of purity by admitting the Depressed Classes into his temple. Moreover, those three days are the most sacred days for the Vaishnavites and, during those days, people from all parts of the country congregate for His worship. The purification ceremony is performed not only in this particular temple, but in all temples after the annual gathering. My friend, Pandit Sen, pleaded ignorance to all this and now he comes and says something. In all other temples in which Depressed Classes are not allowed, there also such ceremonies are performed. Sir, in my humble opinion, the purification ceremony is performed not because the Depressed Classes are admitted inside the temples, but because Brahmins and non-Brahmins, clean and unclean, are all admitted without distinction during that period. To my knowledge, similar ceremonies are performed in temples to which Depressed Classes have no access. Again, Sir, Raja Bahadur Krishnamachariar found fault with me for saying that temples in South India belonged originally to the Depressed Classes, who were subsequently expelled by the cunning Brahmins. Might I ask the Raja Bahadur whether the temples in South India belong to the Brahmins?

M.C. Rajah: I am glad to hear that. Sir, I assert once again that temples in South India did belong to the Depressed Classes, the ancient Dravidians, otherwise called the Adi-Dravidas. In this connection, let me tell my friend, the Raja Bahadur, that Brahmins had no hand in installing idols in temples. Let me quote Professor Max Müller. Professor Max Müller says:

> The religion of the Vedas knows of no idols. The worship of idols in India is a secondary formation, a later degradation of the more primitive worship of the idol Gods.

Again, Sir, Mr. J.C. Ghosh, in his Tagore Law Lectures, says:

> That wave of the influence of the Brahmins and the unpopularity of the worship of fire led to the worship of images which might have been borrowed from the aboriginal tribes and from foreign invaders in ancient times.

Brahmins were even outcasted if they went to worship in temples. This is historically and Vedically true: "We should know", says Mr. Ghosh, "that dedication for the Gods meant dedication for the maintenance of the worshipping Brahmins, who, because they so worshipped, were called *Devalas* and were all but outcastes among Brahmins."

Again, Spence Hardy says: "Image worship is alluded to by Manu, but with intimation that the Brahmins who subsist by ministering in temples were an inferior class."

In Tirumular's *Tirumantiram*, the standard work in Tamil on Agamic cult, runs as follows: "If a Brahmin, as such, does puja to God, it will bring disaster to the king and famines to the country."

Sir, even in Palni itself, remarked Mr. Justice Sadasiva Iyer: "The priest was non-Brahmin till about a century ago. Now the priest is a Brahmin."

From Chanakya it is evident that the position of the Brahmins in Hindu temples today is due to an accident. That great Frenchman Abbeduboix, a century ago, referring to the Brahmins, wrote:

> It was principally for their use that the dancers and prostitutes, who were attached to the service of the temples, were originally entertained and they may be heard to intone the following scandalous line – *Vaishya darshanam punyam papanasham* – which means looking upon a prostitute is a virtue which takes away sin.

While referring to the Sree Rangam Temple, which is situated in the place where my revered leader hails from, the Raja Bahadur has said that this site was bought by Vibhisana. You all know was the brother of Ravana, who was a mighty Dravidian King.

M.C. Rajah: I accept the correction, but how could any site be bought? Did he bring the site from Ceylon? This is a wonderful thing which I do not understand. For the information of my friend, Raja Bahadur Krishnamachariar, who represents the Vaishnavites of the Madras Presidency, let me give a presentation of a paragraph from the Gazetteer of the Trichinopoly District. This is a Government publication. It was published in 1907 and was written by Mr. F.R. Hemmingway, Indian Civil Service.

M.C. Rajah: You quoted Meghasthenes and Fah Hien, what do they know about our Hindu Religion? Sir, let me finish this. With reference to the Sree Rangam Temple, he says: "A local legend states that the image of the god was placed in the temple by Vibhishana, brother of Ravana, who was of great assistance to Rama in his conquest of Ceylon."

M.C. Rajah: As far as I know, Ravana was an ancient Dravidian King.

M.C. Rajah: It is something like saying that Tirupan Alwar was a Brahmin.

G. Krishnamachariar: The Honourable Member is misrepresenting me. I should like to say....

M.C. Rajah: I do not give way to my Honourable Friend.

Mr. President (The Honourable Sir Shanmukham Chetty): No Honourable Member can interfere unless the Honourable Member in possession of the House gives way.

M.C. Rajah: The Gazetteer continues:

> A local legend states that the image of the god was placed in the temple by Vibhishana, brother of Ravana, who was of great assistance to Rama in his conquest of Ceylon. In his gratitude, Rama gave him the image to take to Ceylon; but on the way hither he halted in Sree Rangam and the idol became fixed to the ground there.

So, that was the origin of the Sree Rangam Temple and the image was placed there by an ancient Dravidian, Vibhishana.

Now, Sir, I do not hold any brief for Mahatma Gandhi nor does he require anybody to defend him in this house. Since my revered leader, the Raja Bahadur, had made certain distorted statements regarding the deputation of the Depressed Classes that waited on Mahatma Gandhi in Madras, I find it my duty to place certain facts before the House. The Raja Bahadur says "that one Mr. R. Srinivasan in Madras, a graduate also a Vakil of the Madras High Court, and who had something to do with learning law in Madras, law under Sir C.P. Ramaswamy Aiyar" and, therefore, he said, he is an enrolled Vakil of the Madras High Court. . . .

M.C. Rajah: I hope the Honourable Member means that he can say anything in the world subject to correction. He said, and, therefore, an enrolled Vakil of the Madras High Court gave an unpleasant half hour to Gandhiji. Let me say that, as far as I know, there is no person of this description in the Madras Presidency belonging to the Depressed Classes. But, Sir, it is true that my friend, Rao Bahadur R. Srinivasan, and a number of leading members belonging to the Depressed Classes, met Gandhiji on the 23rd December 1933. It is stated in the newspapers that Swami Sahajananda and Mr. Pushparaj, B.Sc., B.L., protested before Gandhiji while a few others touched his feet and the scene was a striking demonstration of love and affection. In this connection, let me tell the House that Rao Bahadur Srinivasan did not say that he did not want temple entry. What he said was this and I read from the *Hindu*, dated 23 December 1933. He says: "As regards temple entry, we are not opposed to it." With reference to the expression "Harijan", it is true that the Depressed Classes of Madras did not like that term "Harijan", and when that was represented to Gandhiji, his reply was this:

> Lastly to the name "Harijan", you say that the Depressed Classes were not consulted. They consulted me. That is the point. I have visited all parts of India. "Why are we called Harijans", I am asked. Why should they not have a better name? That is the generality of feeling. "For heaven's sake do not call us coolies" they pleaded. At one time this word had a particular significance.

Further on, Gandhiji says:

> It is not, as I said, my coining. An untouchable pleaded with me not to be known by any expression of eternal reproach, Depressed or suppressed reminds them of slavery, he very rightly said. "I have no name to suggest, will you suggest", I asked. Then the man suggested "Harijan". He quoted in support from Narasimha Mehta, the Guzerathi poet who had used it in his works. I jumped at it.

Therefore, Sir, it seems that at the bidding of the Depressed Classes themselves he seems to have given that name. I am not very particularly interested in that at all.

Again, Sir, the other day, while speaking on the Temple Entry Bill, Raja Bahadur Krishnamachariar has said with reference to my friend, Dr. Ambedkar, that he too was not for temple entry. Here is a document in my possession to prove that Dr. Ambedkar is for temple entry. The document is dated 11th January 1930, and it was sent to me from the office of the Temple Entry Satyagraha Committee, Nasik. This circular letter was addressed to me by one Mr. B.K. Gaikwad, Secretary of the Satyagraha Committee, Nasik, and it runs as follows:

I hope you are aware of the Kala Ram Temple Entry Satyagraha of Nasik conducted under the leadership of Dr. Baba Saheb Ambedkar last year. The short summary of the same is as under.

Well, Sir, I need not tire the House with all the details. The request that is made in this circular letter to me is this:

Now, the committee, with the full consent and a sort of order from Dr. Baba Saheb Ambedkar, who is just now sitting on the Round Table Conference, decide to begin again Satyagraha. But this time we do not care to have it only as a local show. It is an all India question, and the honour of all Indian untouchables is in the scales. And I write this letter on behalf of the committee to request you very strongly that you please take up the question and use all your resources for the cause.

Sir, with reference to my politics and the politics of Gandhiji, let me say a word. Politically even myself and Mahatma Gandhi are poles as under and, so far as I know, Mahatma Gandhi does not wish to interfere in our politics. I can assure this House that he had not interfered with our politics till now. Sir, after all, my revered leader, Raja Bahadur Krishnamachariar, was arguing his case in this House as a police court advocate. As he represents the orthodox section of the Hindu community, I am glad to note that he has shown his real feeling and a sense of responsibility when he said that, in his own lifetime, he had seen things which no one expected thirty years ago. He believes that greater changes might follow during the next fifteen years. Therefore, why force the pace, he asks, and thus divide a great community and thus lose a very great chance of uniting together and pulling together to obtain our goal. It seems to me that the Raja Bahadur concedes that what is objectionable now will become inevitable at no later period. Might I ask the Raja Bahadur why delay justice by fifteen years. Justice delayed is justice denied.

Now, coming to my Honourable Friend, Pandit Sen, the high priest of orthodoxy in this House, my honourable friend complained that some of his friends cried "Down with Manu, long live Gandhi". Though this is a new slogan to Pandit Sen, I find I have been hearing of another slogan "Down with Manu and burn the Code of Manu" for the last 25 years. I myself presided over huge meetings in various parts of the country where resolutions were passed and sent to Government to expunge the Code of Manu from the list of legal authorities on Hindu customs, and in certain meetings resolutions were passed to burn the Code of Manu, and in some meetings copies of "the Code of Manu" were actually burnt and reduced to ashes.

Pandit Sen is just like the frog in the well. He does not seem to know what is happening in the country. Pandit Sen denounces not only Mahatma Gandhi as being a non-Hindu, he denounces Dr. Tagore and Sir P.C. Ray as being non-Hindus. At the same time, Pandit Sen is working in the City College, founded, financed and conducted by Brahmos! After all, Pandit Sen and the so-called Sanatanists quote Shastras in support of their contentions. I also base my vehement opposition to untouchability on the same Shastras by which these men swear. There are very learned men who have just as much right or perhaps a better right to interpret the Shastras as the so-called Pandits.

Coming to the question of authority, so far as social and moral arguments are concerned, they have been exhausted and even the orthodox people are inclined to accept them. The fact that they seek shelter in Shastras shows that on pure moral grounds, on grounds of reason and justice, not to speak of patriotism and progress and nationalism, they are not able to justify untouchability. They seek shelter of authority, and when the Shastras are not able to speak with a certain and unmistakable voice, they fall back upon custom, knowing that custom possesses legal sanction and that the Courts will uphold it when the existence of the custom is once proved. As things exist at present, it is law that sustains custom, not even the Shastras that sustain untouchability. That is to say, in the ultimate analysis, it is law that sustains untouchability. If it is law that sustains untouchability, it is only law that can deprive it of its binding power. In the name of law and order, untouchability is maintained. Recent research has indicated that untouchability has but a shadowy support in ancient Hindu scriptures and that its strength lies in its observance and the latter day Smritis. Now that the recognition has come, untouchability is a foul blot on Hinduism. What should be the aim of everyone concerned in the welfare of Hinduism? The aim should be its abolition. Sir, the Shastras were written thousands of years ago. These pernicious customs and usages were introduced into the Hindu society thousands of years ago when there were no Muslims and Christians in India. Those who were responsible for these customs and usages did not know what would happen now. They merely adopted them to suit the then existing conditions. They had not the wisdom to follow the practice after (say) about 2,000 years, when the world has completely changed. Would Pandit Sen's and Pandit Jha's grandfathers have ever dreamt that their grandsons would travel in railway carriages dressed in the latest fashion with shirts, coats, collars, ties and shoes? Would they have dreamt of aerated waters manufactured by our Shudra brethren or would they have dreamt of the banquets attended by our orthodox friends in Hotel Cecil or the Government House where food and eatables are prepared and served by Muslims, Christians and members of the Depressed Classes? God has given us enough foresight and intelligence, we are not going to be bound down any more by the ante-diluvian, stupid customs.

There is absolutely no meaning in assuming that all the best has manifested itself in the past. God's manifestation is progressive. Men must look forward and wait for the revelation and jump into it setting fire to every part of his life – political, intellectual, social and religious, – until he is prepared to say that he had perfect life, perfect bliss and perfect knowledge. Religion must march with the times and this has been one of the essential characteristics of our Hindu religion, which distinguishes it from other religions, namely, that it expressly admits the possibility to suit altered circumstances. A careful study of the history of Hinduism would clearly reveal that there had been every now and then, whenever necessary, such movements for purifying the Hindu society and Hindu religion in the past, which had been led by religious reformers whose lead had been accepted without any question by all sections of the community. For instance, let me remind my orthodox Vaishnavite friends in this House of the religious revival of Sree Ramanujacharya. Did he not give *Mulamantram* to all persons in spite of the protests from his *Guru* who said that he would go to hell if he only did so? But what was the reply of Sree Ramanujacharya? Did he not say, "Let me go to hell, but let these thousands go to heaven by the benefit of the *Mulamantra*"? Again, did not Sree Ramanuja, who is worshipped by true Vaishnavite devotees even to this day, increase the Brahmin fold by recruiting into it barbers, weavers, potters and toddy drawers and give them the appellation Tirumanis, by giving them *Diksha* and converting them as Vaishnavite Brahmins? And Sree Ramanuja did this in one generation without the necessity of any re-birth.

I have already pointed out that the Shastras did not sanction caste or untouchability, and untouchability is not religion but irreligion. The present-day caste cannot be identified with those of the past. It should be borne in mind that the division of Hindus into four castes was based merely upon division of labour and that there was no hard and fast rule that one caste should not adopt the profession of another. The so-called untouchables or Depressed Classes do not come under the term Chandalas as Pandit Sen seems to think. Fah Hien also refers to Chandalas. Nothing can be further from the truth. The term 'Chandala', contemplated by the Shastras, means an illegitimate son born of a Brahmin woman with a Shudra paramour. If the number of such erring Brahmin women was so great as to produce such a large community as the Depressed Classes who form nearly one-sixth of the population of India, then such a Brahmin community is not worth having and every Brahmin will be ashamed to call himself as such. The origin of the Depressed Classes through such a source is physically impossible because if the contribution to the Depressed Classes went on at such high rate in olden times, we do not see even a minute fraction thereof taking place nowadays. Nor do we even hear of such cases now. It may be conceded that a few such Chandalas might have been foisted upon the Depressed Classes and the Depressed Classes might have been compelled to take them into their fold and a few such Chandalas might have merged therein. But to brand the whole community of the Depressed Classes as Chandalas is a strange misreading of history and a misinterpretation of the Shastras. Mr. V. Kanakasabai Pillai, in his work *Tamils Eighteen Hundred Years Ago*, published in 1904, has stated that there was a class of people known as "Pulaiyars" even in *pre-Aryan days*, i.e. *pre-Shastric days*. Mr. P.K. Arunachalam Pillai, M.A., of the Annamalai University, in his article of the "Historical Importance of Tholakappiam", has stated the same thing. Mr. P.T. Srinivasa Ayyangar, in his work on pre-Aryan Tamil Culture, has also stated the same thing. Dr. P.S. Subramanya Shastri, M.A. (Oxon.), Principal, Sanskrit College, Tiruvadi, who is now making researches in pre-Aryan Tamil literature, said in one of his lectures at Tiruvadi that there was a class of people known as Pulaiyars even before the advent of the Aryans into Southern India, and he quoted "Chalappadikaram" as his authority therefore. In support of the above, Mr. S. Somasundara Bharathi, M.A., B.L., Professor of Tamil, Annamalai University, in his lecture on "Untouchability and Social Lift", delivered at the said University on the 7th September 1933, states as follows: "The genesis of the system of untouchability was to be found in a historic accident and not in the religious gospel."

Chandalas are mixed castes like the Vaidyas to which class my friend, Pandit Sen, belongs.

M.C. Rajah: I have got records to prove when I say that Vaidyas trace their origin to a degraded Brahmin marrying a low caste Shudra woman. I will not tire the House by reading them, but I will give the references. I will refer my friend to Risley's *People of India*, pp. 116-17, and also the *Census of India Report, Bengal and Sikkim*, vol. V, p. 456. And then there is his great authority, the *Code of Manu*, which says that the Vaidyas are Antyajas, pp. 404-05. Let my Honourable friend read through all these.

Sir, we belong to an independent race and we are an ancient people. We had our own advanced civilization long before the Aryans came to India. We reached the agricultural stage many centuries before when the Aryans were still in the pastoral stage leading the life of nomads.

Sir, my Honourable Friend, Mr. Amar Nath Dutt quoted chapter and verse from a book recently written by Sir Albion Banerjea. I think Sir Albion Banerjea was also connected with the Mysore State. If you refer to the *Indian Antiquary*, vol. 3 of 1874, p. 191, you will see stated there:

> It was well known that the servile castes in Southern India once held far higher positions and were indeed masters of the land on the arrival of the Brahminical races. It is not so well known that the Brahmin, who considers himself polluted by the touch of an Adi-Dravida, will not be allowed to enter the *cheri natham*, or the dwelling of the depressed classes. Should a Brahmin ventures into a *cheri*, water with which cow dung has been mixed is thrown on his head and he is driven out.

It is also stated in the *Indian Antiquary*, 1873, vol. 2:

> The Brahmins of Mysore consider that a great luck will await them if they can manage to pass through the Hiliya (Depressed Classes) quarters of a village unmolested and that, should a Brahmin attempt to enter their quarters, they turn out in a body and slipper him.

These are from records published in 1873 and 1874, and not my own inventions. I can cite instances after instances of the greatness of Adi-Dravidas. Pandit Sen says that untouchability, as practiced in India, is the mildest of all, as if he has traveled throughout the world and studied the conditions of untouchables in other parts of the globe. Let me tell him that a little knowledge is a dangerous thing. Untouchability, as practiced in India, is nowhere found in the globe. In India, untouchability is based on man's arrogance, while in other parts of the globe, it is based on the economic position of a class. In

India, the Depressed Classes owe their miserable condition to social, economic and religious rules operating against them through centuries. The peculiarity in the case of India does not lie in the existence of such a class, but rather in the means employed to keep that class permanently under the blockade set up by the usurpers of power and influence.

Pandit Sen said that if the House passes this Bill, he will create a position in India just like the Mutiny of 1857. No one is afraid of the threats of Pandit Sen, the priest of orthodoxy. If he really means what he says, the Depressed Classes will not in any way lag behind to take up this challenge. But I can assure the House and the Government that we are a peaceful and law abiding people, but we are also a martial race; and if my friend, Pandit Sen, engineers a mutiny and creates confusion in the country, I say, the British Government should either take proper steps to restrain these people or allow both the parties to decide the issue by a trial of strength.

Sir, every human being is divine material, to be made and moulded into the highest perfection, both physical and intellectual. People only exaggerate differences. What are exceptional endowments of a few are in the main due to differences of opportunity. Every individual ought to be given the fullest opportunity to develop his capacities to the utmost. It is opposed to the teachings of our Hindu religion to say that each man must live and die in the environment into which he is born. By birth alone one does not become superior to another, and birth alone did not make caste. The glories of your birth and state are shadows, not substantial things. It is said in the *Mahabharata* that if they found qualities in a Shudra adorning a Brahmin, he should be regarded as a Brahmin, and if they found the qualities of a Shudra in a Brahmin, he should be looked down upon as a Shudra. Only actions of the just smell sweet and blossom in the dust.

Sir, what the law can do for the removal of untouchability is answered by the statement that wherever untouchability is brought up for recognition before the tribunals of the land, it can authorize these tribunals to refuse to recognize untouchability on any ground whatsoever. While it is difficult to enumerate all the forms in which untouchability operates in the life of the country, few facts are more conspicuous than the extent and depth of its pervasiveness in Hindu society. In economic pursuits, in social dealings, in religious worship, even in the satisfaction of the elementary amenities of life of the Hindu people. Any attempt to change the existing state of affairs is immediately resisted; and if the resistance is resented, the arm of the law, through Civil and Criminal Courts, is invoked. Established authority, when appealed to, always takes the side of those who want to maintain the *status quo*. The weapon most often used for this purpose is section 144 of the Criminal Procedure Code so far as the police and the magistracy are concerned. As for the Civil Courts, custom is one of the laws which they have to administer.

As observed by Sir James Colville, in delivering the judgement of the Judicial Committee of the Privy Council in the Ramnad case:

> The duty of a European Judge who is under obligation to administer the Hindu law is not so much as to enquire whether a disputed doctrine is fairly deducible from the earliest authorities, as to ascertain whether it has been received by the particular school which govern the district with which he has to deal and has there been sanctioned by usage for under Hindu Law clear proof of usage will outweigh the written text of law.

This is exactly what Sanatanists are claiming when they want the country to follow not the Shastras as they are, but the Shastras as "traditionally interpreted and followed". The Courts are helping them to do it. That is also why Mr. Mayne is constrained to remark in his book on Hindu Law that the advent of British Courts has helped to arrest the progress of Hindu society and petrify social customs by throwing over them the mantle of judicial recognition with the powerful sanction enforced by the British Courts of Law. It is only for the Honourable Law Member that I am saying this. It is claimed by the caste Hindus that few customs have had longer standing than untouchability. The Courts have recognized untouchability as a legal institution with respect to more than public places and institutions.

It is, therefore, imperative that the Legislature should intervene and say distinctly that the Courts of Law will not recognize this custom any longer. Public recognition that Courts and public institutions will not countenance untouchability will go a long way to help in its removal, both by encouraging the Depressed Classes and by discouraging those who want to preserve it. With these words, I resume my seat.

M.C. Rajah: Sir, I accept the motion.

Hindu Temple Entry Disabilities Removal Bill, 23 August 1934*

M.C. Rajah: Sir, at the outset, let me assure my Honourable Friend, Raja Bahadur Krishnamachariar, that I have great regard for him, not only for his learning, but also for his age. Moreover, he is a Vaishnavite like myself, and let me also tell him that it is stated in Tirumalay that even a Brahmin versed in Vedas and Shastras, if he thinks or speaks low of his devotee, to whatever caste he may belong, instantly becomes a *pulaya*. The punishment meted out to a Brahmin, however learned he may be, for questioning the caste of a Vaishnavite, however low he may be in birth, is the same as the punishment meted out to him for questioning the substance with which the idol in the temple is made of. Raja Bahadur Krishnamachariar has said that God likes everybody. He said that God likes him and Mr. Ghuznavi and I suppose God likes me also.

M.C. Rajah: If God likes us also, then why deny us entrance into His House? Let me answer him from the Vaishnavite sacred books. Shri Ramanuja, nearly 900 years ago, called the Depressed Classes Tirukulathars, men belonging to the Holy caste. Do you deny that also?

M.C. Rajah: I am answering some of the points that he has raised, and that is why I said in connection with Nandanar that the Brahmins give different interpretations to the sacred texts as it suits them. In the interests of the peace and order of the Hindu community and in the interests of the stability of the Hindu society, I want my revered friend, Raja Bahadur Krishnamachariar, to make himself bold and courageous to hug the Depressed Classes.

Sir, this morning, three speakers made three appeals to the House. My friend, Mr. Ranga Iyer, in his speech appealed to the Sanatanists to build separate temples for the Depressed Classes. Sir, let me tell my friend, Mr. Ranga Iyer, that the Depressed Classes do not want separate temples for themselves just as they do not want Separate Electorates.

*Speech in the Central Legislative Assembly.

M.C. Rajah: No, Sir, I am speaking for the Depressed Classes in general. Moreover, the idea of the Depressed Classes is that they want to enter these temples as an integral part of the Hindu society. I come next to my Honourable Friend, the Raja of Kollengode. He appealed to the Government to be neutral in this matter. I welcome that appeal. If only the Government remains neutral, I am sure all the temples will be open to Depressed Classes tomorrow. I then come to my friend, Sir Maulvi Muhammad Yakub, who made a welcome appeal to the Depressed Classes to embrace Islam. I am thankful to him for that appeal. We have also considered that question and my friends are of opinion that we should fight to the last to get the entry into the Hindu temples. Next I come to the Honourable Home Member. Sir, I am very thankful to him for his frank and straightforward reply. I recognize, and my community also recognizes, that in the face of voluminous opinion against the Bill, it is not possible for any Government to support a measure of this kind. Moreover, the Honourable Home Member has mentioned some of the facilities offered to the Depressed Classes in the various Provinces of India. Sir, I have on many occasions, on the floor of this House, thanked the Government for their beneficent activities as regards the Depressed Classes and let me also take this opportunity to say that the elevation of the Depressed Classes in India is due more to his Excellency Lord Willingdon than to any official in India. It was in 1919, when His Excellency was the Governor of Madras, that he inaugurated a Special Department, called the Department of the Protector of the Depressed Classes, which was meant for the amelioration of the condition of the Depressed Classes in that Province. Since that time, that Department had been doing marvelous work. In this connection, I should also like to thank the European Christian Missionaries who have taken up this work. They were the first and the foremost in the field and they were the pioneers in the amelioration work for the Depressed Classes in India. Sir, we are thankful to Government for giving us civic and political privileges and I sincerely hope that the Government will continue to do even greater things for us.

Sir, Mr. Ranga Iyer suggested that there should be a combined car festival in various localities. But, may I inform my friend, Mr. Ranga Iyer, that without the help of the Depressed Classes the car festivals cannot take place.

M.C. Rajah: I am referring to the car festival that takes place throughout India. It is a device, I think, made by the so-called high caste Hindus to allow these Depressed Classes to pull the ropes of the car because they are not strong enough to pull the car themselves. Moreover, it is said that a Brahmin who pulls the rope along with the Depressed Classes should not and ought not to bathe when he goes home because there is no pollution there.

M.C. Rajah: They (Brahmins) do and they do touch the rope. Now, Sir, coming to the merits of the Bill, I should like to make a few observations. Sir, all adverse comments are based on the assumption that the Bill threw open the temples to the Depressed Classes. Nothing of the kind is proposed to be adopted in this Bill. The Bill only makes a provision for a machinery to find out the wishes of the people in the matter. The Bill does not interfere with religion at all. If, in any locality, the caste Hindu worshippers come to believe that they could open the temples to the Depressed Classes, then the Bill enables them to do so. It is merely a Temple Entry Local Option Bill. It is argued by my Honourable Friend, the Rajah Bahadur, that by admitting the Depressed Classes into temples the purity of the idol will be defiled and polluted.

M.C. Rajah: If temples are spiritual power houses and places of purity and sanctity, then they cannot be polluted by the presence of the Depressed Classes. On the other hand by being allowed to come to the presence of God, the Depressed Classes will be purified and spiritualised. (Hear, hear.) If the idea that purity is one which will be affected be correct, then such a powerless purity is not worth anything at all. When Saint Tiruppanalwar was taken to Srirangam temple, the idol was not considered to have been polluted. When the Mohammedan Princess died at the feet of the idol at Malekot, the idol was not considered to have been polluted. As a matter of fact, an image of her was made and installed under the feet of the idol of Ramapriya for daily worship as Tulukka Nachiar (Mohammedan Goddess Consort). A similar idol for this goddess is in the Srirangam temple. Sir, temples are the home of God and in God's home nobody could be treated as an untouchable, since God is the common father of all. (Hear, hear.) The Hindu temples play a most important part in the life of the masses. Among the Hindus there is more devotion to God than in any other people, and, in the lower classes especially, the devotion is stronger than in the higher classes. Though this devotion may be blind, yet it is powerful. Temple worship as an institution came into existence for the purpose of providing for the community as a whole a mode of approach to the Supreme, suitable to the understanding of the unintellectual and unphilosophically minded. To men of higher understanding going to a temple is absolutely of no value; as my Honourable Friend, Mr. Ranga Iyer, himself had said. When they go to a temple and discharge a function connected with it, they do so for the benefit of the community as a whole. So, I ask, why keep out the real men for whom all this is intended and enacted? Why then rob the lowly among you of what is their due by right of true benefit? Is temple worship not the worship of the Almighty God? Did the God of the Universe disclose His form only for some specified classes to the exclusion of others? Is there no room for real worship on the part of these simple devotees? Are there not innumerable instances where such prohibitions have not been put into practice? Many of the saints of South India have been originally persons of the Depressed Classes and have been admitted into the temple and the idols of some of them are now being worshipped by the most orthodox Brahmin. I tell you, Sir, to decline wholesale spiritual food to the poor innocent people is a great crime against God and humanity for which you shall have to answer before the Lord Who makes no distinction between the members of His creation. You say that the campaign should be diverted towards the removal of their economic disabilities. Yes, that is true. The question of temple entry is only one of the many items in the campaign for the eradication of the curse of untouchability. If untouchability is corrected, the economic uplift would follow. The opening of temples to the Depressed Classes will give a new life and a new hope to them. You call them unclean. Their unclean habits are entirely due to you, as you keep them away and give them unclean quarters and not give them light, water, enough to drink and bathe. You are the sinners. You have degraded them and then have the audacity to use their very degradation against their rise. Not contented with your past unrighteous actions, you have now the audacity to say that they are not anxious for the reforms. In judging a community and its aspirations you should realize that it speaks through the most enlightened of its members. Sir, in this connection my Honourable friend, the Raja Bahadur, has quoted some opinion from one Mr. Ratnavelu Pillai who, he says, holds the position of a District Judge. Equally eminent men of the same standing have given quite contrary opinions. Does he accept those opinions also?

M.C. Rajah: I am not giving way.

M.C. Rajah: I am not at all asking for answers from my Honourable

Friend. I am simply meeting the points raised by my Honourable Friend. I hope he will not be excited. Another thing I wish to say is that my Honourable Friend just now said that the Depressed Classes think that their going into the Hindu temples will upset their whole family life and so on. He also said that the Depressed Classes say that they would be visited by diseases if they enter a Hindu temple. Sir, this reminds me of a story which I am sure you, Sir, also know. In a village there was a Depressed Class man who was serving under a zamindar. The wife of this Depressed Class man gave birth to a son and his father christened the child as "Perumal", meaning God. Then one day the zamindar went to the village and heard the father of the boy calling his son as "Perumal". The zamindar was taken aback. He asked the Depressed Class man as to what he meant by calling his boy as "Perumal". He said: "You, fellow, give your son some other name. If you call him "Perumal" the wrath of God will be on you and the boy will die tomorrow. So call him by some other name, such as black or white or mud or clay or anything else". The Depressed Class man was an intelligent fellow and next day he called his son "Peria Perumal" meaning Great God. Next day when the zamindar went to that village to see his Depressed Class servant, he was nonplussed to find that his son was called "Peria Perumal". Similarly, my Honourable Friend, the Raja Bahadur, says that if the Depressed Classes go to a temple they will be infested with all sorts of diseases. Sir, I have got very little time now and so I can not narrate at this late hour all the anecdotes that I have got in my possession. I am very sorry to say that these so-called Sanatanists do not know these people. One who had moved with these untouchables in their cheris, mohallas and slums would have found in them dissatisfaction of their lot rankling in their hearts, a really burning desire and an unquenchable thirst for their amelioration – their education, economic advance and the satisfaction of their spiritual hunger. In this connection, with reference to the quotation which my Honourable Friend, the Raja Bahadur, gave from Mr. Ratnavelu Pillai's opinion, let me also tell the Raja Bahadur that a great seer, the Saint Ramanuja, nearly 300 years ago, hugged the Depressed Classes. Sri Ramanuja's heart surged with love and compassion for these unfortunate people. Ramanuja devoted himself entirely to the service of the Lord by serving man, His own image and has always been a friend of the poor, the needy and the helpless and genuinely interested in the redemption of all the downtrodden. It was he that first worked for the amelioration of their condition and it was he that first wanted to take them into his fold. Sir, these episodes are somewhat worthy of note. Ramanuja specially warned his disciples against pride of caste, pride of wealth and pride of learning as the three great dangers for the unwary to fall into perdition. When Ramanuja was old and weak, he used to lean on somebody's shoulders and walk into the river for his daily ablutions. While going to the bath he used to lean on one of his Brahmin disciples but while returning after his bath he would walk leaning on the shoulder of one of his Depressed Class disciples. The orthodox people were greatly incensed at this practice. They said he may lean on this low caste man before bath but why should he lean on him after bath. Ramanuja said, "I lean on this low-born person when returning after ablutions because this is the way to wash off my pride of birth which I cannot remove by ablution with water."

Sir, how different from the superstitions of his present-day followers! It is an irony of history that among those who claim to represent Sri Ramanuja's authority and to follow the creed of Ramanuja are some of the stoutest opponents to the movement which he initiated 900 years ago. . . .

M.C. Rajah: Very good, Sir. This one episode is enough. I have many with me. Raja Bahadur being a Vaishnavite he must know them. We have been witnessing, Sir, during the past few months a tidal wave on the surface of Hindu life, Sanatanists holding meetings throughout the country vehemently opposing this measure, to thwart and defeat the legitimate demands of a vast majority of their fellow caste-men. Sir, I welcome this unrest among the Sanatanists. It is a part of the plan of the world that some kind of unrest should be the precursor of everything that is most useful and beneficent. Just call to mind how the setting in of the rains which are needful for the support of every form of life and of all that makes natural life enjoyable is always preceded by storm or other forms of atmospheric disturbance. I cherish indeed the hope that it may be instrumental in making India what the God of all the nations intends it to become. The fact that a cause is righteous does not guarantee its immediate success. All history testifies to this. The final triumph of good causes is for the most part long delayed. Even should our path immediately before us be marked not only by delay but by disaster for a time, I am quite confident that our cause will conquer in the end. I trust that it will conquer in our own hands, but even if it does not, yet in worthier hands than ours hereafter.

I shall conclude by telling this House the chief ground on which my confidence is based. "Blessed are the meek for they shall inherit the earth." Observe that this promise to the meek is not of some mystical possession in the clouds, it is not even the Kingdom of Heaven. That also may be theirs, but what the saying tells of is the inheritance, the possession, the rule and the guardianship of this familiar earth. Sir, man looketh on the countenance, but God looketh on the heart. Lincoln, when he overheard a woman in the crowd exclaim, "Why, what a common looking fellow he is!", retorted, "God likes common looking fellows or he would not have made so many of them!".

Sir, the greatest religion is the religion of love. That is the be-all and end-all of all Vaishnavism, that is the creed of Shaivites too. Disinterested service to one's fellowmen is the essence of the message of Madhava to mankind. You probably remember, Sir, the story of Abu Ben Adhem. He awoke one night from a deep dream of peace and saw within his room the beautiful vision of an angel writing something in a book of gold. When asked what she was writing, the angel replied: "The names of those who love the Lord". "And is mine one?" asked Abu. "Nay, not so", said the angel. "Then write me down as one that loves his fellow men" said Abu. The angel wrote and departed. When next night she returned and showed the names of those whom the love of God had blessed, lo! Abu Ben Adhem's name led all the rest.

Sir, in conclusion, let me remind this House that the first efforts of the man who means to build a tower is directed not upward but downward. He digs out deep foundations before he puts a single stone or brick upon brick. If he acted otherwise he could never have a tower to show. That is what we have done now and I hope on a future occasion a measure of this kind will be passed.

Provincial Excise, 14 September 1937*

M.C. Rajah: Mr. Speaker, Sir, I must first congratulate my Hon. Friends the Prime Minister and Mr. V.L. Muniswami Pillai for the bold step that they have taken to introduce prohibition in our province. All that I want to say is that immediate total prohibition should be introduced. The talk of prohibition was in the air all along, until that great man, Mahatma Gandhi, took up that issue and made it a live issue in our land. Until then, there was mere talk of prohibition, local option, temperance and all such things. Therefore, we are greatly indebted to Mahatma Gandhi for the inspiration he has given to this movement. We are also thankful to the Hon. Mr. Rajagopalachari for faithfully carrying out that policy. Through Gandhiji it has become not only a live issue but practical politics.

Prohibition has been my cry for a very long time, ever since 1917. The Hon. Prime Minister will bear this out. It was in the year 1920, during the Minto-Morley Reforms, I moved a resolution in the Legislative Council asking the government to close down toddy and liquor shops on the roads largely used by labourers proceeding to or coming from centres of labour. But I could not succeed. I hope under the present Government I will be able to see that object achieved.

All that I want to say is that prohibition should be started all over the Presidency, not only in Salem. Especially, if you want to try prohibition, you will have to try it in a city like Madras, and that would be the proper test for you to introduce prohibition all over the Presidency. Then, you will be able to carry public opinion with you, and that will go a great deal to help you in this policy. I do not believe in piece-meal introduction in one place. Prohibition requires a big step to be taken all over. I hope steps would be taken to reduce the number of shops at present existing by half or one-third by the next budget and the remaining shops might be dealt with in the following years. By this process we will be able to introduce prohibition throughout the province. I know, Sir, that liquor shops have been

*Speech in Madras Legislative Assembly.

located close to the places inhabited by the Depressed Classes and the labourers. The Government ought to do something to suppress this evil.

The Government ought to do something to suppress this evil; they should respect the feelings of the people; it should be the business of Government to keep a high sense of duty, and therefore it is absolutely necessary for them to change their present policy. I hope for great things under the present Government; prohibition, untouchability, moneylending and races, all go together; they form one organic unit. Prohibition will certainly raise the standard of living and with that the standard of the people will rise. Government has in the past made many laws to protect the poor from the moneylender. But if they could abolish the liquor shops they would be conferring a greater boon on them than any number of laws intended for their relief. Making money out of the vice of people should not be the policy of the Government. It is for the furtherance of the morality and purity of the nation that we want prohibition to be introduced. To rescue people from the grip of misery and ruin is a noble mission. As regards revenue, we can in the meantime find out new sources for meeting the deficit.

One thing I want to mention. Side by side with progressive prohibition, we must also introduce certain attractions for the people who are accustomed to drink. That is a most vital thing. I will suggest one attraction for the consideration of the Ministry. Side by side with taverns there should be drinking restaurants, where a sort of rice conjee with sambhar and sharp pickles could be sold cheap. At the start by way of demonstration they should be doled out free. Government must help the local bodies as well as private people with certain grants to give this conjee free for a few weeks. I understand that the present Government is going to introduce a Bill – I have not seen the Bill; but I have also given notice of a Bill – for introducing total prohibition within three years; and I hope the Government will embody some of my suggestions in their Bill, so that it may be acceptable to all sections of the House.

Bill to Provide for the Removal of Social Disabilities Among Certain Classes of Hindus, 29 September 1937*

M.C. Rajah: Sir, I beg to move for leave to introduce a Bill to provide for the removal of social disabilities among certain classes of Hindus.

Mr. Speaker: As there is no opposition, the leave is granted.

M.C. Rajah: Sir, I introduce the Bill.

SUBSTITUTION OF DISTRIBUTIVE SYSTEM OF VOTING FOR CUMULATIVE SYSTEM

M.C. Rajah: Sir, I move the resolution standing in my name, viz.:

This assembly recommends to the Government to make a recommendation to the Secretary of State for India to do away with the cumulative system of voting in the general constituencies of the Madras Legislative Assembly, wherein seats are reserved for the scheduled castes and to substitute the system of distributive voting instead.

Sir, in commending this resolution to this House, I need not make a long speech. The main object of the Poona Pact is to prevent any division in the Hindu community and to preserve Hindu solidarity so as to keep the scheduled castes within the Hindu fold. The cumulative system of election, Sir, is quite contrary to the provisions of the Poona Pact. It is human nature, Sir, that communities always tend to strengthen their own representation. As a matter of fact, in the recent elections, some of us observed that caste Hindu voters were always inclined to plump their votes in favour of caste Hindu candidates, and the scheduled caste voters were also inclined to plump their votes in favour of the scheduled caste candidates. This, Sir, is quite contrary to the essence of the Poona Pact. Moreover, Sir, the cumulative method of voting lends itself to new forms of corruption. In as much as a candidate was permitted to canvass not only for one

*Speech in Madras Legislative Assembly.

vote but also for all the votes which a voter was qualified to give, it was a greater incentive for a rich man to buy up all the votes, and also it was a greater incentive for a voter to sell his votes for a higher price. Hon. Members who are sitting here are all legislators who are subject to passing through an election. As a matter of fact, this system of cumulative voting has been criticized by most of the Hon. Members during the last elections and even before. Therefore, Sir, it is not necessary for me to explain the system of elections and its disadvantages. The only system which will be of advantage to all and which will carry out the intentions of the Poona Pact is the system of distributive voting, whereby the caste Hindu voter will be forced to give one vote in favour of a Depressed Class candidate, and so also the scheduled caste voter will be forced to give one of his votes to the caste Hindu candidate. If this system is adopted there will be greater cordiality, there will be more friendly feelings between the Harijan voters, the Harijan candidates, the caste Hindu voters and the caste Hindu candidates. On these grounds, I commend this resolution for the acceptance of this House.

M.C. Rajah: Sir, my task has become easier, for this motion before the House has been supported by all sections of the House and by all sexes also here. Sir, attempts have been made in the past to do away with this system of election. As a matter of fact, when I appeared before the Provincial Franchise Committee, I objected to the present system; when again I appeared before the Hammond Committee, I put forward my views advocating the distributive system. Then, in the Central Legislative Assembly, we tabled a motion favouring the introduction of this system of distributive voting. Afterwards, I think my Hon. Friend, Mr. V.M. Ramaswamy Mudaliyar, also gave notice of a motion to that effect in the Madras Legislative Council. Sir, we have not succeeded; now, we find greater support. Since we are all creatures of the last elections, it has been our experience at the last election that this system is disastrous and that opinion is very much stronger in favour of the distributive system. The present system of election cuts at the very root of the Poona Pact and instead of unifying the different sections of the community, it disintegrates the society; and that is the very reason why we are all against this system. My friend, Mr. Muniswami Pillai, has already pointed out how we have been trying to get rid of this system and how we have not succeeded. Our Premier has said that different sections of the House and different parties of the House and all the Harijan members have supported this motion. Myself, Mr. Muniswami Pillai, Diwan Bahadur Srinivasan and Rao Sahib Guruswami, have all fought against this system of election, and we now hope, Sir, that the present Government which is a popular Government, representing particularly the poor Harijan people, will take action in this matter and request the Government of India to immediately give effect to this system of distributive voting.

Sir, I think to-day is a Harijan day, because I had the good fortune of moving this morning a motion for leave to introduce a Bill to provide for the removal of social disabilities among certain classes of Hindus; and now, Sir, I am glad that the House has unanimously and universally supported this most important motion which I have moved now. I have nothing more to say, Sir, except to thank the various parties, on behalf of the Harijan community, for their support to this motion.

A Bill to Provide for the Removal of Civil Disabilities Among Certain Classes of Hindus, 17 August 1938*

M.C. Rajah: Sir, I move that the Bill to remove the disabilities of the so-called Depressed Classes in regard to entry into Hindu temples be referred to a select committee.

I shall give the names of the members later on. Mr. Speaker, Sir, in moving this motion I wish to remind the House that my Hon. Friend Dr. Subbarayan moved a resolution in the Madras Legislative Council on the 1st of November 1932, six years ago, for temple entry for Depressed Classes. The resolution reads as follows:

This Council recommends to the Government that they may be pleased –

(1) to recognize the strong and growing public feeling in the Hindu community that disabilities hitherto imposed by usage on certain classes of the community in regard to social intercourse and common worship at temples should be removed and justice rendered to them;

(2) to take advantage of the great impetus given in this respect by the settlement arrived at Poona among the leaders of the communities and the consequent agitation in the country that places of public worship should be thrown open to the so-called Depressed Classes; and

(3) to bring up legislation setting at rest and removing, if necessary, the doubts and disabilities which trustees and other persons holding authority in the administration of Hindu temples feel in regard to throwing them open to the said classes, with necessary safeguards for the making of regulations for maintaining order and cleanliness in temples and also the performance of ceremonies according to the usage of the temples.

This resolution was accepted by the Council without a dissentient voice. Dr. Subbarayan in his opening speech spoke as follows:

Mr. President, this resolution is not being brought forward by me as a mere pious wish to admit our depressed brethren into temples. If this resolution is accepted by the House, I mean to go on with legislation in this respect also, if the Government do not seem to do it. Because, Sir, I do feel that the time has come when we must recognize the growing public feeling in this

*Speech in Madras Legislative Assembly.

country and also we must recognize the sentiment of our depressed brethren. We cry hoarse about nationalism and nationality.

Mr. Speaker: Is the Hon. Member going to read the whole speech?

M.C. Rajah: No, Sir. I am going to read only the relevant portion.

I would like to ask Hon. Gentleman sitting on the other side as well as my Hon. Friends on this side of the House whether this cry is going to be only of nationalism for ourselves, so that we, the higher castes, may dominate this country, or is it going to be a common nationalism by which we are all going to be one with the growing sentiment of our depressed brethren that their place in the Hindu community should be recognized. I do not think we can get away from the fact that in spite of all that has been done during the last half a century by reformers in this country, we, caste Hindus have not done our duty to our depressed brethren.

I would like to read more, Mr. Speaker, but I do not want to do so.

True to his words Dr. Subbarayan presented a Bill to the Government of Madras on the 1st of December 1932. This was the Madras Temple Entry Bill. The principle and the object of the Bill were the same as of the Bill now before this House. That Bill would now have been on the statute book and there would have been no need for the present Bill if the Governor-General had accorded sanction for the introduction of the Bill in the Madras Legislative Council. But he accorded sanction for the introduction of the Bill in the Central Legislative Assembly, where as you all know, myself and Mr. C.S. Ranga Ayyar introduced it in 1933. I was not able to pilot the Bill through as I had left the Central Assembly and entered this House.

Let me point at the outset that this Bill is not a piece of compulsory legislation. It only provides for the practical expression of the people's desire when they wish to allow Depressed Class people to join them in worship in their temples. To describe this as an interference with religion is to misrepresent it altogether.

May I request you to read the Bill carefully? The Bill does not throw open the doors of temples to Depressed Classes all at once, whether the worshippers like it or not. This is a kind of Local Option Bill for removing the legal impediments to reform and puts no compulsion whatever on the caste Hindus. The Bill seeks to give every congregation of Hindu worshippers the right of deciding the question of opening the temples to Harijans instead of being dictated to by a minority.

In this country usages and customs have become hardened into law and reform has become difficult. The British courts and British law have enforced the established usages and customs of the Hindus and prevented the natural growth and evolution of Hindu customs. Any departure from the custom has been prevented and penalized by the law. Reformers, when they obtain for their proposals the consent of the majority of people in any area, have been unable to give effect to their object, if even a single dissentient rushed to the courts to block the reform. I need not say that customs which have become part and parcel of law cannot be altered except by legal enactment. Such being the state of the law, it becomes necessary to seek the aid of legislation. This Bill seeks to enable Hindu opinion when it has become liberal enough to be translated into action, to express itself without any legal impediment. In fact we want the help of the courts to be refused to the practice of untouchability which, as you all know, is interference with the elementary rights of a vast section of the Hindu community. To check this interference, cannot be described as interference at all.

This Bill is intended to create a machinery for the education and ascertainment of public opinion and for giving practical expression to it, where opinion is predominantly in favour of the reform. If in any locality the majority of the caste Hindu worshippers decide to open any of their temples in that area to the Depressed Classes, this Bill enables them to do so, even though a small minority may object to it. If the majority of the people do not favour this view, the Bill will compel nobody to throw open the temples to the Depressed Classes.

I am against coercion of any kind in matters of social and religious rights whether the party concerned is a majority or a minority. No doubt minorities should be protected, but when the minority is coercing the majority we need protection for the majority. What we want legislation for is for the removal of the existing legal obstacles. Laws could be changed only by laws. An act for the removal of the impediment is but the barest justice due to the Depressed Classes.

I have pointed out that public opinion has already been registered by the vote of the Madras Legislative Council in 1932. The Congress has always advocated Temple Entry to Depressed Classes and the Bill gives effect to a vital of the Congress programme as embodied in the Poona Pact.

Sir, the Tamil Nadu Congress on the 19th January 1938 met at a place called Batlagundu and unanimously passed a resolution that a Bill like this should be passed in this Assembly. The resolution was published in the 'Hindu' of the 19th January. The resolution asked that suitable legislation be undertaken to remove all legal obstacles in the way of Harijans entering Hindu temples and urged upon the Government and the Legislature to take the necessary steps in this matter. Sir, I need not again repeat to you the statement of Mahatma Gandhi with reference to public opinion in this matter because I have already quoted that in the speech I made while referring my other Bill to the select committee.

Temples, Sir, are meant to be spiritual power houses and places of purity and sanctity. Temples are places consecrated for devotion and worship. They were intended to be available to all devotees in spite of differing manners and customs, and can not be closed against even the most wretched amongst us who stand in greatest need of religious consolation and purification. Temples are not the sole property of any section of Hindus. Temples are the most catholic of Hindu institutions. Caste distinctions should be forgotten inside temples. Temples should be unifying forces and not disintegrating factors.

In the second statement, dated 5th November 1932, issued by Mahatma Gandhi soon after his memorable fast, he expressed his foremost desire that there should be a complete merger of the Depressed Classes with caste-Hindus. He wrote thus:

> What I wanted and what I still want is their complete merger in the caste-Hindus and that of the latter in the former. It is my deliberate opinion, not likely to be altered by any fresh fact that may come to light, that the more the suppressors give the suppressed the more they gain.

Sir, the people on whose behalf I approach this House with this Bill are not treated as out-castes by Hindus alone. The bar that has been put upon them in the Hindu society affects the psychology of other classes as well. The Depressed Classes are treated as unfit for close association by the Mussalmans, Christians and other communities, among whom they live. I hear Mrs. Yakub Hasan say, "no". Mrs. Yakub Hasan does not know the existing conditions in the village parts. Sir, the removal of this disability is therefore not merely a Hindu question, but a national question. So long as the Hindus act in the spirit of the Poona Pact, the merger will take place and the Depressed Classes will be numbered amongst them. If at any time there should be a departure from the spirit of that Pact, they will become and behave as a separate community, and this will not be their fault, and the Hindus will have to thank themselves for it. I have only to call your attention to the state of things in Bengal where the scheduled classes remain apart from the Hindus and their strength is cast on this side or that. The Temple Entry Bill which I had the honour to introduce and which I have no doubt you will accept and pass into an Act, is a kind of social and religious insurance against any such fate overtaking us in this Presidency.

I request this House, Sir, to give its considered opinion to this Bill and pass this motion without any dissentient voice.

M.C. Rajah: Sir, I am amazed at the attitude of the Hon. Prime Minister Mr. C. Rajagopalachari. Now, I would like to place certain facts before this House. Six years ago my Hon. Friend Mr. C. Rajagopalachari drafted this Bill and sent it to me.

Mr. Speaker: Is not the microphone working?

M.C. Rajah: No Sir; even the lights on the other side are off. Sir, these lights and these phones are not working as they also feel the gravity of the situation. (Laughter) They also resent the attitude of the Hon. the Prime Minister today.

Sir, the Hon. the Prime Minister has anticipated what I am going to say and he has replied to it all in his own inimitable way. He says that I had introduced this Bill with his consent and at his request. Quite so: but what was the request? When he handed over the draft Bill to me, he told me and he told the country that the country was ripe for this measure. And now, six years afterwards, he comes and asks me to withdraw the Bill or to withhold the Bill. Is it right for him to do so, Sir? I have been deceived in this matter. I believed what the Hon. the Premier said then: I took him at his word that the country was ripe for this reform. I can prove that in a minute. I introduced the Bill with great trepidation. I had to fight the Government of India and I had to fight some of my Hon. Friends in the Indian Legislative Assembly including the Hon. Member Raja Bahadur Krishnamachariar who was then the leader of the Central Party of which I was the Secretary. Why did I do it? I did it because I believed what the Congressmen said, namely, that they knew the country well and that the country was behind them. They said that public opinion was ripe then. Did not my Hon. Friend the Premier tell me that public opinion was ripe then? Did he not tell me that this measure cannot wait for a day more? I will quote chapter and verse to prove this. I have got all the papers with me. Now, he comes and tells me, "Withdraw the Bill". And what is the suggestion? The suggestion is that it can come up in the next session and then be killed. Is it not so, Sir? If I withhold the Bill now, what is going to happen to it? The Bill is not going to come before the House again. He is going to supplant it by another smaller Bill.

"Sir, six years ago the Hon. Mr. C. Rajagopalachari told me that the country from the Himalayas to Cape Comorin was ripe for a Bill like mine. Did he not say so, Sir? But now when I want to introduce this Bill, not for the whole of India, but for a smaller area, for our province, he comes and says 'No, no, you cannot do it.' But what does he say? He says: 'Let us have a Bill for Timbuctoo or Malabar and not for the whole province.' Sir, I am surprised that my Hon. Friend Mr. Bhaktavatsalam Mudaliyar is laughing."

M.C. Rajah: I am standing here all alone and they think they can play their tricks with me. Sir, I have been subjected to too many interruptions. For ages we have suffered like this. When we want to place our grievances before the House, they shout and howl. Why should they do it? They think by this, they can suppress me. They are mistaken.

M.C. Rajah: Sir, only the wearer of the shoe knows where it pinches. Hon. Members do not know to what position they have driven me to-day by asking me to withhold the Bill. They have no feelings. Swami Sahajanandam feels with me and the Harijan members on the other side also feel like me, but they cannot express their feelings; as my Hon. Friend Mr. Prakasam said just now, they are under discipline. You have no business to exercise discipline over the Harijan members there. They joined the Congress subject to certain conditions laid down by Mahatma Gandhi. I am not going to touch my Hon. Friend Mr. Muniswami Pillai. He is under discipline. He will clear out. . . .

M.C. Rajah: I was making reference to a speech which Mr. Muniswami Pillai made just now. I said that I am not going to criticize him, because he belongs to my community. I am not going to criticize him also for the reason given out by the Hon. Mr. Prakasam just now, viz., that the Harijan members are under the discipline of the Congress party. . . .

M.C. Rajah: I would like you, Sir, to get the reporter read his notes. Anyhow, Sir, what I wanted to tell you was that when Mr. Mahboob Ali Baig spoke on this motion and said that there were three members who could speak on the subject but dare not do so, the Hon. Mr. Prakasam said: "No, they dare not speak, because they are under discipline.". . .

M.C. Rajah: Sir, my friend, Mr. C. Rajagopalachari always speaks in parables, and to-day he said he who wants to go into the jungle must go wearing shoes and he who wants to ascend a mountain must take with him a stick. He is quite right, Sir, if the mountains and the jungles are actual mountains and jungles; but Sir, as regards the mountains and jungles which we are going to pass through and ascend, with reference to this Bill, I say, we have cleared the weeds already and made the paths safe. Public opinion has been created during the last twenty years. There are no weeds, no wild beasts also, and therefore we can walk there quickly and safely without shoes or sticks. Sir, then, what did he say? My friend, Mr. Rajagopalachari said: this was not action taken by the whole Cabinet. Till last week he was in favour of the Bill. But only last week, something flashed through his brain. I do not know what it was and immediately he called the Cabinet and said, "you must all agree to this Bill being withdrawn". If this is the considered opinion of the Cabinet and also the considered opinion of his party, I can very well understand it. But I cannot understand this flashing through his brain. Something flashed through his brain! Then he says: "Mr. M.C. Rajah must withdraw his Bill," and gives his command like Hitler, "Do not budge an inch." Sir, something might flash through his mind next week. I do not know what it would be. It may probably be to kill this Bill. Flashes might be coming to him every month, nay, every week. We are not going to accommodate ourselves to these flashes. Sir, he said that he is introducing prohibition, district after district. It is all right. We should like to know the reason for his going to confine the Bill to Malabar only. He says, it is not rupees, annas, pies, but difficulty. At one time he says rupees, annas, pies. At another time, he says "No; it is not rupees, annas, pies but difficulty." Which is true? Whenever it suits him, it is rupees, annas, pies. Otherwise, not money, but difficulty. But here he says it is not rupees, annas, pies but time. I can also say the same thing over and over again. And then, Sir, as regards the Government piloting a Bill, I should like the House to know that before I introduced this Bill, I sent a letter to my friend, Mr. Rajagopalachari on the 7th of January 1937 in which I wrote. . . .

M.C. Rajah: I never said I was anxious to introduce the Bill. I offered my Bill to Government to take it as the Government Bill. I preferred the Government taking up the Bill and piloting it as their own, so that they may pass it as a Congress measure before the end of the official year. It would give me great pleasure to support it as such on behalf of the Depressed Classes. Sir, I was not at all anxious to pilot the Bill myself. But for his asking me to do so in the Legislative Assembly, I would not have done it. Sir, let me read his reply to my letter. It is this: "Yours of 7th January. You may depend upon me to do all that is useful and good for your community. So you need not be anxious about such legislation as you want to get through. There will be no non-official day in the present short sitting, but I shall provide you facilities after the budget is over. I do not approve of your amendment of the Criminal Procedure Code." Sir, I wanted to introduce a Bill to amend the Criminal Procedure Code also, because the Premier said that he was giving facilities for this Bill. . . .

M.C. Rajah: And then, Sir, if the Hon. Premier had told me that he was opposed to the introduction of the Bill, I would not have introduced it. Because he gave me every hope till last week, I was sure of his support. And then, Sir, with reference to this Bill, I asked the Premier to give me facilities to introduce the Bill, and at the same time move a motion for consideration. For that the Premier wrote on the 18th March as follows: "The Government after careful consideration are of the opinion that it would be desirable that the normal procedure should be followed in this case, that is to say, the leave of the Legislative Assembly should be obtained for the introduction of your Bill." So I introduced the Bill last session. And I am now bringing the motion for reference to the Select Committee. Moreover, Sir, I should like to tell this House that I brought this Bill in this Assembly at the request or invitation of the Premier. It was on the 15th May 1937, just before the Premier took up office, speaking at Tanjore to the Tanjore Circle Temple Committee. The Hon. Premier said, it is reported in the Madras Mail, that he could not rest at peace for a minute longer without securing temple entry for Harijans and invited Rao Bahadur M.C. Rajah to introduce a Bill in the Madras Assembly and assured him of popular support for the measure. . . .

M.C. Rajah: I will take your ruling, Sir. Now the Premier says, the time is not ripe and therefore, I must withdraw the Bill. May I ask, Sir, how often has not public opinion been ignored and even set at defiance when you were anxious to pass a Bill on which you have set your heart. What about the Prohibition Bill? What about the

Debtors' Relief Act or compulsory introduction of Hindi in schools? Did you heed to public opinion? Is there not agitation now through out the country? There will be agitation of every kind. What sort of public opinion does the Premier want? Is it the enlightened public opinion or the ignorant public opinion or the orthodox public opinion? Sir, are our rights to be sacrificed simply because a set of people priding themselves on imaginary religious superiority are to be humoured and their so-called religious scruples which are really fetters with which they seek to enslave us to be cajoled and left undisturbed? Is the Congress Government, Sir, in order to pacify the religious scruples of a handful of orthodox Hindus going to sacrifice the rights and privileges of the Depressed Classes who are the ancient sons of the soil? Is caste arrogance to receive Congress recognition? Is the Congress Government going to countenance the doctrine of touch pollution? There seems to be, Sir, absolutely no justification for the Congress government to ask me to withdraw this Bill. This Bill has been most widely circulated and public opinion has been perceived in its favour. You are anxious, Sir, that I should finish. I am not going into details. I wanted to tell you the reason why we subscribed to the Poona Pact. We thought there will be total removal of untouchability. That was the promise given to us then. But now, Sir, we understand from the attitude of the Government that the Poona Pact was intended only as a political manoeuvre and not for the eradication of the wrongs. When the Poona Pact was signed, Mahatma Gandhi said: "But if these vital conditions of the Poona Pact are not carried out by the caste Hindus, could I possibly live to face God and Man? I ventured even to tell Dr. Ambedkar, Rao Bahadur Rajah and other friends belonging to the suppressed group that they should regard me as a hostage for the due fulfillment by caste Hindus of the conditions of the pact." . . .

M.C. Rajah: I should like to know if Gandhiji was consulted in the matter, or the Working Committee? Because Gandhiji is the central figure in this. I should like to know this, Sir. May I pause for a reply? . . .

M.C. Rajah: The Hon. the Premier said that there is toughness, ignorance and something more. I want to know when he found out that there is toughness and ignorance. I have been under the impression that there has been this toughness and ignorance for the last so many centuries. Only the rigour of the toughness and ignorance has been gradually waning. My friend Mr. Prakasam said and my

Friend Mr. Muthiah Chettiyar appealed to me, "when 250 members ask you to withdraw the Bill; why not you do it?" May I tell them that 250 million people asked me to pilot this Bill in the Legislative Assembly? If I now accede to the request of 250 people here what am I to tell my friends outside? The whole country from the Himalayas to Cape Comorin asked me to pilot this Bill and I did it. If to-day 250 members here ask me to kill this Bill, am I to kill it? Am I to be played with like this, Sir, and be subjected to the whims and fancies of 250 members here? There is only one more point, Sir, and I will finish, because you are anxious that I should finish soon. The Hon. the Premier said that in my district of Chingleput during a fire-walking ceremony, an Adi-Dravida was killed. True. May I also tell him, that in my district, in my own place, Alandur, during fire-walking ceremonies Depressed Classes are allowed to participate in the ceremony. If, Sir, we are going to withhold this Bill now henceforth caste people will say, "you dare not come in here". Some of the temples as you all know are now thrown open to the Depressed Classes. If you are going to withhold the Bill to-day, do you know what will happen to-morrow? Caste people will not allow the Depressed Classes hereafter to enter into these temples and will say "You dare not come in here; you go to Malabar." Is it right, Sir, to withdraw the Bill? Are you not going back? Where is the plighted word given to me and to my people? . . .

M.C. Rajah: Sir, Mr. Prakasam is a very good friend of mine. Three or four years ago when he came to Simla he paid me a visit and assured me of his support for all these measures. But to-day, Sir, he has disappointed me and Mr. Prakasam is under discipline.

Then again, Sir, coming to the question of the Harijan Members, I must certainly make an appeal to them. The Harijan members of the Congress party are all members of my community. I do not attack their present attitude, because the Hon. Minister for Agriculture has said that they are under discipline. (Hon. Members: he never said so.) I mean the Hon. the Minister for Revenue.

(At this stage the Hon. Mr. V.L. Muniswami Pillai rose in his seat.)

I tell you Mr. Muniswami Pillai, I am not going to touch you. Sir, during the elections when the Congress party wanted the Harijans to join them, there were negotiations; and then, Sir, I wrote to Mahatma Gandhi on that point.

M.C. Rajah: Sir, I am not at all interfering with any other party's discipline. I am only referring to my Harijan party discipline and the condition that Mahatma Gandhi gave me. Mahatma Gandhi said that the Depressed Classes might join the Congress on certain conditions. Why did those Hon. Members join the Congress? (An Hon. Member: 'But you did not join'.) Ah: I did not join. Yes. Because I wanted to test the sincerity of the Congressmen still further. I have tested them now. I will test them further. Sir, the condition is this.

M.C. Rajah: Sir, I am not saying anything about the bulls which the party might have issued, but I am only concerned about my friends, the members of the Depressed Classes belonging to the Congress party, because I was in a way instrumental in making some of them join the Congress, because I then agreed with Mahatma Gandhi and his conditions. The condition is this: Harijan members of the Congress party will have full freedom of opinion and vote in respect of matters specially affecting the Harijan community where they differ from the policy adopted by the party should any such difference arise. I say this, Sir, because some of the Harijan Congress members came and told me that they were not in agreement with the Premier. I may tell them, Sir, that they are not bound by the discipline of the party in this matter, because they have joined the party only on the condition I have mentioned and they are therefore free to vote with me if they agree with me. . . .

M.C. Rajah: Only one word more, Sir. I am not going to be a party to this unholy alliance. I am not going to withdraw this Bill nor withhold this Bill till the next session. If I withhold the Bill what will happen? If my Bill is not going to function what is the use of keeping it in agony for one month more and then killing it? If you want to kill it, kill now. Why keep the Bill in agony?

Sir, this is the last thing I want to say. I expected very many things from this Congress party and at one stage I even co-operated with it in the hope. . . .

M.C. Rajah: Sir, but for our Interim Ministry you would not have been here to-day. We paved the way for you; we made you accept the Ministry. Sir, I expected many good things for my people from the Congress. In the first attempt I made here I am disappointed. The other Bill which we have passed of course may go a little way. My friend Dr. Subbarayan says "A long way". But he did not say that in 1932 when he moved his Bill. My friend is a very good man. He has made a lot of propaganda on behalf of the Harijans. Wherever he went he took votes-in Tanjore, Negapatam, and Rajahmundry. I have got the notes here. But Mr. Speaker, you would not allow me to deal with them, Sir. Sir, he has been taking votes. He said that our province was ripe. But to-day he cannot go against the discipline of his leader; he is also bound by discipline.

Sir, I have only one more word. I am disappointed. I say, Sir, that I am deceived also. I am very sorry to say that but I feel that I have been deceived in this matter. If I had known that six years hence you would go back to your old position....

(The motion was put and declared lost.)

The Malabar Temple Entry Bill, 1938, 2 December 1938*

M.C. Rajah: Deputy Speaker, Madam, I have already spoken on this subject of temple entry and the House is well aware of my views on this subject. Last night we heard the eloquent speech of the Hon. the Premier in defence of the opening of temples to the excluded classes, while introducing the Malabar Temple Entry Bill. I am not surprised at the speech because I have been listening to a number of similar speeches which he has been delivering for the last seven years in the very same strain. I understand he made the speech to convince some members here, but I doubt very much whether he is convinced that this question is very important and immediate. It is something like saying, "Do as I say, but not as I do." That has been the order of the day nowadays.

As a matter of fact, when I moved for reference to the Select Committee the Madras Temple Entry Bill which was drafted by no less a person than the Hon. the Premier himself, and which was introduced by me in this Legislature, there was no such opposition as we see here to-day. What is all this opposition due to? Is it not due to the Premier killing the Bill on the floor of this House with the mechanical majority he has in his hands? If he had accepted that Bill then, and extended its provisions only to the district of Malabar, he would not have had to face the music to-day in this House. My friend, Mr. Palat, who supported my motion that day and voted with me, is opposing it to-day. . . .

M.C. Rajah: It is the fault of the Premier. I do not blame my friend, Mr. Palat, because he made it quite clear that his heart is with the Bill but that he spoke on behalf of his constituency. One cannot expect this son of the great man, Sankaran Nayar, a great social reformer, to come and oppose this Bill, and that in the year 1938. He has done it for his constituency. His constituency gave him a mandate to express its view before the House, and he has done it. In that connection, I should like to correct Mr. Palat, when he said that the mass of Harijans are against this Bill. He quoted the fact

*Speech in Madras Legislative Assembly.

that 27 members belonging to the Depressed Classes who are in the Congress party voted against the Bill. When a similar question was put to the Hon. Premier some time back, he answered by saying – let me quote his own words, because that will be a fitting answer to my friend, Mr. Palat, "Some say that the untouchables do not desire to enter our temples. This is because we have trained them to do it as we train bullocks and horses. If a step-mother ill-treats her step-child, he will go to the neighbour. Is it an excuse for the mother to say that the boy does not come home for food?" So, Mr. Palat should know that the Premier is as good as any trainer of horses or of any other animal. You know how they train animals, in the circus. The Premier has trained them to do so and therefore they have voted against the Bill. Do not be under the impression that you can browbeat me by these interruptions. Deputy Speaker, Madam, if they are going to interrupt me, I am prepared to answer every member of the House, but it will take the time of the House, and you may pull me up saying that I have taken too much of the time of the House. . . .

M.C. Rajah: Sir, my friend, Mr. T. Viswanatham, the Parliamentary Secretary, interrupted and seemed to raise a point of order. He said that I called some members of this House bullocks and horses. I did not call them so. It was the Premier who called them so. I am merely quoting his own words. . . .

M.C. Rajah: I was answering my friend, Mr. Palat and defending the Premier as regards this Bill. I am doing his work. It was his business to answer Mr. Palat. I am answering for the Prime Minister. Instead of thanking me, Sir. . . .

M.C. Rajah: Then, Sir, Mr. Palat said, "Why hurry" "Wait." Even this, I want to answer and help the Priemier by giving quotations from his own speeches. I think I can effectively answer Mr. Palat by quoting what the Premier said on another occasion. He said, "You want Swaraj. You all want Self-Government. The Britisher would feel very grateful to you, if you could wait for a little more time, till he settles his economic difficulties. Would you wait? Is it not enough that you had been under the British rule for the last 150 years? The same answer I shall give to Mr. Palat in this connection. Why should we wait any longer? Where there is a proved or admitted wrong, there is no justification to keep it going any longer, even for a single day. Mr. Krishna Rao who also opposed the Bill said that public opinion is not in favour of the Bill. But there is ample evidence to show that public opinion is in favour of the Bill."

But what has happened in the interval between the 17th August 1938 and to-day is that public opinion has gone backwards. That was due to the attitude of this very House. That was due to the attitude this House took with reference to the other Bill which was introduced on the 30th march 1938. Till I moved to refer the Bill to a Select Committee on 17th August 1938, there was no public opinion against the Bill. Not a single dissentient voice was raised here either on behalf of the members here, or on behalf of the Sanatanist opinion outside. . . .

M.C. Rajah: Even so, Sir, public opinion against the Bill has developed still more now. It is because of the attitude of this House in killing, stifling, that Bill. Mr. Krishna Rao said that even Diwan Bahadur R. Srinivasan is against temple entry. I may correct him by saying that it is not so. Diwan Bahadur Srinivasan has published a leaflet in which he says that important temples in South India belong to the Depressed Classes. . . .

M.C. Rajah: The statement published by Diwan Bahadur R. Srinivasan, if I remember correctly, states: "We, the Depressed Classes, are not going to worry with the temple entry problem. It is the duty of caste Hindus to open the temples for us. When they are opened, then we shall see whether we should enter or not." That was what Diwan Bahadur Srinivasan had stated. I am glad that Mr. G. Krishna Rao accepts this. If he does not believe what I say, I shall make a present of a copy of the pamphlet, so that he may read Diwan Bahadur Srinivasan's opinion.

Coming to this Bill, Sir, I do not believe that the Hon. the Premier has acted wisely in this matter. When a person wants to sow, the first thing he does is to select the softest soil, the soil that is congenial to the growth of the plant and then he sows the seed. In such a case he will get a luxuriant harvest, pleasant to look at, and beneficial not only to himself but to others as well. As you all know – and I dare say that the Hon. the Premier also will admit it – Malabar is the most difficult of all the districts in this Presidency for a measure like this. Nowhere in the whole presidency is the stigma of untouchability more perceptible than in Malabar, aggravated as it is by feelings of unapproachability and unseeability. So much so that Swami Vivekananda described Malabar as the "lunatic asylum of the Presidency". I shall be glad to know that his description of Malabar in respect of the treatment accorded to the Depressed Classes there is wrong, and that Malabar has outgrown the times in which that description was made.

But what I know is that untouchability has been in the grossest and most inhuman form in Malabar. There, even the look of a Depressed Class man is supposed to pollute, and not merely the touch and the shadow. What has happened in such a place as to merit the Hon. Premier choosing it – a rocky place to sow his seed? There was a silent and passive consent on the part of the orthodox people of that place over this question until the other Bill was killed in this House, and now they have come forward with their objection. I say that this is all due to the activity of the Hon. the Premier during the interim period. I have been closely watching the several speeches he has made during his tours through the districts. In one place he had said that the country had gone backwards. Sir, is it right for the Hon. Premier who is to pilot this Bill, to go round the country and only say to the people that the country has gone backwards. It is nothing but an optical illusion. When we travel in a railway train and the train actually moves, we see the objects around moving, and then we think, the objects are all moving along with us. Sir, it is the Hon. the Premier who has gone backwards, he thinks that the country has gone backwards too. My illustration may not suit you but your parables will suit you.

Sir, he again goes to another place – I am sorry I cannot quote all his speeches – and tells that the women of the country are averse to this. Here I would like the Hon. the Deputy Speaker of this House to come to my help when I say that I had an occasion to speak at a meeting of ladies that was presided over by her, where a resolution was passed supporting the Bill, and if I am not mistaken, even the Madras Women's Association has supported the Bill. Even the ladies of Mylapore whose photograph appeared in the *Madras Mail*, some time ago, held a meeting and supported the Bill. That being so, I do not know what kind of ladies our Premier refers to when he says that the women are averse to this.

Sir, on the other hand, what do I see in the case of the other Hon. Ministers, such as the Hon. Dr. Subbarayan, the Hon. Mr. Gopala Reddi, the Hon. Mr. Ramanathan and others? They have been consistent throughout and they have been sincere in their work. Wherever they go, they create a favourable opinion and take decisions by asking the people who are in favour of the measure to raise their hands. That is the sort of work that these Ministers have been doing, and I thank them and congratulate them on the work they have been carrying on.

With reference to prohibition, my friend, the Hon. the Premier, has chosen the right soil, and I am glad to see that prohibition is said to be a success in Salem. He ought to have applied the same principle with reference to temple entry also. Had he taken the City of Madras first, where the members of the Depressed Classes also have got franchise to elect trustees to the Sri Parthasarathi Temple at Triplicane, had he taken a soil like this, there would have been no opposition to the Bill at all. Or he might have taken Salem. Perhaps he might say, 'why bother me!' I say Salem, because we have got there our Premier, and fortunately the Hon. Dr. Subbarayan is also there – a double barrel gun, as it were in Salem. The prospect of bringing into force this measure effectively there is very bright. Or take other districts. Why not your own district, Sir – East Godavari – where your influence and sincerity would achieve better results? As a matter of fact, East Godavari has been already ploughed by able social reformers like the late lamented Veerasalingam Pantulu and Dr. Sir Venkataratnam Nayudu. Take Krishna; there is Dr. Pattabhi Sitaramayya doing his great work in this direction. I now come to Guntur, where there is Mr. Konda Venkatappayya: does he say that he does not want the Temple Entry Bill to be put into effect there? There are other places like Trichinopoly where there is Dr. Rajan who had been long associated with the work of the Harijan Board. With regard to this district, I might say that the Tamil Nadu Harijan Sevak Sangh has already passed a resolution asking for temple entry there. Such being the case, why brush aside all these earnest demands, and go to a rocky place like Malabar to sow your seed there? Perhaps you will say, "I have got all the charm there!"

Sir, the other day, the Hon. the Premier gave an illustration to show why he has chosen Malabar. He told us how an old woman who offered a steaming plate of gruel to a Mongol warrior, asked him to put his finger at the edge and not at the middle of the plate where the gruel was the hottest. The Premier expected me to follow the advice of the old woman, that is to say, his own advice not to tackle this problem at the thickest and hottest part where the opposition is likely to be at its height but to go from the edge to the centre. Apart from the confession of his being an old woman in this affair, what is he doing but to put his finger at the hottest and thickest part of the gruel of temple entry? Hon. the Premier. . . . Apart from the confession of being an old woman. . . .

M.C. Rajah: I stand corrected. Apart from the desirability of testing the gruel of temple entry in the hottest part, there is this aspect of the question. Our thoughts are about the present and the future generations alone. Here we are enacting a measure that will affect both the present and the future generations. We are not concerned with the past generation. So let us not bring these antiquated grandmother's stories into our problem. Sir, he says, Malabar is contiguous to Travancore. But what do we see in the Travancore Proclamation? The Travancore Proclamation is only a proclamation and not an expression of opinion of the people of Travancore. It is only a fiat of a ruler, which is met with opposition in Cochin and Malabar. If the people of Travancore did not raise any cry of protest against it, it was out of deference and respect to their Ruler. But, all the same, God alone knows what is going on in Travancore! The report is that temple entry in Travancore is a success. I get other reports also saying that it is a failure. But I am not a judge of these contradicting reports. All I would say is that this Travancore Proclamation has not helped Malabar in any way to be prepared for a Bill of this kind. I am glad that my friend, Mr. Karunakara Menon, has said that temple entry, if it should be a success in Malabar, needs much spade-work. I am glad he says that, and it shows how much of hard labour it requires there to sow the seed. So, why should we go and place ourselves in the midst of the stoutest opposition, in the district of Malabar, instead of putting our finger in the coldest part of the gruel of temple entry?

Sir, you should know that I am not against the present Bill. There is a proverb which says, half-a-loaf is better than no bread at all – and I may say here that this Bill is not even half-a-loaf but very much smaller than half-a-loaf, something like the one-twenty-fifth part of a loaf. But still I shall cooperate with the Hon. the Premier. I shall show some of the difficulties, and I shall try to help him, but I will not be responsible for the result.

Sir, when the Hon. the Premier made his final speech on the subject at the last session, towards the concluding portion of his speech, he seemed to have imagined certain things which I did not say. It is a very, very, gratifying sign to see the Leader of the House coming forward to defend the Leader of the Opposition against something which he says I said or thought of the Leader of the Opposition. From the official report of the proceedings, I find that he said: "I can understand the Hon. Mover's disappointment and anger with us – or with me in particular – it is very unfair for him to have said or even thought all the things he seemed to think about the Hon. Leader of the Opposition." I have vainly turned the pages of the proceedings to find out if there was anything, that I said in the course of my speech about the Leader of the Opposition. I had said not a single word against the Leader of the Opposition, nor did the Leader of the Opposition say anything against me. It is very unfair for an Hon. Minister, a responsible Minister, to work up a situation which did not exist. Taking advantage of the position that I had no right to reply after him, he said that; and further he said that the Leader of the Opposition had supported him and did not support me; whereas, as a matter of fact, the Leader of the Opposition supported me and not him. Sir, coming to the point. . . .

M.C. Rajah: Not at all. It is very clear; any man who knows English will understand it. Read your speech in the proceedings of the Assembly.

Sir, coming to the provisions of the Bill, I must at the outset say that this Bill is for the Sanatanists and not for the Depressed Classes. I shall substantiate my statement in a few words. Sub-clause (4) of clause 2 of the Bill requires that a temple should have an annual income of not less than Rs. 5,000 under section 69 of the Madras Hindu Religious Endowments Act, 1926, to come within the purview of this measure. . . .

M.C. Rajah: As regards voters, the Depressed Classes have been excluded from the voter's list. I would bring to the notice of the house one particular point. If the Bill were ever to come to Madras, and if you are to exclude the Depressed Classes from the vote, then you will be excluding a very large number of Depressed Classes who have already got their votes with regard to the election of trustees to the Sri Parthasarathiswami Temple. When you say that this Bill is intended for the Hindus, why do you exclude the Depressed Classes from the list? Are we not Hindus; are we Christians; are we Muslims; and if we are not Hindus why should we agitate for temple entry? Clause 5 says that where after fifty voters sign a requisition and send it on to the trustee of a temple, if just two clear days before the date of the referendum, not less than 25 persons who signed the requisition apply for its withdrawal, then the proceedings shall be deemed to have been cancelled, and then the question cannot be raised for two years to come. The implication of this clause is this: supposing 50 Sanatanists join together and sign a petition and 25 of them withdraw their signatures the whole proceedings would automatically drop and the question will be closed for two years. Then why should a 2-year limit be fixed, when in these days public opinion is developing very fast? Will not six months do? Clause 5, sub-clause (2) is unnecessary. It runs thus:

> The Provincial Government may, at any time, before the results of any reference to the voters are announced, order that all further action in respect of such references shall be suspended and upon such order all previous proceedings relating thereto shall be deemed to have been cancelled.

This is unnecessary, as it takes away with the left hand what is given by the right hand.

The Hon. Premier told us yesterday that he was going to make rules and regulations for the maintenance of order, etc., in the temples. I would like to know whether those rules and regulations are intended for the worshippers of the Depressed Classes or for other classes of worshippers as well. It is not clear in the clause. . . .

M.C. Rajah: Yes, Sir. As I have said, I will cooperate with the Hon. Premier in this matter; but I want him to say in his reply what the other districts are, to which he is contemplating to bring a similar Bill next, and when that will be. In one of his speeches in Madras he made it perfectly clear that he would go to Madras next. He said that in a public meeting; and I want to know whether this advance will be to Madras or elsewhere? . . .

M.C. Rajah: It appeared in *The Hindu*, dated the 31st October 1938. *The Hindu* which is a great advocate of the Sanatanists, in 1932 supported the Bill and it went to the extent of saying that the bureaucratic Government should support the measure. But in 1938, it has gone back on that statement. It says, Mr. M.C. Rajah's enthusiasm outruns his sense of justice. Perhaps *The Hindu's* ardent enthusiasm of 1932 dwindled away in 1938.

To continue what I said, it was a speech delivered before the Malayalees of Malabar; it was presided over by Mr. Gopala Menon. At the conclusion of the meeting it is said "Mr. Gopala Menon thanked the Premier for his 'lucid exposition' of the proposed legislation and assured him that the people of Malabar would do all they could to make the measure a complete success. Answering a question raised by a member of the audience, the Premier said that he had fully explained on the floor of the Assembly why he suggested to Mr. M.C. Rajah to hold back for a time his Bill." He said, "It is because I want the reform to get through, I want the cause to succeed as a whole, that I implored Mr. Rajah to suspend his motion and allow me to get through Malabar first. From Travancore let us progress to Malabar and thence to Madras and other parts of the Province." May I present the Hon. Premier with a copy of this? Sir, I do not wish to detain the House any further. My only fear is that this Bill will not succeed; if it succeeds, well and good.

Sir, I support the motion.

8 DECEMBER 1938

M.C. Rajah: Mr. Speaker, Sir, it was not my intention to intervene in this debate at this stage. But since some of the previous speakers in their speeches have unnecessarily dragged my name into the debate, I think it is my duty to reply to some of them. First of all, I should like to request my friend, Mr. Palat, to be a little more conciliatory. We have done the best for him in the Select Committee; but for his persuasion we would not have made the provisions under sub-clause (4) of clause 2; we also added, Sir, a new sub-clause to clause 11 [sub-clause (2)], only due to his efforts in the Select Committee. And I think Mr. Palat was entirely pleased with us. I think he said on a previous occasion he was the spokesman on behalf of the orthodox section to-day. Perhaps he wants to pacify them by making another speech here to-day. I think we can forgive him that.

And then, my friend, Mr. Krishna Rao, has made some reference and said that the Congress party – of course since the Premier has already asked for my cooperation, I am going to help him in this, – has not mentioned temple entry in the programme which it placed before the electorate. True, they have not; but Mr. Krishna Rao should know that one of the main planks in the Congress programme was the removal of untouchability. . . .

M.C. Rajah: Now, Madam, Mr. Krishna Rao says that the voters did not know it. But the voters who voted for the Congress must have been Congressmen and therefore they must have known the Congress programme. . . .

M.C. Rajah: It is their mistake if they voted for the Congress. Non-Congressmen have no business to vote for the Congress candidates and if they had done so, they will have to suffer for it.

Mr. Krishna Rao then referred to a statement of mine issued some time back with reference to the Harijan Advisory Boards recently constituted by the Government. He has spoken of that, and I also should like to say – I am not going to contradict him at all on that point: that was my view and I still hold that view – that the transference of the hostels from the management of the labour commissioner to the Harijan Sevak Sanghs is gradually going back to the days of Manu because I am afraid, when the caste Hindus are taking up the management of the hostels, whether they will treat our boys properly and will not infuse into the tender brains their principles and policies.

Madam, I come next to my friend, Mr. B.S. Murti, the Parliamentary Secretary. He said that the Harijans do not want temple entry but all that they require are food, raiment, education and appointment. As against that, the Hon. the Premier. . . .

M.C. Rajah: I am grateful to Mr. Murti for making my position very clear indeed. Mr. Murti says that the Harijans outside this House are not for temple entry, while those 30 members in this House are very anxious for it. If that be the case, why did they kill my Bill on the last occasion? That would have been the best opportunity for them to show their anxiety and they should have supported the Bill. The fact that they opposed it and killed it, is in itself a very clear indication to show that these 27 or 26 Harijans there, were not for temple entry but that the country was for it. Because as a matter of fact, I have been getting a number of resolutions passed in the Andhradesa whence my friend, Mr. Murti comes, stating that they were going to take communal disciplinary action against those Harijan Congress members who voted against my Bill. Only against Harijan Congress members, because in the case of other members they cannot do that. That shows the volume of opinion in the country. . . .

M.C. Rajah: I am cooperating with you so far as this Bill is concerned, and if I make these observations, it is because I am only correcting some of the misconceptions that are lurking in the minds of some members. Just as you, as the Leader, can control them, teach them and give them good advice, I think, I too can give them some good advice to the extent I can – and I claim to possess some capacity which entitles me to do so.

I am glad on the other hand, my friend, the Hon. Sri Muniswami Pillai, who also belongs to the community, has come forward and said that the volume of Harijan opinion in the country is in favour of the Bill. I am very glad that he has now advanced in his views. Two months ago he was not in favour of the Bill and said that the country was not for it, and now he has changed his view – and I thank him for that.

With reference to Harijan Advisory Boards, my friend, Mr. Murti, unnecessarily brought in the name of Mahatma Gandhi. Mahatma Gandhi did not say, "hand over all the Depressed Classes hostels that are now being managed by the Madras Labour Department to the Harijan Sevak Sanghs". Did he ever say that? I do not think he has ever said that. What he said was that Harijan Sevak Sanghs also should work in the same direction as the Congress Government, just as a double-barrel gun – two independent bodies working together to bring this ameliorative work to success as early as possible. He never said that the Harijan Sevak Sanghs should get into the shoes of the Labour Commissioner, take over the hostels managed by the Commissioner and force their policy and principles on those young men. He did not say that at all.

I have nothing more to say at present, but shall try to say something more when the motion for passing this Bill into law comes before the House. . . .

M.C. Rajah: Mr. Speaker, Sir, this is a stage in which benedictory speeches are generally made on the passing of the Bill. But before doing that, I would like to remind the house of a famous saying of Babu Surendranath Banerjee, one of the founders of the Indian National Congress, the fruits of whose labours the present Ministry is now enjoying. He was fond of saying, Sir, while thanking the British Government for all the benefits conferred by them on the people of this country, that gratitude was a keen sense of favours yet to come. In this case, of course, it is no favour which the Prime Minister is bestowing on the Depressed Classes; he is simply doing his duty, and for that of course I am grateful to him, but with the proviso and hope that this Bill will soon be followed up by a larger and more comprehensive measure like the one which I had the honour to introduce and which the Hon. the Premier had the honour to oppose.

Sir, I agree with this Bill so far as the principle of temple entry is concerned; but as far as the machinery set up and the limited locality for the application of the measure are concerned, the Premier alone is responsible for them. In my speech on the last occasion, I asked the Premier to state definitely in what other districts he was going to introduce similar legislation; he omitted to answer the question perhaps in the excitement of the discussion; but now that he has had ample time to think about it, I hope, Sir, he will give us an indication, by taking the House into his confidence and telling us the several districts in which he is going to extend the application of this measure.

Sir, I have already stated that the whole Presidency, taking all the districts together, is ripe enough for a permissive measure like this. Sir, now I may mention to the Hon. the Premier once again about Andhradesa. I think that some of my friends who are sitting on the opposite side and who belong to the Tamil districts are afraid of a measure like this. I am very glad to hear that, but why did you oppose my Bill then? I hope some of you will get up after me and ask the Premier to extend it to the Tamil districts. But, so far as Andhradesa is concerned, I know it is not only willing but also eager to remove untouchability and to effect temple entry. I must here give my thanks to the late Mr. Viresalingam Pantulu, Mr. B. Venkataratnam Nayudu, to yourself, Sir, the Hon. Speaker of this House to my bold and frank friend the Hon. Mr. T. Prakasam, to Dr. Pattabhi Sitaramayya, and last but not least, my late lamented friend Mr. Nageswara Rao Pantulu. Sir, I do not know if the Hon. the Premier has witnessed the Telugu talkie which is running its course in one of the local talkie houses in Madras, called *Malapilla*. It is the result of the ingenuity of the Telugu people in the Andhradesa; it is clearly brought out in that film how untouchability could be easily abolished. If I remember correctly, that film is dedicated to the late lamented Nageswara Rao Pantulu. If I understand the film correctly. . . .

M.C. Rajah: Sir, in these days of democracy, I am sure these talkie houses are going to solve the difficult social or religious problems confronting us. The immense popularity of this Telugu play not only in Andhradesa but also in the Tamil country shows that the country would welcome a measure like this. As a matter of fact, I would like each and every member of this House to see this film *Malapilla* and also the films *Mahatma* and *Chandi Das* of Bengal. My humble request is that the Hon. the Premier must see these films. . . .

M.C. Rajah: But I wish to tell him, Sir, that I am not the proprietor of any of these film houses, nor am I the agent or the manager.

Sir, in fine, I want the Hon. the Premier to give us an indication as to what district he is going to take up next for extending the application of this Bill. With these words, I thank him for his labours, and I thank also the members of the Select Committee for coming to an unanimous understanding. Sir, I support the motion and I wish the Bill success.

Miscellaneous Departments, 28 March 1939*

M.C. Rajah: Sir, I beg to move – '*that the allotment of Rs. 21,34,800 for Miscellaneous Departments be reduced by Rs. 100.*'

Sir, while speaking on this motion I will confine my remarks to the portion relating to the work of the Depressed Classes and the policy of the Government towards the amelioration of the condition of the community. The Hon. Prime Minister while replying to the general discussion of the budget referred to page 379 of the budget. When I spoke on the general debate I also referred to the figures on page 379 and I placed before the House the fact that the present Government has not done anything over and above the last year's budget. But the Hon. Prime Minister said that they have given a considerable amount of grant under this head for the education of the depressed classes in the next year's budget. It is not so. And then, he goes on quoting that in the year 1937-38 he set apart a sum of Rs.10,41,611 and then he jumps on to 1939-40 overlooking the fact that he had also set apart an amount of money in 1938-39. The Prime Minister wants us to understand that for the coming year he has given us over and above the current year Rs.1,27,000. And out of that he has set apart Rs.17,500 for the Chidambaram School. Practically he has given us only Rs. 4,500 over and above last year's budget. That is what I say. . . .

M.C. Rajah: I am glad, Sir, the Prime Minister has put the question to me. I am not treating Chidambaram as nothing at all. If he only had a little more patience, he would understand that the case of Chidambaram is quite different. Chidambaram is an existing institution. For Chidambaram institution, the Government have been already paying a substantial amount of grant and therefore Rs.17,500 which is said to have been given to Chidambaram this year is not Rs.17,500; it is 10,000 or so. I think that formerly Chidambaram had been getting a grant of about 4,000 or 5,000 rupees and therefore you cannot wholly claim, in the exuberance of your heart, that you have given

*Speech in Madras Legislative Assembly.

17,500. Chidambaram is a very important institution and we want the institution to be permanent. I am glad you are taking it up. It is your duty to do it, instead of subsidizing it. Instead of giving money to private agency, you are taking that in your own hands. I am glad you are doing it. In that connection, Sir, the Hon. Premier asks us whether we should not appreciate the little mercy shown. But what about the bombastic claims you set forth as Congressmen, posing as benefactors of the Depressed Classes? Compared with the bombastic claims, I venture to say that it is absolutely nothing. Sir, in that connexion, the Hon. Premier has also questioned us by saying, "is it to catch votes that we have done it? Have the scheduled classes voted us into the position that we hold? Not at all. Let there be no mistake about it." I am surprised to read this statement of the Hon. Premier. I know, Sir, the Premier is not an ordinary gentleman; he is an intellectual prodigy and not a baby. And I am surprised to hear from the Premier that the scheduled classes. . . .

M.C. Rajah: If I begin to explain, it will take time and therefore let me go to the point. Sir, what I say is the Hon. Premier has evidently forgotten the Poona Pact and the Joint Electorate in which the Depressed Classes were roped in with the Hindu electorates as against the Muslim electorate and also he does not seem to attach any special value to the 28 votes that he commands in this Assembly from my own community. Perhaps he thinks that these 28 votes are mere ciphers which by themselves have no value, but added to certain figures, they enhance the value of the figures and that the Depressed Classes have not also helped the party that came into power. I do not claim that we alone have set the party in power. There are also others the non-Brahmans, whose representatives are now in jails. They have also voted for them. What I say is this: To make a statement on the floor of the House that we of the Depressed Class have not taken part in the elections and have not voted. . . .

M.C. Rajah: Well, I am not afraid to speak the truth. If I had said so, I will accept it; I would not fear anybody in the world. It was because the Premier said, "You have not put us into power; you are nowhere in the world; we have come of our own strength," that I ask, "have not the 28 members supported him and his party?" They are all human beings. . . .

M.C. Rajah: I want the Hon. Premier to understand that those 28 votes are precious to him. That is what I am driving at. But he does not seem to understand it. I shall read what he had said. It will make the position clear. It does not give me pleasure to attack anybody in this House; it pains me. . . .

M.C. Rajah: Well, I will read. The Premier says, "Is it to catch votes that we have done it? Do the scheduled classes vote us into the position that we hold? Not at all. Let there be no mistake about it." Certainly we did vote you into the position. I say you are entirely mistaken. You are there in virtue of the fact that the scheduled classes have also voted for your party men in 152 electorates. That is exactly what I am driving at. . . .

M.C. Rajah: The next point I want to speak about is the Labour Department. The Labour Department has been in existence for the last two decades and still it is a disgrace to say that the department is not made permanent. The other day when I put a question the Government gave me the answer that the general staff in the Madras Labour Commissioner's office are all permanent men. I understand even the departmental staff in the districts are permanent. But the poor teachers who are carrying on the actual labour work, the educational work and the ameliorative work are not made permanent. They are treated as mere ordinary outcastes. They are left alone in the district. Their conditions are precarious. The educational rules governing them are also quite contrary to the education rules that govern the other schools. As regards salary, they do not get their salary – they are very poorly paid teachers – even on the 20th; sometimes they get it the next month. Then, how do they send the salaries to them? They are sent by money orders. The money order commission is also deducted. I am speaking on behalf of the poor people, not rich people. A labour school teacher who gets 15 or 16 rupees, if he gets his salary on the 20th or 30th of the month, how is he going to live at all? On the other hand, I understand that the Government enforces a certain rule on the capitalist, the mills and the factories. They say, in mills and factories the labourers should be paid on the 7th of each month; but here the Government, who are employers of large labour, themselves do not pay the poorly paid teachers even on the 5th or 6th of the month and I want the Government to look into the matter very carefully. The labour officers carry on their work as mere automations. They are not at all interested in the elevation of Depressed Classes. . . .

The next point, Sir, is that whereas teachers employed in ordinary schools get half holidays on Saturdays and full holidays on Sundays continuously, these teachers are given half holidays on Wednesdays and full holidays on Sundays. It is because they do not want to give them continuous holidays on Saturdays and Sundays. They are treated differently, not as human beings. As regards the methods of teaching, they are not at all looked after. The labour officers in the districts are drawn from the revenue department. They are not educationists, they know nothing about the methods of teaching, they know only how to fine and transfer the teachers from one place to another and harass them as much as possible. But they do not take any interest in the educational work.

The next point is about the lady teachers employed in the schools. The other day I brought to the notice of the House that they are not treated properly, that they are not given maternity benefit at all. As Mr. Langley pointed out the other day, the lady workers in the mills are given maternity benefit. Factory owners are compelled by Government to give these facilities to lady workers, whereas this Government, which is supposed to look after the lady teachers, treats them with scant courtesy. They must be given maternity benefit. Sir; I hope the lady members in this House will take up this question.

Then so far as elementary education is concerned, very little progress has been made with reference to the education of these scheduled class boys. Sir, all these labour school boys were given midday meals. They have now stopped it. You must know it is difficult for these poor boys living in rural areas to get meals. For want of meals, they are not able to educate themselves. Even now the Public Service Commission says that though there are graduates, they are physically weak and therefore they are not selected for public services. As Mr. Reid has said, people get only half-a-meal a day. As regards my community, they do not get half-a-meal even. The school children are not given the benefit of medical inspection. I hope the Government will consider the question of the periodical medical examination of the boys in the labour schools.

In the matter of higher education, they have absolutely made no headway. I want the Government to attend to this. Unless they give higher education to the Depressed Classes, how will it be possible for them to compete with others for the posts which seem to be open to them?

As regards the S.S.L.C. course, I want that course to be free to the scheduled classes. As regards hostels I would ask the Government to pursue a policy of having a network of hostels all over the Presidency.

There should be at least one hostel in each district on the lines of the Paddison Hostel, Madras.

I have been for a very long time agitating for a hostel for girls in Madras City. I am just rushing through all the items without enlarging upon each item and taking up the time of the House. I trust the Government will consider this also.

Then, Sir, as regards the management of the hostels I suggest that it should be entirely in the hands of the Labour Department and not in the hands of any political party. That must be borne in mind very carefully. The present policy of giving grants to the Harijan Sevak Sanghs and entrusting these hostels to their charge is opposed to our principles and we protest strongly against this new policy. As regards the Advisory Boards also I want the Government to be more cosmopolitan and more liberal. They should not tie these boards down to one political party. In regard to this matter the Hon. the Premier says at one place that these Harijan Sanghs are not political bodies and at another place he says that they are. Last year in Kodambakkam the Hon. Premier said that the Harijan Sevak Sanghs form part and parcel of the Congress in the country. I take him at his word and say that we do not want any political party to get the funds that are intended for our hostels.

Lastly, Sir, I want to make a submission. We have been called by all sorts of names by all sorts of people that come into existence in this world. We have been protesting against the new name given to us. There is a bad odour about that name. I do not know whether most of the Members of the House know how we got the name Adi-Dravida or Adi-Andhra. In the year 1922 in the Madras Legislative Council a resolution was passed and from that day forward the community has been styled as Adi-Dravida or Adi-Andhra. That resolution was passed on 20th January 1922. . . .

M.C. Rajah: I was only trying to emphasize the fact, Sir, that the Depressed Classes were not consulted when the name "Harijan" was chosen for them and that large and influential sections of our people resent the name "Harijan". Sir, if a name is to be given to a particular community, it is but right that the community should be consulted. It is not right for you, at a moment's notice, to say: "Oh, we are going to call you Harijans." It is our right to select a name for our community, as the Congress party rightly says: "it is our right to frame our Constitution. We must have a Constitution framed by ourselves." We say, similarly, we must have the right to choose our name and not you. You must consult us. My point is this: You may call us by any name, but in Governmental records how can you introduce it? You have cunningly produced a book with the heading "The Harijan Uplift". I take objection to it. You must have consulted us and then by common consent adopted a name. Now, what does this name "Harijan" mean? It means "Sons of God". Are you not sons of God? What is the difference between you and me. Do you call yourselves Harijans? If so, there is no mistake at all. But you call yourselves "Brahmans" – a very holy name and you call yourselves "Kshatriyas", and so on and so forth. We strongly protest against this name "Harijans". I am not going to suggest a name. I want my community to suggest a name for itself. It is their right and not yours. . . .

M.C. Rajah: In this connection I want to tell the Government that my community has selected a name for itself and that the Legislature has accepted the name "Adi-Dravida", "Adi-Andhra", and "Adi-Karnataka". My friends may read the literature on it if they are interested in the community. In conclusion, Sir, I must say that I am glad that the department is now in the able hands of the Hon. Mr. V.V. Giri. He is a labour leader and I know him intimately. He is safeguarding the interests of labour. My community is akin to labour and I hope he will take note of all the suggestions I have placed before the House and speedily redress all our grievances.

Temple Entry Indemnity Bill, 1939, 3 August 1939*

M.C. Rajah: Mr. Speaker, I heartily welcome this Bill. I am glad that it is recognized that there is and has been a growing volume of public opinion demanding the removal of the disabilities imposed by custom and usage on certain classes of Hindus in respect of their entry into and offering worship in Hindu temples.

The important thing here is not so much that such a volume of opinion exists, as the fact of its existence being recognized by those who have it in their power to remove the disabilities imposed by custom and usage. The recognition of the volume of public opinion in this matter is a fact on which on the principle "better late than never", the Hon. Mr. Rajagopalachari deserves to be congratulated.

Sir, this Bill is not a piece of direct legislation nor even of permissive legislation. No elaborate machinery such as is found in the Malabar Temple Entry Bill is set up to give effect to public opinion. The public opinion which exists is allowed to act naturally, through individuals like a temple trustee, or a priest, or a Government official or any other person connected therewith, who is free to exercise his judgment and give effect to it in spite of a certain measure of inevitable opposition. In all cases of social and religious reform, there will always be two parties and two sections of public opinion, one demanding the reform, the other opposing it. The points to be considered in introducing legislation for securing the reform are (1) the justice and desirability of the change to be effected, and (2) the existence of a sufficient and growing body of progressive opinion in favour of it. I say, a sufficient and growing body of progressive public opinion, because the reform is not a matter to be decided by considerations of majority and minority. The thing to be considered is whether the progressive section is sufficiently big and whether it is a growing body holding in its hands, the future generation of the country; whether the conservative section, however numerous and influential

*Speech in Madras Legislative Assembly.

it may be for the present, is not a diminishing quantity, whether it is not like a waning moon, losing its size and lustre day by day until at last it disappears from the sky. Thus while, if you look into the past, you may or may not find authority in the *shastras* for throwing open the doors of temples to all classes of people alike, is there anybody who will venture to deny that the spirit of the times demands that there should be no exclusion practiced against those who wish to worship God in any manner and in any place they choose? So far as we Adi-Dravidas are concerned we may set up our own temples and *bhajana kudams* and prayer halls and give spontaneous expression to our feelings of devotion to God in more sincere forms than is possible in the existing temples. But it is the principle of exclusiveness and discrimination that we protest against and wish to see renounced and relinquished, so long as there is a desire to count us among the Hindus. If we are regarded as Hindus, we must be treated as Hindus in all respects and on a footing of equality with every other class of Hindus. The principle involved is one which applies not only to the so-called Depressed Classes but applies to all other classes of Hindus. There should be no boundaries set up between God and man, no lines of demarcation between one body of worshippers and another. All are equal in the eyes of God. All are His children and let us behave as brothers at least in His presence however much we may quarrel outside His House. A true God will say, "Come unto me, all ye who labour and are heavily laden and I will give you rest." He will say it particularly to the labouring classes among whom the Adi-Dravidas are most prominent. It therefore behoves all those who wish to save Hinduism from extinction, to support this Bill, which seeks to support and protect those functionaries of Hindu temples, who, becoming aware of the justice of the desire of the Adi-Dravidas to worship in Hindu temples and of the strength of the public opinion among Hindus in favour of their demand, venture to give expression to that progressive growing opinion, in spite of the opposition of a gradually diminishing and dwindling conservative section, however numerous that section may inevitably be.

One thing I may say. This Bill is intended to replace the Indemnity Ordinance which has been promulgated in the name of His Excellency the Governor. This ordinance is no doubt an extraordinary procedure especially in a matter which concerns the social and religious customs of the people. There would have been no need for such an ordinance and for such a procedure if the permissive Bill which I introduced in this Assembly only last year had not been torpedoed by my friend the Hon. Mr. Rajagopalachari. But wiser counsels have since prevailed and we should congratulate him upon this none too early attempt at reparation and we should also thank his Excellency the Governor for so promptly coming to the rescue of the Premier.

Sir, the Bill is very simple and contains no elaborate machinery. This is its supreme merit. It simply opens the sluice gate for enlightened, progressive, patriotic and forward looking Hindu opinion to flow into the social and religious life of the people of all castes. I say *social* advisedly, because once the religious equality of all Hindus is recognized, the social equality will follow, and the barriers of caste will naturally crumble down. Finally, I request all parties and communities represented in this Assembly and in the Presidency to co-operate in making this temple entry a real success. Let there be no make-believe or eye-wash about it. Let no party make political capital of it. It should be remembered that this measure has come into being in the fullness of time. It is the result, as is said in the preamble to the Bill, of a growing volume of public opinion. To this growing body of opinion, various agencies have contributed; to mention only a few, the Hindu social reformers of the 19th and 20th centuries, the awakeners of the Depressed Classes both within and outside the community, the critics of the Congress Party, and last, but not least, Gandhiji – all these have done their share in bringing about this result. Let not the Congress Government claim a monopoly of the credit. A proportionate share of the credit is due to my friend Mr. Rajagopalachari, but the major portion of the credit should go to the hundreds and thousands of persons of all parties who have created the growing volume of public opinion to which this Bill seeks to give effective expression. Sir, I support the motion before the House.

Resolution on the War Situation, 26 October 1939*

M.C. Rajah: Mr. Speaker, I stand to oppose this resolution. My reasons are these.

The Governor-General has done nothing which he is not authorized to do under the Government of India Act of 1935 which is the constitutional basis of the British Government in India at present and under which the present Legislative Assembly functions. He is specially charged with responsibility for the prevention of any grave menace to the peace and tranquillity of India. What he has done to fulfil these responsibilities is quite in order and quite opportune; delay or omission on his part would have been dereliction of duty and exposed India to grave danger. For these thoughtful and timely acts the people of India ought to be really thankful. If any section of the people regard themselves as non-participants in these and other defence measures, it is not to their credit; but anyhow they will enjoy the safety which the British Army and Navy and Air Force will secure for them, whether they acknowledge it or not. The other sections of the people are, however, grateful and will regard it as a privilege to participate in defending the country and securing the safety of persons and property for the people of India as a whole. The people of India recognize and realize that the war in which Britain is now engaged has been undertaken by her at stupendous self-sacrifice for promoting the cause of freedom and democracy in the world. It is not democracy to suppress the opinions of people by this kind of interruption. You must allow every member in this House to express his views. . . .

M.C. Rajah: This requires no testimony or testing and nobody will question it except Herr Hitler and his group. It is the recognition of this fact which prompted Gandhiji to say that he would give unconditional support to the British Government in this war. If the Congress had followed his lead in this matter, and if Gandhiji had followed his original insight without trying to follow his followers, a resolution like this would not have been introduced in this Assembly

*Speech in Madras Legislative Assembly.

to-day. And as for the application of these principles of freedom and democracy to India, are they not being applied in an increasing measure from year to year? The very fact of the various Councils and Assemblies functioning in this country with powers they had not possessed before and the fact that the various Congress and non-Congress coalition Ministries are exercising large powers in the land are but the application of democratic principles to the government of this country. The truth of the matter is that so far as Britain is concerned, the Government of India is becoming more and more democratic and less and less imperialistic. Imperialism is of two kinds – the exploiting kind and the safeguarding kind. The tendency of recent British legislation is to make the exploiting kind of imperialism which has always been silently active in times of peace has now become more and more evidently active at this time of war. For this safeguarding kind of imperialism we ought to be thankful. And if democracy is not more firmly established in India, it is due to the lack of cooperation and absence of unity among the people; and this lack of unity has become more evident and more operative since the various Ministries have taken charge of Provincial Governments, and after the Britisher has moved aside giving the reins of power to Indians. Then reason for this increased disunion is internal rather than external, and there is no guarantee that more power would bring about greater unity. The defect is in ourselves; it is in the communalism and sectarianism of the leaders which is reflected in the actions of Ministries. Communalism is not merely a matter of hatred. It is a matter also of partiality and prejudice and contempt; and I challenge any member of this Assembly to say whether he is free from this mischievous and more potent kind of communalism. What is the use of saying that India should be regarded as an independent nation when she is not, due to internal conditions which retard progress and freedom among the people. It is easy to ask for independence in the sense of freedom from external control; it is not so easy to secure freedom for the different classes of people from the tyranny of other classes. If we have the latter kind of social, religious and economic freedom, the former kind of freedom from external control will automatically follow. Even as matters stand, what is there to prevent the various parties in the country from meeting together and framing an agreed constitution and asking the British Government to accept it? The Congress fights shy of an All-Parties Conference because it knows it cannot impose its will upon the different sections of the people. It does not want other people to think for themselves, and it does not want to cooperate with other parties and groups. It wants to impose its will upon them; if they do not agree, they do not count at all. Is this the way to lead the country? I do not see why the Congress should object to the Viceroy getting into touch with persons and parties who do not belong to the Congress. Is such impatience and intolerance consistent with their professions of democracy? Does not democracy demand the study of the wishes and aspirations, of the views and judgments of all classes of people? What right has the Congress to claim to represent the wishes of those who do not agree with it?

It is true its professed aim is to unite all classes. That is its *aim*. But what is its achievement? Has not the gulf widened between the various communities since it accepted office – between the Muslims and Hindus throughout the country, and the Brahmans and non-Brahmans in this Presidency and the Congress and the Scheduled Castes in India? It is only in recent weeks that the Congress has opened its eyes to the existence of minorities whose interests deserve to be studied; all along it prided itself upon its representing the whole country without distinction of majority and minority.

Sir, I wonder what purpose is meant to be served by the present resolution. I am sure it will not serve to unite the people. It will on the other hand divide them into hostile camps. Is it intended to prevent contribution to the war in the shape of men, money and materials? The people know who will better secure their safety – the Congress or the Government. The resolution is drafted evidently to impress those innocent friends of India in Britain who, standing at a distance know very little of the hardships and injustice which ordinary people undergo at the hands of their own country men. That is why the Congress does not want the suffering groups and classes to speak out. Mum is their word for them: but the sufferer knows where the shoe pinches, and he will cry out whether you like it or not. What we want in India is not so much independence as true freedom and democracy. I say this because recent experience has shown that while the Congress professes to have given my community facilities which are our birth-right and which have long been withheld from us, we have been deprived of the most vital thing, namely, freedom. We who have hitherto been economic serfs, social outcasts, religious untouchables, have now become political slaves as well. We have been deprived by the Congress of the right of thinking for ourselves and acting together as one body in the interests of our community.

Sir, I say this because at a time when Gandhiji undertook "the fast unto death" in order to compel the Depressed Classes to give up their demand for a Separate Electorate and join the Hindus in a Joint Electorate, the Depressed Classes representatives at Poona sacrificed their demand which they had felt would alone give them political strength, in order to save Gandhiji's life. What has been our reward for this generous act of self-abnegation on our part? The Poona Pact was devised in order to preserve our political independence even when we cooperate with the Hindus. But when the Congressmen agreed to accept office and were coming into power, they forgot their solemn pledge, and set up Congress candidates even in the Panel election and created a split in our community and thus managed to commit political dacoity among my people and kidnapped 28 men who have been ready to do the bidding of the Congress party as was evidenced by these men walking like sheep behind their shepherd, the Premier, into the slaughter-house in which the Madras Temple Entry Bill of 1938 was massacred. I am aware that some of these men will be commandeered to repudiate my statement of fact, but that cannot be avoided, seeing that they are not their own masters. You will then hear repetitions of "My Master's voice".

The present Temple Entry Indemnifying Act, though intended to be friendly to the Depressed Classes, is from a Hindu point of view a coercive measure, and as such calculated to provoke, if not to perpetuate, hatred of the Depressed Classes by the orthodox section of Hindu society. This Act is no substitute for a straightforward permissive measure which would bring about the desired result. . . .

M.C. Rajah: Thank you, Sir. I referred to that because there is no democracy here. The Congress has divided my community piecemeal. It is for that purpose that I said that.

It is interesting to note the publication of a notification that the Congress Ministry has given the Scheduled Classes members of the Congress party liberty to vote on this resolution without the pressure of party whip or discipline. During the 28 months this Ministry has been in office, this is the first time that such freedom has been publicly given to the Depressed Classes members. I would remind the House that this is not however any special favour done to these members. Before the last general election, a pledge was given to the Depressed Classes that they are not bound to vote with the Congress in their non-cooperating resolutions. Now is the time for those members to assert their right to vote against this resolution without minding any private or personal instruction given to them by any Congress member, whether Minister or not. I know full well, being one of themselves, the flesh of their flesh and the bone of their bones, that their soul revolts against this resolution which is so much at variance with their traditional loyalty to the British; but will they have the courage to vote against it and assert their manhood? Sir, I oppose this resolution.